The Autobiography Manuscript
of
Major Amos Stoddard

Deluxe Edition with Color Illustrations

The Autobiography
Manuscript
of
Major Amos Stoddard

Edited and with an Introduction
by
Robert A. Stoddard

Robert Stoddard Publishing
11031 Via Brescia
Suite 306
San Diego, CA 92129

First Edition: December, 2016

Printed in the United States of America

Library of Congress Control Number: 2016920056

ISBN-13: 978-0-692-81485-7

DEDICATION

In loving memory of my father, John Spencer "Jack" Stoddard

Stoddard Family Coat of Arms
Silk woven embroidery with gold and silver thread done by either
Esther Stoddard (1738-1816) or Prudence Stoddard (1734-1822)
Daughters of Colonel John Stoddard (1682-1748)
Northampton, Massachusetts
Circa 1750-1760
Photo and Permission Courtesy of Historic Northampton, Northampton, Massachusetts

2d U. S. Artillery Regiment, 1812-1813

H. Charles McBarron, Founding Member, The Company of Military Historians
Military Uniforms in America Series, Plate No. 9, 1949
Used with Permission – The Company of Military Historians

CONTENTS

ILLUSTRATIONS

A NOTE ON THE AUTOBIOGRAPHY MANUSCRIPT TEXT

No attempt has been made to change the spelling, orthography, or syntax of the original text of the autobiography manuscript of Major Amos Stoddard. The spelling, punctuation, capitalization and paragraph structure are the author's own. Only the most untampered and unmodified transcription of the original text is provided.

Due to illegibility of a few words of the original text, or due to paper damage and loss and missing text, allowances had to be made. These are few and rare. Where a word has been used or substituted due to the aforementioned conditions, it is acknowledged through the use of brackets. Missing text due to damage is more prevalent in the last few pages of the manuscript.

In one case, on page 139, the author crossed-out part of a paragraph. This crossed-out text, mostly still legible, was included within brackets. These words are the author's own —as best as could be transcribed. They help convey the intent of the thought within the paragraph interrupted due to missing text.

In other cases, missing words have been added, or words have been added to provide clarity. These words are again provided within brackets. The use of brackets indicates that the word or words provided have been substituted and are not the author's own. These were used sparingly and are few and rare.

Words within parentheses are the author's own. No use of adding text within parentheses has been provided.

In order not to try to speak for the author, some missing words or text could not be substituted without the risk of changing the meaning of what the author intended to convey. In these cases, several words of missing text is identified through the use of [Missing Text] and a single missing word (or possibly two) is shown as [?] whenever inclusion of a word (or words) by the editor could materially alter the original meaning. In these cases, the reader can best decide what words the author may have originally used or intended.

ACKNOWLEDGEMENT

After discovering the autobiography manuscript of Amos Stoddard, and after completing its transcription, it became apparent that his story needed to be published and shared with researchers, historians, history aficionados, and curious descendants of a collateral family line. It is hoped that publication of his autobiography and the introduction to his life will help elevate this man, citizen, soldier, and author to the forefront with other great Americans who significantly contributed to the development of this country.

I would like to first extend my thanks and appreciation to my wife, Vera Stoddard, for her love, sacrifice, and encouragement in this effort and support towards its completion.

This book would not be possible had it not be for cooperation and assistance of Molly Kodner at the Missouri History Museum Library and Research Center in St. Louis, Missouri.

I would also like to thank and acknowledge the contributions and efforts of: Charles M. Province, author, *Patton's Third Army* (and many others), for his sage advice and guidance; Michael Haynes, artist, for the use of his beautiful painting of the scene of recruitment at Ft. Kaskaskia; Jaime Bourassa, Missouri History Museum Library and Research Center; Katherine Kominis, Howard Gotlieb Archival Research Center, Boston University; Amanda S. Vaughan and Zachary Chappuies of the Maumee Valley Historical Society; Dan Woodward, Fort Meigs: *Ohio's War of 1812 Battlefield*; Miriam Touba, Patricia D. Klingenstein Library, The New-York Historical Society; Janet Bloom, William L. Clements Library, University of Michigan; Dave Sullivan, The Company of Military Historians; and Arthur House Jr., Chamisa Redmond, Tomeka Myers and Amber R. Paranick at the Library of Congress.

A special "thank you" is extended to Deena Stoddard for proofreading and pointing out punctuation and grammatical errors. She helped make the use of capitalization and punctuation more consistent. Any remaining errors are the oversight of the editor.

Introduction to the Autobiography Manuscript
of
Major Amos Stoddard

This autobiography manuscript, reluctantly written by Major Amos Stoddard in 1812 after apparent lengthy encouragement from an unknown friend, is a unique and revealing piece of American history and biography. In it, Amos Stoddard provides us a glimpse of his family and his ancestry, an account of himself as a sixteen–year–old boy enlisting in the Massachusetts militia with the intention of becoming a soldier, a detailed description of his life as a revolutionary soldier, and his post–war efforts at what he refers to as placing himself, "on a course of business adapted to my means and capacity, and endeavor to become, what is called, settled in life."

While others also penned versions of their exploits and experiences during the American Revolution, some did so with the intended purpose to defend their honor or to portray their feats and exertions in the most favorable light. Amos Stoddard, who started in the Revolutionary Army as a private in the infantry and later become attached to the artillery as a matross, a rank below gunner, responsible for loading and sponging the guns, provides us a simple account of events "in which I had been a humble actor." Major Stoddard makes no effort to aggrandize his role. In fact, Amos Stoddard is so modest and unassuming during his entire life that his name is more of a footnote in the events of history in which he was a participant —even those in which he played a significant role.

Amos Stoddard, the first child of Anthony and Phebe Stoddard, was born on October 26, 1762 in Woodbury, Connecticut. Soon after his birth his parents removed to Lanesborough, Massachusetts. In 1769 his father sold his property in Lanesborough and bought a farm 12 miles south in Lenox, Massachusetts where Amos grew up. As a boy, he discovered he possessed a powerful memory —and a dislike for farming. While in school he responded positively to the praise of his schoolmaster which motivated him towards learning and helped set his future course in life.

At the age of 16, Amos enlisted in the Massachusetts militia at Lenox in July 1779 and mustered in at West Point, New York. After serving for four months in the 12th Massachusetts Regiment of Infantry, Amos transferred into Col. Crane's Regiment, 3rd Continental Regiment of Artillery, Capt. Henry Burbeck's Company, in November 1779. He grew to know Henry Burbeck as a friend and mentor for the rest of his life, and would serve under him again during a time of peace.

Amos later transferred into Col. John Lamb's Regiment, 2nd Continental Regiment of Artillery, Capt. Joseph Savage's Company, where he served under the overall command of Major General Marquis de Lafayette during the Southern Campaign of 1781. Amos was discharged at the end of the war in the spring of 1783 while stationed at West Point, New York.

After the war, Amos became employed as a school master at Lenox before being retained as a clerk by Charles Cushing, the Clerk of the Supreme Judicial Court of Massachusetts, in Boston in 1784. He later studied law with Judge Seth Padelford of Taunton, Massachusetts and was accepted to practice law in the Supreme Judicial Court of Massachusetts in February 1796. He them moved to Hallowell, Massachusetts (today Maine) and started a law practice. On May 28, 1798 his name was submitted to the United States Senate by President John Adams and on June 4, 1798 he was commissioned as a Captain in the 2nd Regiment of Artillerists and Engineers.[1, 2]

While there are depictions of Capt. Amos Stoddard in some historical and ceremonial drawings and paintings associated with the transfer of the Upper Louisiana in 1804, there are no known paintings or drawings of him from real life. This unpretentious trait was largely true for the Stoddard family as a whole. The only portrait of a Stoddard ancestor of Amos Stoddard known to exist is of Anthony Stoddard from the beginning of the 18th century. The problem is there were two Stoddard men named Anthony Stoddard —both born less than two months apart in the same year (1678) and both of whom graduated Harvard College in the same year (1697). They were first cousins. One is Reverend Anthony Stoddard of Woodbury, Connecticut, son of Solomon Stoddard and a direct ancestor of Amos Stoddard; The other is Judge Anthony Stoddard, Esq. of Boston, Massachusetts, son of Simeon Stoddard, the younger brother of Solomon Stoddard.[3, 4] The portrait, however, is that of Judge Anthony Stoddard of Boston (1678–1748), and not that of Rev. Anthony Stoddard (1678–1760) the great–grandfather of Major Amos Stoddard.[5]

This introduction is intended to provide a more complete portrayal of Amos Stoddard's life than is covered in his partial and incomplete autobiography. Major Stoddard stated in the first paragraph of that manuscript: "...I will fulfill what I owe to friendship, and commit to your care a short but faithful narrative of my life." This editor, from his sense of ancestral duty, provides you his faithful narrative of what was discovered from his research regarding the life and times of Amos Stoddard. The editor uses many excerpts of letters and correspondence from the period to tell the story and refrains (as much as possible) from presenting his own opinion. The introduction does not read like a novel. The editor has primarily taken many different (and scattered) bits and pieces of information and weaves them together in an attempt to provide the reader historical knowledge and a better understanding of Amos Stoddard and the life he led. The introduction has covered nearly very year of the life of Amos Stoddard since he first joined the Continental Army in July 1779 until his death in May 1813 —some years in more detail than others. It represents the most complete biography on Major Amos Stoddard to date.

I. How the Autobiography Manuscript was Discovered

An explanation of how the original, handwritten manuscript made its way into this publication is a worthy starting point in this introduction of its author —the subject of this section. The first knowledge of the existence of the autobiography manuscript of Amos Stoddard by this editor came about completely by coincidence. This editor was researching family genealogy unrelated to Amos Stoddard when he stumbled across a repository of documents relating to Amos Stoddard that were held in the Missouri Historical Museum archives. One item in that collection that caught his attention was described as "Genealogies of the Stoddard family." So, this editor requested photocopies of those items in the collection which he felt might provide answers and clarifications to gaps in his family history, as well as a copy of the Amos Stoddard autobiography manuscript.

Upon receiving the copies he found the items identified as Stoddard family genealogy concerned another related family and were not particularly useful except to members of that collateral family line. However, the copy of the Amos Stoddard autobiography manuscript looked extremely interesting. There was only one problem: it was not transcribed. It consisted of roughly sixty pages of 18th century handwriting that was difficult to read in its photocopy form and extremely hard to decipher due to its ancient writing style. However, the decision was taken: the only way to unlock the story within was to transcribe it. This required going over each page, every sentence, each word, and sometimes every letter, in a slow and methodical yet determined manner. And so the task began.

Within a few weeks, as each page was completed and the testimony emerged, the fascinating narrative slowly began to reveal itself. The deciphering process began to go more quickly as the writing style became more familiar. Within a few months the full account had unfolded. What was disclosed was a compelling, personal, eyewitness account to historical events that, in the opinion of this editor, necessitated that the material should indeed be made available to relatives, researchers, academics and students. Hence, the course was set for its publication.

The truth is the autobiography manuscript (or at least an excerpt of it) was previously published by William Cothren in his book *History of Ancient Woodbury…Volume I* in 1854. Mr. Cothren provides rather lengthy "sketches" of Major Amos Stoddard and his second cousin, Colonel Henry Stoddard (1788–1869) in this volume.[6] Within the sketch of Major Amos Stoddard, Cothren uses sections of Amos Stoddard's actual autobiography manuscript text. Regarding the sketch on Major Amos Stoddard, Mr. Cothren says:

> *"The foregoing sketch has been compiled from copious minutes kindly furnished the author by Col. Henry Stoddard, of Dayton Ohio. He obtained them from the papers of Major Stoddard, which came into his possession after much inquiry for them for many years. His military chest, containing these papers, shamefully mutilated, and many of them partially destroyed, was found at the house of a nephew of his in Mahoning county, Ohio. Others have been found among the papers of the late Judge Lawless, of St. Louis, Mo. Many of them, are of much historic value, and are to be sent to an appropriate place for preservation, by Col. Stoddard."[7]*

It is most likely that the military chest and papers were found at the home of Amos' nephew, Daniel Stoddard (1808–1850), in Boardman, Mahoning County, Ohio. Daniel was the son of Amos' youngest brother, Eliakim Stoddard (1784–1815), who married Sally Evitts of Kent, Connecticut in 1807, and who died in Boardman, Ohio at age 31 in December 1815.[8] [9] Henry Stoddard was not unfamiliar with Daniel Stoddard [10] or his wife Margaret.[11]

Major Amos Stoddard died at the siege of Fort Meigs on May 11, 1813 during the War of 1812. Major Amos Stoddard had been stationed in Pittsburgh, Pennsylvania in September 1812 until January 1813. It is approximately 65 miles from Pittsburgh to Boardman. It is known Major Stoddard passed through the Boardman area on his way to Cleveland (and ultimately to Fort Meigs) and saw his youngest brother Eliakim five months before his tragic death, as evidenced in an excerpt of a letter Amos' brother Eliakim wrote to their mother, Phebe Benham, then living in Camden, New York, on March 28, 1813:

> "Dear Mother: —I received your letter of December last in a few days after date, and I also received yours of March 5 yesterday. I was in hope of receiving a letter from Amos before I wrote you; but I have none. He was through this town on the 8th of January last, on his way to the army. I met him, and accompanied him four miles. He did not come to my habitation; his business and great haste would not admit of it, as the time was then out he was to be there. He reached the Miami of the Lake just the instant that Gen. Winchester was defeated at Frenchtown, on the River Raisin, between 20 and 30 miles distant from the Rapids, so that they could distinctly hear the cannon. I heard from him the first of this month, through a young man of my acquaintance, who returned from the army, and informed me that he was well acquainted with Amos, and that he was as fine an officer as there was in the army. He told me Gen. Harrison regarded him as a wise counselor." [12]

This letter would seem to indicate that Major Stoddard arrived at the Maumee River on or about January 18, 1812 —about the same time that General Harrison arrived at the rapids and made his encampment there.

While Eliakim knew his brother was headed into harm's way, he probably didn't realize at the time that this brief four mile encounter with him was going to be the last time he would ever see his brother Amos.

Later, after learning of the death of his brother at Fort Meigs, Eliakim wrote to the military post inquiring about Amos' personal effects. His letter received a reply from Capt. Eleazor Darby (E.D.) Woods on June 30, 1813. Capt. Woods stated that his personal possessions were in the hands of the commanding officer (at the time, Brigadier General Green Clay of Kentucky) and would be sold at auction and that the proceeds would be held and turned over to the administrator of the estate. While this may sound cruel today, it was the common practice at the time as it was a way of recycling needed clothing and equipment for the Army. It was also easier to hold and transfer money than it was to hold or send personal items. Capt. Wood reported he had already collected $328. He went on to say, "I have likewise a watch and a spye glass in my possession belonging to the estate both of which will be sold with the other effects and accounted for." In a postscript, he wrote, "P.S. You can visit this post with perfect safety. There are no Indians in the neighborhood, a very few at all events. E. D. W." [13] This was actually rather bad advice —as there was a second attempt by the British and the Indians to capture Fort Meigs between July 20 and 27, 1813.[14]

It is also known that Amos' cousin, Asa Stoddard (1762–1842), father of the aforementioned Henry Stoddard, arrived at Fort Meigs with supplies on June 13, 1813.[15] Asa Stoddard (the son of Amos' uncle Israel) and Amos were the same age.[16][17] However, had Asa Stoddard taken possession of Amos' military trunk at Fort Meigs, his son Henry would not have spent the next 35 years looking for it.

In any case, the military chest belonging to Major Stoddard was likely given to his brother Eliakim Stoddard by the Army, as he was the closest relative, and it was later found by Henry Stoddard at the home of Eliakim's son Daniel in Boardman, Ohio after his death in 1850. The trunk may even have been retrieved by Amos' brother Eliakim at Fort Fayette in Pittsburgh —as it is possible that the trunk did not go on to Cleveland and Fort Meigs in January 1813 with Amos: the priority at the time was the artillery train and supplies.

It also appears that Henry Stoddard never got around to providing the manuscript "to an appropriate place for preservation." Somehow, the autobiography manuscript of Major Amos Stoddard made its way to sisters Emmeline C. Smith (Mrs. J. Edward Agenbroad) and Ellen M. Smith of Dayton, Ohio, the great–granddaughters of Henry Stoddard. Those ladies donated the autobiography manuscript to the Missouri Historical Society for preservation in September 1958.[18][19] The manuscript must have been passed to them through their father and mother, Fowler and Ellen Smith. Fowler Stoddard Smith was the son of Samuel B. Smith and Eliza Jane Stoddard,[20][21] the daughter of Henry Stoddard. Today, the autobiography manuscript can be found within the *Amos Stoddard Papers* collection of the Missouri History Museum in St. Louis.

There were yet even more surprises encountered in the process of publishing this autobiography manuscript in its entirety for the first time in over 200 years. While researching the archives of Yale University Library catalog, the editor came across a document on microfilm that by its description sounded exactly like the autobiography manuscript:

> Notes: *Microfilm. New Haven, Connecticut, Yale University Library. 1946.*
>
> *Originals in the possession of Henry Holt & Co.*
>
> Summary: *The papers consist of a typescript of an incomplete text of the autobiography of Amos Stoddard. In the seventy–five pages, Stoddard describes his military service in the Revolutionary War and during Shays' Rebellion and also describes a trip to England.*

The questions that began to be formulated in this editor's mind were: What exactly was this? Was this a copy of the manuscript? Was this the "copious minutes" provided by Henry Stoddard to William Cothren? The microfilm was ordered, loaded into a film reader, and reviewed. What was revealed came as a real surprise: the archive document on microfilm in the Yale University Library collection was yet another transcription of the original Amos Stoddard autobiography manuscript!

An attempt was made to contact Macmillan Publishers Company (the current name of the former publishing company, Henry Holt & Co.) to determine if they indeed possessed the original, typed transcription found on microfilm at Yale Library —and more importantly —to try to determine from where and from whom this transcription had originated. The response was that they had "moved and consolidated many times over the years" and they did not know anything about it. The only clue is a handwritten note on the top of the first page of the typescript, which reads:

> *"Armenal,*
> *Pages 16 to 30 Cover the campaign by Lafayette against Cornwallis & the siege & surrender at Yorktown.*
> *Fowler"*

It is most likely that "Fowler" was Fowler S. Smith (1876–1947), the son of Eliza Jane Stoddard Smith (1843–1928) who was the daughter of the aforementioned Henry Stoddard. Further, it is most likely that "Armenal" was Armenal Wood Patterson (1895–1962),[22] the daughter of Anna Stoddard Wood (1872–1961)[23] and granddaughter of John W. Stoddard (1837–1917) of Dayton, Ohio[24] who was the son of Henry Stoddard and the brother of Eliza Jane Stoddard. In other words, Fowler S. Smith and Anna Stoddard Wood were first cousins. It appears Fowler sent the typed transcript to his cousin's daughter, Armenal, who likely expressed an interest in it.

While it is only wild speculation, it seems Armenal Wood Patterson was probably the one who sent the typescript copy provided to her by Fowler Smith to Henry Holt & Company in the hope and desire for it to be published. Nothing was apparently done with it, and in 1946 it was put onto microfilm for preservation. The original typescript was probably lost or destroyed over the years. It can further be speculated that the typed version was probably produced by Fowler S. Smith around the time typewriters became widely available and affordable circa 1920.

This typescript from film was cross–referenced against this editor's transcription, and while there were mistakes and errors in both versions, the result is that the reconciliation of the two versions has provided for the best possible transcription for this publication. Indeed, the autobiography manuscript of Major Amos Stoddard has finally been brought out of the shadows of archive folders and microfilm obscurity and made available to family members, historians, researchers and history aficionados.

Besides the Major Amos Stoddard autobiography manuscript, there are numerous other papers related to Major Amos Stoddard, primarily consisting of letters and documents from the period 1803–1805, that make up the bulk of the *Amos Stoddard Papers* collection of the Missouri History Museum, which were apparently once in the possession of Col. Henry Stoddard. These documents were probably also found in his military chest or "among the papers of the late Judge Lawless, of St. Louis, Mo." Judge Luke E. Lawless of St. Louis represented some of the entitled heirs of Amos Stoddard after his death in the matter of property.[25] However, the Missouri Historical Museum has reported no record as to who donated these papers, or even when they were donated to the Missouri Historical Society.

A chronicle of the transcriptions of some of these papers and documents involving Amos Stoddard's role in the transfer of the Upper Louisiana territory from Spain to France, and from France to the United States, was published in St. Louis in 1935 by the Missouri Historical Society in a pamphlet titled, *Glimpses of the Past*. That essay begins with the transcript of a letter Capt. Amos Stoddard received, dated November 7, 1803, in which he is notified and ordered by Secretary of War Henry Dearborn (who served eight years in that capacity during the Jefferson Administration) that he is "hereby authorized" to take possession of the Upper Louisiana.[26] The publication ends with a letter, dated September 30, 1804, from Amos Stoddard to Charles Gratiot, a prominent fur trader and "President of the Committee of St. Lewis," a civilian group of Louisianans. In this letter, Amos (in his typical modest manner) expresses his thanks to the committee for their approval of his official conduct but gives credit to his subordinates and the distinguished citizens of Louisiana for their contributions.[27] Captain Amos Stoddard was appointed the first civil commandant of the Upper Louisiana for the government of the United States on January 24, 1804 and served in that capacity from March 10, 1804 until September 30, 1804, after the acquisition of the territory from France by the Jefferson Administration in what is known as "The Louisiana Purchase."

Henry Stoddard is a particularly interesting and important kinsman when it comes to telling the story of Amos Stoddard and the autobiography manuscript. He should be credited with finding, retrieving, and ultimately preserving these valuable documents for posterity.

Henry was the only son born to Asa Stoddard and Armenal Prindle in Woodbury, Connecticut.[28] Asa Stoddard, Amos' cousin, was the son of Israel Stoddard and Elizabeth Reed Stoddard. Amos' aunt Elizabeth was his mother's sister, and his uncle Israel was his father's brother. Asa's sister (and Henry Stoddard's aunt), Elizabeth Stoddard, married Taylor Sherman. They had a son, Charles Robert Sherman, who then married Mary Hoyt. The sixth child born during that marriage was William Tecumseh Sherman, the famed Civil War general.[29] Henry Stoddard, Major Amos Stoddard, and the Stoddard family are mentioned in the General's autobiography published in 1875.[30]

Henry Stoddard first married Harriett L. Patterson. She died leaving him one son, Asa P. Stoddard. He then married Susan C. Williams, with whom he had several more children. One of their sons was John Williams Stoddard, who started the Stoddard Manufacturing Company in Dayton, OH.[31] John Williams Stoddard first became wealthy producing farm equipment. His company then manufactured bicycles at the end of the 19th century, but he finally abandoned both farm equipment and bicycles, and the Stoddard Manufacturing Company became the manufacturer of luxury automobiles under the brand name "Stoddard–Dayton" in the early 1900s.[32]

Henry Stoddard became a successful lawyer after being admitted to the bar at Litchfield County, Connecticut in 1815. He opened a law practice in Kent, but he soon left to seek his fortune in the "far west," arriving in Dayton, Ohio around 1818. About 1825, Henry learned of a large estate of land that was left by the tragic death of his second cousin, Major Amos Stoddard, from those relatives entitled to inherit it.[33] Over the next twenty–five years, he, and later with the assistance of his son Asa P. Stoddard, also now a lawyer, pursued the recovery of this land, located along the Missouri River, which had over the years significantly increased in value. These legal cases and challenges were long and arduous and went all the way to the United States Supreme Court where Henry Stoddard was ultimately successful.[34]

The only negative aspect of these victories in the U.S. Supreme Court by Henry and Asa P. Stoddard was the fact of some apparent fraud that was perpetrated by them on their relatives. The method of acquiring the rights to the land in a trust from these other entitled Stoddard relatives was apparently not entirely altruistic. He and his son provided misleading estimates of the value of the land to these entitled Stoddard relatives.[35] While some of them were indeed aged, and probably needed whatever money they could get at the time, and whereas Henry had already invested a significant amount his own money and valuable time pursuing this legal case on their behalf, with no guarantee of securing the property for them, it was disingenuous of him to apparently deceive their relatives about the current value of the land. However, the many legal cases and challenges are so long and complex that only a mention of them, without prejudice, can be made.

II. Hereditary and Genealogical Influences

To write a biography in an attempt to get to know Amos Stoddard, an examination of his family and ancestral influences are essential. Amos tells us that those relatives who came before him formed a benchmark for him in his life: "When young, I prided myself on my ancestry, and used to exclaim to my schoolfellows, "Don't you know, that I have the blood of the Stoddard's in me!" In 1787, after being embarrassed by the Reverend Ephraim Judson for not making a more impressive representation of himself, Amos demonstrated an inclination to measure his behavior against that of his predecessors. He relates that as time went by while he was based in Taunton, Massachusetts, and as he got to know Reverend Judson better, "I endeavored to convince him by my conduct, that I was not unworthy of the name I bore." Therefore, a cursory examination of the ancestry of Amos Stoddard is required in order to provide an account of the legacy that Amos found important to mirror in his own life.

There is a considerable recording of the life of Amos' great–grandfather, the Reverend Anthony Stoddard (1678–1760) of Woodbury, Connecticut, and his great–great–grandfather, the Reverend Solomon Stoddard (1643–1729) of Northampton, Massachusetts. Both were important and influential men in their respective and growing colonies. There is also a wealth of knowledge about Reverend Solomon Stoddard's father, Anthony Stoddard (1606–1687) of Boston, Massachusetts, the first Stoddard to arrive in America. The story of the family history is based on information that is well–researched and known.

Little information is available about Amos' grandfather Eliakim (son of Reverend Anthony Stoddard), or Amos' father Anthony (son of Eliakim). They were simple farmers who did not make a significant mark in the world. Therefore, little detail can be shed on their individual lives.

Both Reverend Solomon Stoddard and his son Reverend Anthony Stoddard greatly benefited from their Harvard College educations. However, the opportunity for this type of higher education was apparently not afforded to Reverend Anthony's sons. There is no record of any of Reverend Anthony's sons benefiting from a university education. It wasn't because Reverend Anthony Stoddard couldn't afford it —he was one the wealthiest men in Woodbury, Connecticut at the time. At least he was wealthy and prosperous in terms of the amount of property he owned and the amount of land he could farm.[36]

Reverend Anthony Stoddard was a 1697 graduate of Harvard College in Cambridge, Massachusetts,[37] and in September 1738 he was elected a succeeding trustee of Yale University, in New Haven, Connecticut, a position he held until his death in 1760.[38] The reason for not sending any of his sons to his alma mater, or to nearby Yale University, where he served as a trustee, is not known. It is unimaginable that Reverend Anthony did not at least consider a Harvard or Yale education for his sons. It simply might have been that his sons, especially Amos' grandfather Eliakim, did not demonstrate the capacity or inclination for higher education. It is possible Eliakim preferred an occupation of muscular endeavors and working the land rather than studying books and writing.

Regarding Amos' father, Anthony Stoddard, and his lack of a secondary education, it can be considered that his father Eliakim died in 1749, at the age of 44, before most of his sons came of age. Amos' father Anthony was just 15 years old at the time. Since nearly all of Eliakim's sons were minors at the time of his death (the oldest, John Stoddard, was 19 years old), we will never know whether he intended for his sons to receive university educations or not. In any case, none are known to have graduated from Yale, Harvard or any other college.

Israel, the second son of Eliakim, and two years older than Amos' father Anthony, was Amos' uncle. He was also known as Dr. Israel Stoddard. In a short biography of him it was said that he, "prepared himself for the practice of medicine, and settled in Judea (now Washington, Connecticut, but then a parish of Woodbury). He was a jovial, and a good–natured man, somewhat addicted to free–living, and died young." [39] Where he studied medicine, or whether he received a formal education, has not been determined. He and Amos' father Anthony married sisters (Israel married Elizabeth Reed on the July 4, 1759, and Anthony married her sister Phebe —presumably in the next year although the date has not been determined), and therefore the men and families were likely closer than they were with other members of the family. In fact, Amos in his autobiography mistakenly names Israel as his grandfather.

In any case, neither of these two Stoddard men, Eliakim nor his son Anthony, pursued education as a means of extraditing themselves from physical labor, and they were apparently happy and satisfied with being patrons of husbandry.

The following sections break up the descendant relationships to Major Amos Stoddard in order to make his genealogical connection to them more convenient to the reader.

Anthony Stoddard (1606–1687)

Anthony Stoddard was the first of this family to arrive on the North American continent from England. Anthony was born in the year 1606 and was baptized at the church of St. Michael le Querne, a parish of London,[40] but the family origins can be traced back to Rushton Spencer, Staffordshire, England, a rural farming community approximately 160 miles northwest of London.[41] Anthony had a brother, William. The two brothers were members of the Skinners Guild, founded in 1327, one of twelve merchant guilds in the City of London.

Anthony and William's father's name was Anthony (or Antonie) and his brother's name was William — which can be very confusing to their posterity. They also had a brother Francis. These three brothers were also all members of the Skinners Company, with William being a wealthy merchant and an especially prominent member of the Guild.[42]

When Anthony decided to leave London and start a new life in the Massachusetts Bay Colony in 1639, he sailed on the ship Endemion from London. This was a merchant ship and not a passenger ship. In the Port Book, Anthony had trading goods and his passage booked on this ship scheduled to depart London February 22, 1639. Perhaps intending to set–up a merchant trading shop in the colony he was bringing with him the prerequisite trading goods? [43]

There were at least three distinctly different Stoddard men that arrived in the English colonies in North America around the same period of time: a John Stodder of Hingham, Massachusetts Bay Colony, arrived in 1638; [44] a John Stoddard of Wethersfield, Colony of Connecticut, around 1638–9; [45] and Anthony Stoddard of Boston, Massachusetts Bay Colony, arrived in 1639, from whom Major Amos Stoddard descended.[46] There has never been any concrete evidence found of a family connection between these three Stoddard men or of their common origins back in England. All three families, however, appear to have made claim to the same coat of arms originally granted to a George Stoddard, a wealthy merchant of London, England, in the 16th century. A coat of arms granted to a man named Stoddard can only be used by his descendants. Therefore, it is possible these men were related in what Amos Stoddard refers to as "a collateral branch." A collateral branch of family is a relation by blood but not through a direct line of ancestry.

Anthony Stoddard, in a short period of time, became one of the most important men in the Massachusetts Bay Colony. He was admitted a citizen of Boston on August 26, 1639 and admitted to the church on September 28, 1639. In May 1640 he took the oath of allegiance to the colony and became a freeman. This gave him the right to open his trading shop. He was frequently referred to as "Mr." Stoddard in early colony records, a title only bestowed on men of wealth and prestige.[47]

It has been speculated that Anthony may have been married prior to leaving London, but there has never been any evidence found of such a marriage. He did, however, soon after arriving in Boston, marry into the family of Emmanuel Downing through his marriage to Mary Downing.[48] Mary's mother was Anne Ware, the daughter of Sir James Ware, of Dublin, Ireland. The year after Anne's death in 1621, her father married Lucy Winthrop, the sister of John Winthrop, who became Governor of the Massachusetts Bay Colony. Emmanuel Downing brought his family to Massachusetts in 1638. Mary's half–brother, George Downing (his mother was Lucy Winthrop), graduated from the first class of Harvard College in 1642.[49] He returned to England in 1645, and on July 1, 1663 he was made 1st Baronet of East Hatley in the County of Cambridge by King Charles II, hence he became known as Sir George Downing. Downing Street in London is named after him.[50]

The exact date of the union between Anthony Stoddard and Mary Downing is not known, but their first child, Benjamin, was born in August 1640.[51] This marriage alone was evidence of the astronomical rise in prominence Anthony had attained in the colony. He not only quickly became a wealthy merchant of Boston, but he became politically active and served the colony as constable, recorder, selectman, and representative to the General Court during his life.

Mary Downing Stoddard died in 1647, likely from an influenza epidemic. They had three sons together: Benjamin, who died shortly after birth; Solomon, born in September 1643 (who will be covered more in this section); and Sampson (1645–1698).[52]

Anthony next married Barbara Clapp Weld, the widow of Capt. Joseph Weld of Roxbury, soon after the death of Mary. In those days, remarriage after the loss of a wife was deemed a practical necessity, especially when young children required care. Barbara also had three young children of her own from her marriage with Capt. Weld. She inherited a sizable estate upon the death of her husband which she was able to use to encourage the marriage. They had five children together but three of the children died young. His wife Barbara died in April 1655.[53]

Anthony then married Christian Eyre with whom he had nine more children before she passed in 1683. He then married for the fourth and last time to Mary Symmes. They had no children. Anthony died in March 1687, while his wife Mary lived until the year 1710.[54]

Anthony Stoddard created a very prosperous beginning in America for his children and his posterity. He fathered 17 children, of which nine lived to share in his estate upon his death.[55] He left a legacy of risk taking, hard work, and public service. One hundred years after his death, and five generations later, his descendant, Amos Stoddard, knew the exact location where Anthony Stoddard's old wooded shop and home once stood in the merchant district of Boston —and yet he never knew his own grandfather or accurately recalled his name.

Anthony's oldest surviving son, Solomon, a graduate of Harvard College with a master's degree in divinity, who served as the university's first librarian, went on to become arguably the most influential Congregationalist minister of his time in the Massachusetts Bay Colony. Solomon's sons Anthony and John became prominent and important men of their generation. This was quite a start in the new world of America and an exceptional accomplishment for a family that came from humble and meager beginnings as tenant farmers just a few generations earlier in Rushton Spencer, Staffordshire, England.

Reverend Solomon Stoddard (1643–1729)

Solomon Stoddard was the oldest living son of Anthony Stoddard. In 1653, Solomon and his step–brother, Daniel Weld, became boarding students of Elijah Corlet in Cambridge. Master Corlet, educated at Lincoln College, Oxford, England, was perhaps the most eminent schoolmaster in the colony.[56] Solomon, at the age of 15, entered Harvard College in 1658. He received his undergraduate degree in June 1662, and in the fall he entered the School of Divinity.[57] He received his master's degree in divinity in August 1665. On March 27, 1667, Solomon was appointed the first librarian of Harvard, a position he held for several years.[58]

Apparently, Solomon's health was stretched from his years of intensive study, and he traveled to Barbados, where he remained for some time preaching to religious dissenters on the island. The exact years of this trip are unclear, but it might have been between the time he graduated Harvard College in 1665 and the time he was appointed librarian in 1667. There would not have been sufficient time for such travel between his appointment as the university librarian in 1667 and his appointment as church minister in 1669 —unless he only served as librarian for a very short period of time.[59]

Reverend Eleazar Mather, minister of the Congregational Church at Northampton (Massachusetts Bay Colony), after serving as minister just 11 years, suddenly died at the age of 32 in July 1669.[60] The church leaders immediately went looking for a replacement. In those days, when a church minister died, after the town had made a considerable investment in him, and leaving a large extent of land, a house, and a widow of marriageable age, it was nearly a custom to seek a young bachelor to take his place. They came to Boston seeking a replacement, and a local minister recommended Solomon Stoddard as the most qualified candidate available. Apparently Solomon was about to take a trip to England —in fact his belonging were already on-board the ship when the church committee approached him. He was persuaded to accept their offer and immediately cancelled his trip. Fate has a unique way of intervening when it is least expected.

He began to preach on a trial basis in Northampton in late 1669, and on March 4, 1670 he was elected to become their minister, although he was not constituted as such until September 11, 1672. He also married the deceased preacher's widow, Esther Warham Mather (1644–1736), in March 1670.[61]

Reverend Solomon Stoddard, this eldest son of Anthony Stoddard, thus began his nearly 60 year reign as the leader of the church in Northampton, being only its second minister. Northampton was considered "the frontier" in those days, and its population could still be counted in the hundreds. Reverend Stoddard went on became arguably the most influential man in the Connecticut River Valley of western Massachusetts, and was well–known and respected throughout the Massachusetts colony for nearly a half century.[62] His power amongst the people became so great that his critics referred to him as "Pope Stoddard." This reference had a negative connotation at the time by associating him with the Catholic Church.

Amos Stoddard already provides us a descriptive biography of his great–great–grandfather within his autobiography. He was a man of tall stature and unusual piety and ability, and he commanded the respect, confidence and esteem of the people. He was a leader among the clergy of the province.[63][64] Reverend Benjamin Colman, from a sermon given at Harvard University commencement day, which was printed in the Boston Weekly News–Letter, No. 112, February 20, 1729, said of him:

> *"THE most in the Town have been born & bro't up under his Ministry; and scarce any Minister was more reverenc'd and belov'd by his People....HE injoy'd a great measure of Health, and was seldom taken off from his beloved Work by Sickness. His Stature was something taller then the common Size, his Countenance comely, his Presence venerable; his whole Look and Behaviour such as gave those who convers'd with him, occasion to say of him, as the Woman of the Prophet, I perceive that this is a holy Man of God."*[65][66]

While the ecclesiastical influence of Reverend Solomon Stoddard and his impact on religious theology and church doctrine is far too great for this sketch, it is fair to say that Reverend Solomon's positions on church membership, known as the Half–Way Covenant, and on an open admission to Communion, were considered "liberal." His views were even referenced to as "Stoddardeanism." [67] He was opposed by some of the more conservative members of the Synod (the assembly of the Massachusetts clergy) such as Increase Mather, the former minister of the affluent North Church in Boston, a contemporary of Reverend Stoddard, and his son, Cotton Mather, then minister to the congregation at North Church. To make matters even more personal, these two religious men were Reverend Solomon's wife's former father–in–law and brother–in–law! Nevertheless, Reverend Solomon always argued his positions with great civility and dignity.[68]

Upon his death on February 11, 1729, at the age of 86, the position of church minister transitioned smoothly to his grandson, Reverend Jonathan Edwards, perhaps a final indicator of his sage leadership.[69]

Reverend Solomon Stoddard was the father of thirteen children. His second daughter, Esther Stoddard, married Rev. Timothy Edwards. Their fifth child was Jonathan Edwards (1703–1758), who married Sarah Pierpont (1709–1758),[70] whose third child, Esther Edwards (1732–1758), married Rev. Aaron Burr, Sr. (1716–1757), and their only son, Aaron Burr, Jr. (1756–1836), became the third vice–president of the United States.[71] Aaron Burr became infamous for killing his political rival, former secretary of the treasury, Major General Alexander Hamilton, in an illegal duel on July 11, 1804,[72] and for being accused of committing acts against the government of the United States, for which he was arrested and tried for treason but acquitted on September 1, 1807.[73]

Reverend Solomon Stoddard's seventh born, a daughter, Christian Stoddard (1676–1764), married Reverend William Williams (1665–1741). Their son Solomon Williams (1700–1776) had a son they named William. This William Williams (1731–1811) was a Signer of the Declaration of Independence.[74]

The eighth born, Anthony Stoddard, is covered as a continuation of this introduction section. A short biography of his tenth child, John Stoddard (1681–1748), is included as an endnote to the autobiography manuscript.

Reverend Solomon Stoddard is without a doubt one of the most important figures of his time, and within the legacy of the Stoddard family. Through his example, two of his sons, Anthony and John, went on to leave their indelible marks on history.

Reverend Anthony Stoddard (1678–1760)

Anthony Stoddard was the eighth child born to Reverend Solomon Stoddard and Esther Warham Mather Stoddard and the eldest male son. He was born on August 9, 1678 in Northampton, Massachusetts. He graduated from Harvard College in 1697 and afterwards studied divinity with his father in Northampton. Anthony was licensed for the ministry in 1700, and shortly thereafter was asked to come and preach, on a trial basis, at the First Congregational Church in Woodbury, Connecticut after the death of their minister, Reverend Zechariah Walker (1637–1699).[75]

After the trial period, it was voted at a town meeting on August 13, 1700 to make Anthony an offer to be the permanent minister:

> *"At a lawfull Towns–meeting ye 13ᵗʰ of August 1700 in ordr to ye settling of ye Reverend mr Anthony Stoddard amongst us in ye work of ye ministry. And for his encouragemt so to do;"*

They proposed to build him a house:

> *"Wee do also promise, to build him an house here in Woodberry of known Demensions; yt is to say, the Carpenters works & Masons work; hee providing nayles and glass; by building ye sd house, is intended, doors, floures, filling up and playstering and partitions, finishing it as also a well;*

And to provide him lands:

> *"We do also promise to accommodate wth a five and twenty Acre Accommodations Round yt is to say five and twenty Acres of home lott & homelott division, five and twenty Acres of Meadow or lowland; five and twenty Acres of good hill Division, five and twenty Acres of Wood Division. Twelve Acres and an halfe of pasture Division; Foure Acres and an halfe of white–oak–plaine division so Called:"*

Conditions were applied:

> *"The Conditions of this engagement are; That in Case hee, ye sd mr Stoddard, accepts of these or proposalls and engages to lives and Continue wth us in ye Work of ye Ministry six years after ye Date hereof; Then wt is promised as to house and Lands to bee a firm grant to him his Heires and Assigns forever to all intents & purposes wtsoever…"*

And terms were agreed. His home lot in Woodbury was laid out in an area of Woodbury called Foot's Neck. His house was fortified with palisades, a type of log fence, as a defense against sudden Indian attack. His salary was to be paid entirely by provisions. Reverend Anthony Stoddard was ordained at the First Congregational Church in Woodbury, Connecticut on May 27, 1702.[76]

PARSONAGE HOUSE of REV. ANTHONY STODDARD. *Woodbury.*

This house was built in 1702, and was for many years surrounded with palisades as a defence against the Indians

From *History of Ancient Woodbury, Connecticut, Volume I*
William Cothren
1854

Reverend Anthony Stoddard married at least three and possibly four times in his life and fathered twelve children with two wives. He fathered nine children in his first marriage to Prudence Wells (1682–1714) including his fourth child, Eliakim Stoddard (1705–1749), Amos' grandfather. Gideon Stoddard (1714–1780) was the ninth and last child born during that marriage as Prudence died sometime after his birth. Four of the other children from that marriage, including three sons, died during an epidemic in May 1727. This made his son Eliakim, Amos' grandfather, the oldest surviving male.[77]

Abijah Stoddard (1718–1776) was one of three children (and the only son) Reverend Anthony fathered during his second marriage to Mary Sherman (1692[78]–1721).[79] Abijah died in 1776 at Crown Point, New York while serving his country during the American Revolution.[80]

Reverend Anthony's third wife, with whom he had no children, is only known as "Mrs. Hannah, wife of Anthony Stoddard." [81] She died on November 26, 1747 —some 13 years before her husband.

According to William Cothren in his 1879 book of genealogical statistics, there is an "inscription on a monument in the ancient grave–yard at Woodbury, Conn." that reads, "Widow of Rev. Anthony Stoddard, July 29, 1783." [82] There is also a listing of a death in Woodbury on Nov. 16, 1783 for "Anthony Stoddard." [83] However, Reverend Anthony Stoddard died twenty–three years earlier in September 1760. In addition, a headstone lying in the Woodbury South Cemetery, apparently broken, and what can be seen today without disturbing the stone, says, "In Memory of Mrs. Thankfull the wife of Mr. Anthony Stoddard." [84] If Reverend Anthony indeed married a fourth time, her name was likely Thankfull Stoddard. This is highly possible as his wife Hannah died 13 years before him and at his increasing age, and with his prestige, he would probably not have lived alone for that long.

It is worthy at this point to digress into a short but relevant story of Captain Nathan Stoddard, son of the aforementioned Gideon Stoddard, grandson of Reverend Anthony Stoddard, and cousin to Amos Stoddard.

In 1775, Nathan Stoddard enlisted as a private into the 4th Connecticut Regiment. He participated in the Invasion of Canada and the Battle of Quebec during the autumn and winter of 1775 under the command of Colonel Benjamin Hinman. During that time he was captured and taken to Quebec as a prisoner, but with the help of a French woman, he ultimately made his escape —reportedly by swimming the St. Lawrence River. He returned to Woodbury, Connecticut and raised another company for the 8th Connecticut Regiment, under the command of Colonel John Chandler, of which he was appointed Captain. [85] Nathan's brother Anthony and his cousin Eli (son of his uncle Abijah who died at Crown Point) enlisted into his company. Both his brother and cousin were present at Valley Forge during the winter of 1777–8 [86] but Nathan was not.

The 8th Connecticut Regiment and Capt. Nathan Stoddard's Company marched from Woodbury to join Washington's army in Pennsylvania in the fall of 1777. After fierce fighting at the Battle of Germantown on October 4, 1777, Capt. Nathan Stoddard and Ensign John Strong (later, Lt. John Strong, yet another cousin who joined Nathan's Company) went to Woodbury to obtain supplies before returning to action along the Delaware River at Fort Mifflin on Mud Island.[87] There, on November 15, 1777, Captain Nathan Stoddard was killed. He was decapitated by a cannonball. This event was witnessed by Ensign John Strong,[88] who apparently, on frequent occasions, related (somewhat morbidly) that the ball struck his head, cutting it entirely from the body, and that he stood erect, as in life, without a head, before falling.[89]

Private Joseph Plumb Martin, who also served in the 8th Connecticut Regiment, Capt. David Smith's Company,[90] provided an eye–witness account of the events of that very day at Fort Mifflin, in a book written in 1830, *A Narrative of some of the Adventures, Danger and Suffering of a Revolutionary Soldier*. From his account, we can picture the scene while wondering if the "sergeant of the artillery" mentioned in his testimony might not have possibly been the heroic Captain Nathan Stoddard:

> *"Some of our officers endeavored to ascertain how many guns were fired in a minute by the enemy, but it was impossible, the fire was incessant. In the height of the cannonade it was desirable to hoist a signal flag for some of our gallies, that were lying above us [in the Delaware River], to come down to our assistance. The officers inquired who would undertake it; As none appeared willing for some time, I was about to offer my services; I considered it no more exposure of my life than it was to remain where I was; The flagstaff was of easy ascent, being an old ship's mast, having shrouds to the ground, and the round top still remaining. While I was still hesitating, a sergeant of the Artillery offered himself; he accordingly ascended to the round top, pulled down the flag to affix the signal flag to the halyard, upon which the enemy, thinking we had struck, [surrendered] ceased firing in every direction and cheered. "Up with the flag!" was the cry of our officers in every part of the fort. The flags were accordingly hoisted, and the firing was immediately renewed. The sergeant then came down and had not gone half a rod from the foot of the staff, when he was cut in two by a cannon shot. This caused me some serious reflection at the time. He was killed! had I been at the same business I might have been killed; but it might have been otherwise ordered by Divine Providence, —we might have both lived, —I am not predestinarian enough to determine it. The enemy's shot cut us up. I saw five Artillerists belonging to one gun, cut down by a single shot, and I saw men who were stooping to be protected by the works, but not stooping low enough, split like fish to be broiled."* [91]

In addition to the Joseph Plumb Martin recollection, we can also consider the war pension declaration testimony of Deacon Ira Smith, who also served in the 8th Connecticut Regiment, Capt. Jesse Kimball's Company,[92] and who was also witness to events at Fort Mifflin on November 15th, in which he recalls:

> *"[missing text] reference to surrender —and they kept up their fire untill just evening —and there were some killed after we ceased firing among them —Captain Stoddard of the Regular Army and his waiter with one shot. In the following night, our army sent their boats across with muffled oars thro the midst of the British shipping & carried off all that was in the fort —the Artyllermen suffered most tho there was great havoc among the other troops and there was much fewer wounded in proportion —after leaving the fort we lay awhile at the old encampment & from thence we were marchd to valey forge where the Regulars and those whose terms were unexpired wintered and the rest of us were discharged —"* [93]

This version is very similar to the remembrance of Joseph Plumb Martin, and it adds to the distinct possibility that after the flag was lowered and the cannon fire paused, and then the flag was re–hoisted, and the cannon fire resumed again, that it was Captain Nathan Stoddard who was killed —which would make him the officer who bravely climbed the flagpole during the cannonade that day.

The reason for this diversion to a historical account of events indirectly related to Amos Stoddard, in the middle of a short biography of his great–grandfather, is partially to speculate on the possibility of a previously unrecorded heroic act committed by a Stoddard kin, but also to bring to the attention of the reader that all of the progeny of Reverend Anthony Stoddard were distinctly on the Patriot side. Reverend Anthony's son Abijah Stoddard (1718–1776) was the first family member to give his life for the cause of Liberty.[94] His great–grandson Abiram Stoddard (1756–1776) died at Ticonderoga in October of the same year. Nathan Stoddard (1742–1777) died in November 1777.[95] At least nine grandsons (and probably more) served in the Continental Army and fought for the Patriot cause. There were eleven Stoddards at Valley Forge —at least two were directly related to Amos Stoddard while others, such as Orringh Stoddard (1742–1824) of Massachusetts, were likely distant relations. All of Amos' uncles served in some capacity or another during the war. Amos' father left his family to serve at the Battle of Bennington and the Battle of Saratoga in 1777. The military service of uncles and cousins, and their sacrifices, would likely have been known and discussed in his family home. Major Stoddard's life and personality were certainly impacted through the influence of his family as well as the events of his youth. He undoubtedly inherited a strong religious upbringing and a Whig, or Patriot, political viewpoint.

Returning again to the life and times of Reverend Anthony Stoddard, it has been said that his ministry in Woodbury was remarkable for its duration as well as the peace and prosperity which attended it.[96] Under his leadership the ministry was harmonious and prosperous —while other parishes in the colony experienced setbacks and dissention. He was probate clerk for Woodbury for 40 years, and the records of this period are in his own handwriting. He drew up the wills of his parishioners. Yet his ancillary services to his flock never interfered with his higher work as the Lord's ambassador.[97] Reverend Anthony Stoddard served his parishioners faithfully until death.

Reverend Anthony Stoddard passed after two days of illness on September 6, 1760.

It would be hard to summarize the life of so great a man as Reverend Anthony Stoddard better than that provided by Reverend Anson Atwood at the Woodbury bicentennial celebration on July 5, 1859, when he said the following words about Reverend Anthony Stoddard in a speech, *The Early Clergy of ancient Woodbury*:

> *"A part of his name ROMAN [Anthony], but all the rest of him was STODDARD, from the crown of his head to the sole of his foot; and he had a brave, strong Christian heart, that beat full and clear, as it sent out its pulsations through all the channels of the duties of his sacred office. Who was his father? Whence came he? We have the answer. He had an enviable descent, from one of the ablest divines New England had raised on her soil. Solomon Stoddard, of Northampton, Mass., was that father, who had few equals, if any superior, in the ministry of that day. He was of a liberal heart, and he gave to the cause of Christ some large donations. He had a daughter, Esther, much beloved, and he gave her away to be the wife of Rev. Timothy Edwards of East Windsor, Conn., and the mother of the immortal Jonathan Edwards. He had a son, Anthony, equally beloved, and he gave him to Ancient Woodbury."*

"This son honored his parentage. His intellect and furniture of mind were of high order; and one would think from the amount of labor he performed, his mind must have been kept from rusting. He must have had almost a giant's strength, to have, in no unimportant sense, discharged the duties of three professions: that of a pastor, a physician, and a counsellor or judge, while it is said, he neglected no part of his ministry. It was from a necessity of the times that all these labors devolved upon him. It must be remembered, that education was almost with and in the hands of ministers in the early infancy of our colonial State. Hence, they had to do many things that belonged to other professions. To teach school–masters, and to fit them for their work, draw deeds, wills, keep records, and even be judges, in some cases of probate. Many of these burdensome duties pressed upon Stoddard, but he met them cheerfully, manfully devoting soul and body and every energy of his being to the advancement of the best interests of his flock, temporal and eternal, and not without blessed results. A long, prosperous and happy ministry of sixty years crowned his labors. The divine approbations set its seal to his ministry, in permitting him to see almost constant additions to the church through the whole period of his ministry, numbering in all four hundred and seventy–four persons."

"At an advanced age, having served his generation fully, he came to the grave, "as a shock of corn fully ripe," and his record is high." [98]

Amos Stoddard never knew his great–grandfather, Reverend Anthony Stoddard. However, Amos, from his own words, informs us that he was influenced by his ancestors. When, later in his adult life, he met Reverend Ephraim Judson in Taunton, Massachusetts, and when this holy man who knew his great–grandfather tells a story of his strong and powerful character, Amos was reminded that he was a member of this great man's posterity and that he walked in the shadow of his legacy.

In considering the content of Major Stoddard's autobiography, it is apparent that Amos lived a life of austerity, education, self–reliance, and with abiding duty and honor. We never find an incident of boasting or an inclination towards vanity. Instead, we find many of the same personality traits of his forebears: Reverend Anthony Stoddard of Woodbury, Reverend Solomon Stoddard of Northampton, and Anthony Stoddard of Boston.

Eliakim Stoddard (1705–1749)

Little is known about Amos' grandfather, Eliakim Stoddard, the fourth child and second male son born to Reverend Anthony Stoddard and Prudence Wells. He was a simple farmer working the extensive land owned by his father Reverend Anthony. On December 4, 1729 he married Joanna (or Joannah) Curtiss (1708–1768).[99] They had ten children together. There were two sons named Eliakim: the first Eliakim, born 1742, died September 13, 1749, just days before his father's death on September 30; the second Eliakim was born December 11, 1749 after his father's death, and died in Vermont in 1802. Obviously his name was chosen after the loss of his namesake father and brother just prior to his birth.[100] His eldest son was John Stoddard (1730-1795) from whom this editor descends. The next son was Israel (1732-1794), then Anthony (1734-1785), Abiram (1734-1755), and Seth (1744-1828). Eliakim and Joanna's daughters were Joanna (1738 – 1829), Prudence (1740-1829) and Abigail (1747-1803). John Stoddard moved to Watertown shortly after his father's death. Israel became a doctor and resided in Judea (or Washington) in Litchfield County.

Eliakim Stoddard died unexpectedly in 1749. He signed his Last Will and Testament, dated September 25, 1749, just five days before he died. It was probably written by his father, Rev. Anthony Stoddard, who was experienced in such legal matters as the clerk of probate in Woodbury for forty years. Eliakim's wife, Joanna, was appointed the sole executor of his will. She continued to live in the house and raise her children after the sudden death of her husband. However, she remarried as early as 1750 to a Samuel Waller, and removed to Kent, Connecticut with her youngest boys and the girls, where she gave birth to a child, Comfort Waller, in November 1750. Joanna Curtiss Stoddard Waller died in Kent, CT on November 15, 1768.[101]

Eliakim must have been a diligent and hard–working son for his father to deed him land near his own parsonage home and to build him his own house in 1736.[102] At least the land was deeded to him in 1736. The house was likely constructed the year before or the year after and was probably financed by his father.

One of the most remarkable facts of Eliakim Stoddard's legacy is that his original house, built in 1736 on land gifted to him by deed by his father Reverend Anthony Stoddard, is still standing today in Woodbury, Connecticut and is operated as an inn.

However, the commonly accepted historical account of the house, known today as the Curtis House, and that it has been operated as an inn ever since 1754, is based on a marketing myth. An investigation of the facts of its history was conducted. Therefore, a short diversion at this point into an examination of the history of Amos' grandfather's home, on his great–grandfather's property, is warranted.

The details regarding change of ownership of the house after Eliakim's death are a bit murky —primarily because most of the children were still minors at the time of their father's death. The older children chose their own guardians to represent their inheritance interests, while Reverend Anthony was appointed guardian for Prudence and Seth. In the distribution record of the heirs of Eliakim Stoddard, dated March 31, 1752, the house appears to transfer into the name of his son Israel in exchange for the other sons receiving other lands, with the sons' mother, "Joanna Waller," having use of 1/3 of each son's share. This record, using the surname "Waller" for the mother, reflected the fact that Eliakim's widow, Joanna, was already remarried to Samuel Waller by this date. In any case, it appears Israel received sole possession of the house and property through an inheritance consolidation.[103][104] Anthony Stoddard, who was 17 years old at the time of the distibution of the estate, remained in the house at Woodbury. He married Phebe Read in 1760 —the year his grandfather Reverend Anthony Stoddard died. His son Amos was born in his father's house on October 26, 1762, as well as his daughter Phebe in 1764 and son Philo in 1765. Anthony left Woodbury and moved his family to Lanesborough, Massachusetts (then called Framington) in June 1765.

The house remained the ownership of Israel Stoddard until after his death in 1794. The property then reverted into the name of his son Asa Stoddard in 1797.[105] The property was then sold outside of the Stoddard family to William Moseley, by Asa Stoddard, in 1799.[106] For the next 41 years the property had a string of ten different owners, most being owners for only one or two years. This fact in itself seems particularly odd —as people did not buy and sell "homes" at this frequency at the first half of the 19th century.

In researching the string of successive owners, it was discovered that many of these proceeding owners were related by association: many of the subsequent owners of Eliakim Stoddard's home and property between 1799 and 1840 were members of the Woodbury Masonic Lodge —King Solomon's Lodge #7. Many were not just lodge members —but leaders of the Lodge. William Moseley, the first to purchase the property outside the Stoddard family, was the "Worshipful Master" of King Solomon's Lodge #7 in Woodbury, CT in 1798 —the year before he bought the land and the house.[107] Other future owners of the property who were known Masonic Lodge members include Abijah Hatch (ownership 1806–1815),[108] a Junior Warden in 1811, and Nathan Preston (ownership 1820–1836),[109] a Worshipful Master on multiple occasions.[110] Others may have been as well. Abijah Hatch was probably the first Mason known to both own the property [111] and to operate it as a guesthouse for Lodge members and their guests. A Day Book of what appears to be member and guest account records that were kept by Elisha Hatch during 1814–15 has since been found.[112]

The actual record of the first meeting of King Solomon's Lodge #7 in Woodbury was discovered in 1857 and presented in the book *History of Ancient Woodbury, Volume II* published in 1872:

> *"Att a Lodge of Free and Accepted Masons held att the house of Br. Peter Gilchrist in Woodbury, December 27, 1775,*
>
> *Present*
>
> *R.W. Bro. Joseph Perry, Master*
> *" Peter Gilchrist, Senior Warden*
> *" Mitchell Lampson, Junior "*
> *" Delucena Backus, Treasurer*
> *" Aaron Mallory,*
> *" Zimry Moody,"* [113]

Peter Gilchrist was from Scotland and arrived in America circa 1750.[114] He married Damaris Judson June 27, 1752. Nathan Curtiss, the brother of Joanna Curtiss Stoddard, the wife of our subject, Eliakim Stoddard, married Damaris' sister, Esther Judson, on January 21, 1750. Therefore, Peter Gilchrist became related to the Stoddards through marriage.[115] It is clear Peter Gilchrist occupied the house in December 1775 and perhaps as early as 1765 after Anthony left Woodbury with his family to go to Lanesborough, Massachusetts.

Another reference regarding the association of the house to the Freemasons can also be found in *History of Ancient Woodbury, Volume I* published earlier in 1854:

> *"In 1796…In October of this year, David Tallman agreed to prepare a room in Widow Gilchrist's house, and furnish the same for the lodge for twenty–five years, from the first of March 1797, for £114. This was the house now occupied by Lucius H. Foote, as a hotel. Accordingly the lodge convened in this place during the length of time agreed upon, when its meetings were held in Alvah Merriman's building, about 15 years, from which place it removed to the old lodge room for some two years, till the dedication of the present hall in 1839."* [116]

Lucius H. Foote was the owner and operator of an inn located in the former home of Eliakim Stoddard between 1852 and 1857.[117] On March 4, 1856, Lucius Foote, a "Taverner," was found brutally murdered in the horse shed of the nearby Episcopal Church —a crime that had nothing to do with the house or the Lodge.[118]

William Cothren, the author, was redundant on the subject of the location of Lodge meetings in his *Volume II* book published in 1872, but provided some additional information connecting the house with the subsequent string of ownership and its becoming known as "Kelly's Hotel:"

> *"From 1775 to 1797, a period of twenty–two years, the lodge met in an "upper room" or ball–room of Peter Gilchrist's house, now the residence of Geo. B. Lewis, Esq…In Oct. 1796, the lodge voted to remove to a room to be prepared for their use by Bro. David Tallman, in the house of widow Damaris Gilchrist, now the ball–room of Kelly's Hotel."* [119]

These separate statements, found on the same page, appear to relate to different homes and to different owners. However, the home of Peter Gilchrist and the home of "widow Damaris Gilchrist," the residence of George B. Lewis and the site of Kelly's Hotel, were all one and the same location: it was the former house of Eliakim Stoddard.

George B. Lewis was a local Woodbury banker and an owner with Elijah Smith of the property between 1841 and 1852.[120] It is possible he had taken residence in this "hotel" when Cothren's *Volume II* was published in 1872 —although he was not the owner of the property at that time.

"Kelly's Hotel" [121] and "Hotel of F. Kelly's" [122] are names known to have been associated with the property of Eliakim Stoddard. There was praise made at a Masonic celebration in Woodbury in 1865 to "Mr. Kelly's good roasts" [123] and "dear Mrs. Kelly's good dishes." [124] These culinary reviews from Lodge members must refer to Frederick Kelly (and his wife) who was the owner of the former home of Eliakim Stoddard in 1865–66.[125]

It is necessary to conclude and repudiate the commonly accepted story at this time: there is no evidence that this house was ever operated as a hotel or public inn prior to the end of the period agreed on for it to be used for meetings of King Solomon's Lodge for twenty–five years, beginning March 1, 1797 —or until approximately 1822.

Peter Gilchrist died in 1783 [126] while Israel Stoddard died in 1794.[127] Hence, the description of the home as "the house of widow Damaris Gilchrist" in 1796 indicates she remained in the house after her husband's passing (and after the death of Israel Stoddard) and while the "*upper room*" of the house was being used by the Lodge for its meetings. Therefore, it is impossible that the house was ever operated as a public inn or hotel during any of this time.

The expository evidence presented of the association between the home of Eliakim Stoddard and members of King Solomon's Lodge #7 provides a convincing case that the home was used primarily as the personal residence of Peter and Damaris Gilchrist and as a meeting place for King Solomon's Lodge #7, and later, as a meeting place and guesthouse for Lodge members and visiting Masonic guests. It is acknowledged that the house was probably converted into a public hotel or inn sometime around 1823 ("when the lodge removed to a new hall in the building lately occupied by Bros. Chapin and Lathrop where the meetings were held for some fifteen years" [128]) while it continued to serve the needs of Lodge members and their guests.

The first mention of the house ever being used as a public hotel was by William Cothren in 1854, when he mentioned it as being operated as hotel by Lucius H. Foote. It was next seen identified on *Clark's Map of Litchfield County, Connecticut in 1859* [129] as "B. Perkin's Hotel" (although the property was owned by Vincent Judson at the time[130]). The house then became known as "Kelly's Hotel" around 1865, while under the ownership of Frederick Kelly, and was celebrated by members of the Masonic Lodge in that year. Finally, it became known as "Curtis House" at the turn of the 20th century after the nearly thirty–year ownership of Levi Curtis from 1882 until 1909.[131]

The one thing that is abundantly clear is: the house of Eliakim Stoddard was never operated as an inn during any of the time it was owned by the Stoddard family, and it certainly was not operated as an inn by any member of the Stoddard family.

Eliakim Stoddard lived a short life —just 44 years —and he didn't leave us a wealth of information and knowledge about his life. What he did leave his posterity is an ancestral home with an interesting and historical past that still stands today (2016) and should still be standing in its 300th year.

While there is no evidence that Israel Stoddard nor any of Eliakim's sons were members of the King Solomon's Lodge #7 in Woodbury, or any other Masonic Lodge, we do know that Amos Stoddard was a founding member of the Kennebeck Lodge #5 Ancient Free and Accepted Masons (A.F. & A.M) in Hallowell, Maine (then Massachusetts). He joined at their first meeting on May 2, 1796. Amos Stoddard embraced freemasonry principles and wrote and spoke eloquently on them. He delivered "A Masonic Address" to the worshipful master, officers and fellow brethren at the St. John's Day festival in Hallowell on June 24, 1797. His address was so well received it was printed by a fellow brother, Howard S. Robinson. Whether Amos knew his grandfather's house was being used to host Masonic Lodge meetings in Woodbury is unknown.

Anthony Stoddard (1734–1785)

Anthony Stoddard, Amos' father, had to grow up quickly due to the early death of his father at the age of 44 in 1749. Anthony was just 15 years old at the time. Anthony chose his mother's brother, Nathan Curtiss, to represent his interests as his guardian, while his brother Israel chose his grandfather Rev. Anthony Stoddard as his.

On March 31, 1752, when Anthony was still only 17, the distribution of the estate was conducted. Anthony received his share. On November 4, 1760, when his grandfather Reverend Anthony Stoddard's estate was distributed in probate, Anthony and his brothers received their father's share of his intended inheritance.[132]

It is reasonable to assume that Anthony continued to live in the family home after the death of his father and the re-marriage of his mother to Samuel Waller and her removal to Kent (where she gave birth to a girl, Comfort Waller, in November 1750). We can imagine that perhaps all of the older sons stayed living in the family home for some time —under the watchful eye of Grandfather Reverend Anthony who lived nearby. They probably kept active working their grandfather's lands as their father had done before he unexpectedly passed away. Undoubtedly this is how and why Anthony became a farmer in the first place.

It doesn't appear Anthony had an inclination for school although nothing is known about the basic education he received. However, his grandfather would certainly not have let his grandsons suffer idle minds, and it is certain that they received no worse an education than did Amos at their age.

Anthony married Phebe Reed around 1760, although the exact date is not known. It was likely sometime shortly after his grandfather passed away in September 1760 —which would explain why their marriage is not recorded in the church, as the Rev. Noah Benedict, Rev. Anthony's replacement, may not have yet arrived to take his place, or may have simply failed to keep a proper record during the period of transition.

The couple's first child, a son, Amos, was born in Woodbury, Connecticut on October 26, 1762. On June 7, 1765 Anthony bought a 50 acre farm in New Framingham, Massachusetts (the name later changed to Lanesborough). It is not unreasonable to assume that Anthony sold his inherited land tracts in Woodbury in order to purchase the farm. His father and grandfather were gone, and his mother had remarried and relocated to Kent. Perhaps he wanted to make a fresh start away from Woodbury? Then on November 6, 1769, he sold the farm in Lanesborough and purchased a 100 acre farm in East Hoosuck, Massachusetts (the name later changed to Adams) in July 1772. Anthony soon after sold that farm on December 23, 1772 and relocated to Lenox where he purchased a 100 acre farm on February 19, 1773. He purchased the farm from Nathan Mead who had purchased the farm from David Pixley in 1767. Anthony lived and worked the farm in Lenox until his untimely death in 1785. The farm was then divided and distributed to his heirs with the parcels being sold by these heirs from 1787 to 1806. It was discovered in 2019 that the original dwelling house of Anthony Stoddard, with four fireplaces, is still standing on East Dugway Road in Lenox after having been completely restored by owners David and Rori Kanter. The house is a sturdy and beautiful example of colonial-era craftsmanship.

Little is known about Anthony and his wife Phebe. We do know that Phebe's sister, Elizabeth Reed, married Israel Stoddard, Anthony's older brother, on July 4, 1759. The parents of these Reed sisters were Jonathan Reed and Elizabeth Smith. Elizabeth Smith was the widow of Daniel Smith.[133] [134] She and Daniel Smith had one son together, Richard Smith, before Daniel died in 1729. This son married Annis Hurd of Woodbury. They had two sons together —both born in Woodbury, Connecticut: Nathan Smith and Nathaniel Smith.[135] Nathan Smith later became a U.S. Senator from Connecticut,[136] and Nathaniel Smith later became a judge of the Supreme Court of Connecticut.[137]

Amos must have known the Smiths, because in a letter he wrote to his mother (then Phebe Benham, wife of Samuel Benham of Middlebury, Connecticut) from St. Louis on June 16, 1804, he ends his letter by saying, "Remember me to my brother and Sisters, as well as to my other relations —particularly to Mʳ Smith and wife, and you may rest assured that I do not forget my aged mother." [138] It is the opinion of the editor that Amos is probably referring to Nathaniel Smith of Woodbury, his mother's nephew and his cousin, a state senator for Connecticut at that time. Nathaniel's wife, Ruth Benedict, was the daughter of Reverend Noah Benedict, the man who replaced his great–grandfather in the Woodbury church ministry and whom Amos mentions in his autobiography.[139]

Since little is known about Anthony, we can only consider the information provided by Amos and try to give an opinion as to his character. Anthony appears to be a hard–working and diligent man, who stressed education, and who, with his wife, provided a religious–based upbringing for their son. He obviously shared stories of his Stoddard ancestors with his son Amos, indicating he too must have felt a sense of pride in his family roots. He apparently provided well for his family even while intermittently being away to contribute to the cause of liberty as a soldier: He fought at the Battle of Bennington as well as at the Battle of Saratoga in 1777.

Anthony was described by Amos in his autobiography as being a "strenuous Whig" or patriot...and there were British loyalists living among the patriotic men of Lenox to inflame his patriotic passions. So, on May 12, 1782, Anthony Stoddard and other like-minded patriots of Lenox took action: they assembled in the night with their guns, broke into the houses and forced the families of Loyalist neighbors Aaron Wood and Edward Martindale from their homes. Charges were later dismissed in September 1783.

As a father, his dedication to his son can best be exemplified by his actions during the fall of 1779, when he traveled the arduous 120 miles and appeared at the West Point Highlands, and as Amos testifies, "furnished me with money and necessaries, and these probably prolonged my life."

Anthony died of smallpox at the age of 51 on November 16, 1785 while Amos was away in Boston working for Charles Cushing in the Clerk's office at the Supreme Judicial Court. He left eight children, the oldest being Amos at the age of 23, and the youngest being his brother Eliakim, born just the year before. Amos' sister Phebe, just two years younger than Amos, died unmarried in 1800.[140] His second–oldest surviving sibling brother Philo, also a veteran of the American Revolution, was born in 1765. His brother Simeon was born just three years before Amos joined the army in 1779 and his sister Lucy wasn't born until 1782.[141] It is therefore unlikely that Amos spent much time with his youngest siblings.

Anthony was buried on the adjacent farm of Thomas Tracy. The reason: Thomas Tracy Sr. had also died of smallpox some years earlier and was buried on his farm, so Anthony and another man (who died of that disease about the same time) were apparently also buried on the Tracy property (later known as the Stocking farm) "near a big rock.." A search for his burial place is being conducted by the Lenox Historial Society.

Amos' mother Phebe, as a practical matter, then married Samuel Benham (sometime after the death of his wife in December 1787).[142] The year and place of Phebe Benham's death have not yet been determined.

Thus ends the examination of the genealogical factors which contributed to forming the character of Major Amos Stoddard. We shall now examine the results of these influences in the historical record of Major Amos Stoddard from the scant information available.

III. Civilian, Law Student, & Lawyer — 1791 to 1798

As we start to examine the life of Major Amos Stoddard from the ending point of his autobiography, we must adjust the time-line in order to provide the correct starting point. This conflict is acknowledged in endnote 208 of the autobiography manuscript section.

In his autobiography, Amos stated, "I sailed for London, and went on shore at Deal, on the 16th Dec. 1791." He goes on to tell us he spent eight months in England. Therefore, according to this time-line, he would have been in London, England from December 1791 until approximately August 1792.

However, he also tells us he attended the "debates in the house of Commons —particularly the interesting one on the Quebec bill." The Quebec Bill was introduced in March 1791 and was passed in May 1791.

Amos also stated, "Political disputations ran high. Paine had just before published his "*Rights of Man*" in answer to the "*Reflections*" of Mr. Burke." Burke's book, *Reflections on the Revolution in France*, was published in November 1790 and Paine's *Rights of Man* was published in March 1791.

Amos goes on to say, "In the course of my political reading, a pamphlet in answer to Paine, written by Dr. Tatham of Oxford, attracted my attention. The blunders and misstatements of that political divine awakened my resentment, and induced me to write an answer of about 120 pages. This I completed in 4 or 5 days; it found its way to the press and was published." The pamphlet by Dr. Tatham to which Amos Stoddard refers is likely, *Letters to the Right Hon. Edmund Burke on Politics*, consisting of two letters which are dated March 14 and April 2, 1791.

Therefore, it is clear that Amos must have been in London during 1791 and not 1792. However, in order to further prove this correction, the editor of this volume makes the following additional conclusive point.

Amos failed to identify the title of his own political literary work, because, as he says, "I forbear to name the title page, as I am heartily ashamed of that effort at political disquisition —much more, indeed, of the sentiments it contained than of the style and language of the work." We can now say, with near certainty, based on the preceding evidence, that the title of that political discourse was, and is, *The Political Crisis: Or, a Dissertation on the Rights of Man*, which was published by and printed for J.S. Jordan, No. 166, Fleet Street, London, in 1791 (J.S. Jordan also printed *Rights of Man* by Thomas Paine in November 1790).

On the second page of the preface, page *vi*, the author wrote the following:

> "To avoid prolixity, the Writer of the subsequent sheets has seldom noticed the arguments of MR. BURKE; they have been sufficiently answered: He has more particularly paid his respects to those of Dr. Tatham, an Author who is more zealous than just, and who seems to be forgotten; conceiving, that a small tribute is due to the exertions of this political Divine, in support of a cause, which has received additional light, even from the HETEROGENEOUSNESS of his reasoning."

The first hint of the title of this publication came from the book, *Old Hallowell on the Kennebec*, written by Emma Nason in 1909, in which a book title, *The Political Crisis*, published in London, is attributed to Amos Stoddard. This is one of only a few obscure mentions of this book title being attributed to Amos Stoddard which have been found. Further research discovered a book of similar title, printed in London in 1791, *The Political Crisis: Or, a Dissertation on the Rights of Man*, but which does not identify an author.

The conclusive piece of evidence linking the authorship of this pamphlet to Amos Stoddard was thus provided in the preface of this book, with the reference by the author to Dr. Tatham as being the target of his writing —which coincides with Amos' description of his political ire towards Dr. Tatham in his autobiography.

Therefore, Amos Stoddard is indeed the author of *The Political Crisis: Or, a Dissertation on the Rights of Man*. Further, based on the publication year 1791, the ancient pamphlet confirms Amos must have been in London, England during the eight months beginning on December 16, 1790 until approximately August 1791.

Images of the pamphlet's title page and preface page *vi* are presented on the following pages.

THE
POLITICAL CRISIS:

OR, A

DISSERTATION

ON THE

RIGHTS OF MAN.

————it is not a time to mince the matter, through a delicacy that may be as fatal as it is false.

DR. TATHAM'S LET. to MR. BURKE.

The people are seldom wrong in their opinions—in their sentiments they are never mistaken.

JUNIUS.

————to live by one man's will, is the cause of all men's misery.

HOOKER.

————the WISE shall taste
The truths I *speak*—the truths I *speak* shall *feel,*
And, *feeling,* give assent—and their assent
Is ample recompence—is more than praise.

YOUNG.

LONDON:

PRINTED FOR J. S. JORDAN, NO. 166, FLEET-STREET.

M DCC XCI.

Title page, *The Political Crisis: Or, a Dissertation on the Rights of Man*
Published by and printed for J.S. Jordan in London, 1791
Used with Permission. From the Rare Books Collection,
Howard Gotlieb Archival Research Center at Boston University

To avoid prolixity, the Writer of the subsequent sheets has seldom noticed the argu-
ments of Mr. BURKE; they have been sufficiently answered: He has more particularly
paid his respects to those of Dr. TATHAM,
an Author who is more *zealous* than *just*, and
who seems to be forgotten; conceiving, that
a small tribute is due to the exertions of this
political Divine, in support of a cause, which
has received additional light, even from the
HETEROGENEOUSNESS of his reasoning.

The Writers in opposition to the RIGHTS
OF MAN, are actuated more by PREJUDICE
than REASON. When unable to refute an
argument, they descend to personal invective,
and rack their invention to stigmatize the
BIRTH and EDUCATION of those they are
unable to oppose. It matters not whether an
Author can trace an illustrious PEDIGREE,
or whether his BIRTH and EDUCATION were
OBSCURE and ILLITERATE, provided his
CONDUCT and SENTIMENTS tend to pro-
mote the interest and glory of his Country.
THEY alone can explain his MOTIVES and
CAPACITY. THEM we ought to ADMIRE

or

Page *vi* of preface, *The Political Crisis: Or, a Dissertation on the Rights of Man*
Published by and printed for J.S. Jordan in London, 1791
Used with Permission. From the Rare Books Collection,
Howard Gotlieb Archival Research Center at Boston University

Amos Stoddard ends his incomplete autobiography in the summer of 1791 in mid–sentence: "I returned to my studies with vigor," and thereafter, we have to make some educated guesses at the next few years of his life since there is little direct evidence and only a few clues as to his activities.

Obviously, upon his return from England, Amos returned to the law office of Seth Padelford, Esq. in Taunton, Massachusetts, where Amos tells us, "In his office I spent four of the most happy years of my life." We know from his own words, "While engaged in my studies, I was induced to take a trip to England in pursuit of a family estate," that he had already started his law studies with Seth Padelford before his trip to England.

Judge Seth Padelford was the County Treasurer in Taunton in 1783 and was appointed Judge of Probate in Taunton in 1794.[143] Therefore, it is logical that Amos returned to study law with Judge Seth Padelford in Taunton in the early fall of 1791 where he must have stayed for the next three and one–half years, or until nearly the end of 1795 or the beginning of 1796. This time-line perfectly coincides with the date he was accepted to practice law before the Supreme Judicial Court of the Commonwealth of Massachusetts —February 16, 1796. A copy of his lawyerly acceptance signed by Supreme Judicial Court Clerk John Tucker in Boston, Suffolk County, Massachusetts is found on the facing page.[144]

As additional evidence of his time in Taunton, General Joseph Gardner Swift, in his memoirs published in 1890, wrote:

> "By the summer of 1799 I was prepared to enter Cambridge College. It was at this point that there marched into town, and camped on a beautiful site near the margin of Taunton River, the 14th United States regiment of infantry, commanded by Capt. Nathan Rice, composed of two incomplete battalions of the Provisional Army. My father became the temporary surgeon of this regiment, whereas, as his messenger, I became a familiar in the tents of the officers. In a few weeks thereafter Captain Amos Stoddard marched a company of United States Artillerists and Engineers into camp, on its route to garrison Rhode Island Harbor. This officer was an intimate friend of my father's, and had been a student of law in our neighbor, Judge Padelford's office, on Taunton Green. It was very pleasant to me to find that this officer recognized me as an acquaintance." [145]

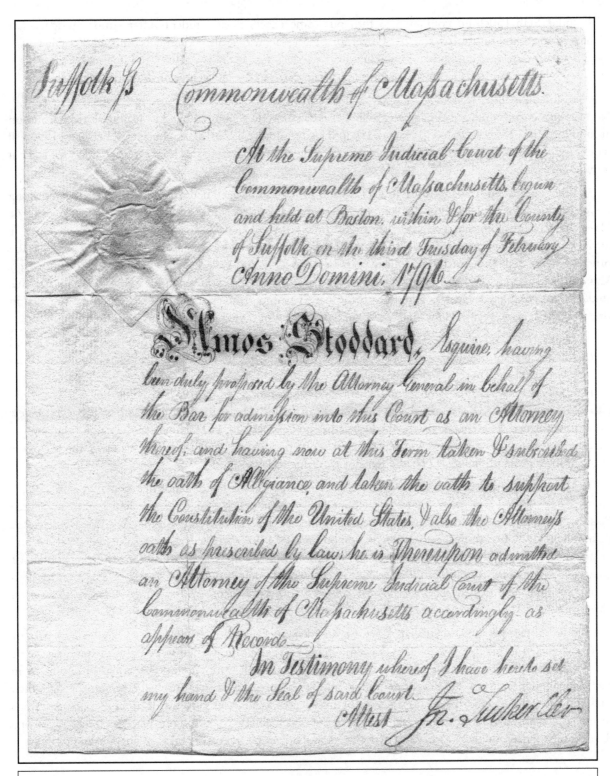

Amos Stoddard, Admitted an Attorney of the Supreme Judicial Court,
Commonwealth of Massachusetts,
February 16, 1796

Used with Permission. Amos Stoddard Papers, Missouri Historical Museum,
St. Louis, Missouri

Judge Seth Padelford continued to turn out some excellent law students after Amos Stoddard left. Marcus Morton, the future 16th and 18th Governor of Massachusetts, also commenced his study of law with Judge Padelford in Taunton before completing his law education at the law school in Litchfield, Connecticut in 1807.[146] Today, Taunton Green is a historical district located in the city center of Taunton, Massachusetts.

In the book, *Old Hallowell on the Kennebec*, it is said Amos Stoddard first arrived in Kennebeck in 1794.[147] No evidence corroborating this has been found. It is far more likely he removed to Hallowell from Taunton around the time he was accepted to practice law in the Commonwealth of Massachusetts in February 1796. All dates point to his arrival in early 1796, including a probate record that notes his legal representation for a client in June 1796.[148]

What compelled Amos to move to Hallowell in 1796 has not been determined. Hallowell, located along the Kennebec River, is located in the state of Maine, but was at that time a part of the Commonwealth of Massachusetts. It was considered the far, northern frontier. It would have been a far cry from the advantages of life in Taunton with its close proximity to Boston. However, another young man who studied with Amos at the office of Judge Seth Padelford during those years between 1792 and 1796, Peter O. Alden of Middleborough, Massachusetts, also moved to Maine (at that time a part of the Commonwealth of Massachusetts) after his studies were completed. He was admitted to the bar at Cumberland in 1797 and started a law practice in Brunswick that same year.[149] He was also a Masonic brother. But perhaps this is all just coincidence?

There are several other pieces of evidence that support that Amos Stoddard arrived in Hallowell around 1796 and which note his activities during that time. One was that he started to demonstrate an interest in politics. He was elected to represent Hallowell, Lincoln County, in the Massachusetts House of Representatives during the November 1796 Session[150] and the January 1797 Session.[151] In fact, in 1797, Hallowell was to be split into two towns, and Amos is credited with suggesting the name "Harrington" for the name of the second, new town to be formed. This change passed the Legislature on February 20, 1797. However, the name "Harrington" soon became a source of derision and was rejected by the people who lived there. The name of the town was changed to Augusta on June 9, 1797, and remains the same today.[152]

Amos Stoddard also served in the Massachusetts militia as a brigadier major between 1796 and 1798.[153] Finally, Amos joined and was a founding member of the Kennebeck Lodge #5, Ancient Free & Accepted Masons, chartered by Paul Revere, in Hallowell. He joined at their first meeting on May 2, 1796 and delivered their first St. John's Day festival celebration oration on June 24, 1797.[154] He later delivered the June 24th St. John's Day oration for the Portland Lodge of Free and Accepted Masons in 1799 [155] [156] and for the Grand Lodge of New Hampshire in Portsmouth in 1802.[157] Amos also accepted other opportunities to exercise his oratory skills during this time: he provided *An Oration, Delivered Before the Citizens of Portland, and the Supreme Judicial Court of the Commonwealth of Massachusetts, on the Fourth Day of July, 1799* for the Portland Independence Day celebration.[158]

While it can be established that Amos Stoddard most likely arrived in Hallowell in the first part of 1796 and started to practice law there at that time, there is no indication whether he enjoyed any measure of success as a lawyer. It is possible that as a new comer to Hallowell, Amos found clients hard to come by in such a small, remote town. He may have dealt in some small probate matters and helped clients prepare their wills and such. In any case, there's no evidence of his success as a lawyer in terms of arguing cases. As Amos seemed predisposed to travel and adventure, or as he calls his inability to settle in one place for long, "my roving disposition," it may simply be that a sedentary career and life as a lawyer soon became unappealing to him.

IV. Military Officer and Garrison Duty — 1798 to 1804

In the middle of 1798, Amos' life took a dramatic turn away from his judicial training and education back towards a life more appealing to his personality: a military career. His name was submitted to the United States Senate by President John Adams on May 28, 1798 for an appointment in the United States Army Corps of Artillerists and Engineers as a Captain.[159] He was commissioned on June 4, 1778.[160] Capt. Amos Stoddard was assigned to command at Fort Sumner in Portland[161] (not far from his home of Hallowell) where he stayed until October 30, 1799 serving in the 2nd Regiment of Artillerists and Engineers.

Actually, the Fort's name *became* "Fort Sumner" at a ceremony on June 14, 1799, as acknowledged in a letter from Capt. Amos Stoddard to Major General Alexander Hamilton on July 9, 1799, in which he wrote, "the ceremony was passed in the presence of several hundred Spectators; and I flatter myself, that the tribute of respect, so deservedly due to the memory and virtues of our late Governor, was not omitted on the occasion."[162]

The long argument over the need for a standing army which began during the American Revolution still ensued in early 1798. During the American Revolution, George Washington had wanted a regular army with long enlistments —while Congress preferred state militia recruits with short enlistments. Washington's point finally won out, but after the war, with the threat eliminated, the mindset returned to militia security.

Since the Constitution of the United States was ratified in 1788, the Federal Government had only a small military force available. It was large enough to fight Indians on the western frontier but not nearly big enough to defend the country from foreign invaders such as England, France or Spain. It was argued that state militias could be called out to fight if hostilities arose. In 1791, a regiment was formed under Major General Arthur St. Clair —but this force was nearly wiped out in an Indian attack in what became known as St. Clair's Defeat.[163] A great number of experienced officers were killed in that battle.

President Washington was angry and embarrassed by the loss. The regiment was reformed under Major General Anthony Wayne, and a second regiment was added, commanded by a newly–commissioned brigadier general by the name of James Wilkinson.[164] General Wayne, who knew Wilkinson from the American Revolution, at first had a friendly relationship with Wilkinson but which later turned confrontational, nasty and bitter.[165] Luckily for Wilkinson, General Wayne died in December 1796. President Washington then promoted Wilkinson to the vacancy left by General Wayne's death before President–elect Adams took office.[166] In 1798 President Adams asked George Washington to return to his military command as senior officer of the Army, which he agreed to do. Lieutenant General George Washington then died in December 1799. Upon Washington's death, his second in command, Major General Alexander Hamilton, temporarily replaced him as senior commander, but his departure in 1800 allowed James Wilkinson to ascend to the post of senior Army officer with the rank of brigadier general in June 1800 in spite of the concerns regarding his loyalty and character.[167]

Thomas Jefferson was narrowly elected President in 1800. Fearing a standing army (and the military in general), and concerned that Hamilton and others had packed the Army full of pro–Federalists, Jefferson did everything in his power to purge the Army of officers who did not support his Democratic–Republican administration. He retained, promoted or replaced officers with men loyal to his government. Lists of officers and their political leaning were literally drawn–up. Serving in the military was now a matter of pledging political loyalty —not loyalty to the country.[168] Joseph Gardener Swift, who had the distinction of being the first graduate of West Point in 1802, recounts in his memoirs how during a dinner in 1806 with Thomas Jefferson, James Madison, and Henry Dearborn, among others, Jefferson asked him, "To which of the political creeds do you adhere?" to which he replied that as yet he had done no political act, but that his family were Federalists, to which Jefferson responded, "There are many men of high talent and integrity in that party, but it is not the rising power." The point was lost on Swift at the time, but Secretary of War Dearborn conveniently reminded him of its importance later.[169]

James Wilkinson was someone whose political preference was to whoever was in power. He believed in the politics of his own self–interest. This apparently suited Jefferson just fine. Jefferson felt Wilkinson commanded the loyalty of the Army, and he obviously felt he could manage Wilkinson. Therefore, by retaining Wilkinson, and promoting him to major general and senior officer of the Army, he could use Wilkinson to insulate himself from his fears of the military turning against the government. However, he selected Henry Dearborn as secretary of war to be the real military leader. Dearborn marginalized Wilkinson and did not allow him to play a significant decision–making role. In fact, he was completely shut off from most discussions, decisions and initiatives. We can vividly see this during the career of Amos Stoddard, primarily from the end of 1802 through 1804, where, as a captain of an artillery company, he is often being ordered and commanded directly by the Secretary of War and without General Wilkinson's knowledge.[170]

Wilkinson retained his senior military position until 1815 in spite of two court martial inquiries in 1811 and 1815. James Wilkinson served four presidents, all of whom were aware of the reports and rumors about his flawed character, his questionable loyalty, and his sinister relationship with the Spanish government. His deceitful and treasonous life story is not widely known. What is most shocking was his ability to dupe four of the Founding Fathers.[171] This was the political situation in the military at the time for Captain Amos Stoddard.

A bill in the House of Representatives to raise an army of 20,000 was debated and passed on May 20, 1798.[172] This coincides with the time President Adams submitted Amos' name to the U.S. Senate on May 28th to be commissioned as a captain of the Artillerists and Engineers in this new Army. The problem was the government was not yet prepared to finance and equip such a large army. There was virtually no infrastructure in place to equip and supply such a force. This undoubtedly led to many problems and frustrations which are evidenced in Capt. Stoddard's early military correspondence.

During the period of his arrival at Portland until at least the middle of 1799, Capt. Stoddard wrote numerous letters to Samuel Hodgdon, Esq. at the Intendant of Stores Office in Philadelphia regarding his desperate need of tents and clothing. On March 10th he wrote Hodgdon, "My men are so crowded in a small building, that warm weather will inevitably breed distempers among them. Thinking it unnecessary to trouble the war office, I have not written to the Sec[y] of War on the subject." [173]

On April 3rd he wrote to Major General Alexander Hamilton a lengthy description of his operational situation, the dire garrison conditions, and in his efforts towards training the men he recruited and enlisted:

> *"Convinced of the necessity of strict discipline, I have endeavored to establish it among my men. When the weather permits, I put them to the exercise of their small Arms, and Artillery —instruct them in the etequette and important details of Guard and Garrison duty, and in the evolutions of the field —teach them the necessity of cleanliness, decorum, and subordination; and I flatter myself that no better men in point of size, nor any more attached to the public service, can be found in the United States. I experience some difficulty from their friends, who mostly live in the vicinity —for I find some base enough to advise desertion. If our services could be dispensed with here, and a rendezvous or station in some other State might operate as an avoidance of the evil, and tend to a more strict and correct discipline.*
>
> *Besides —we labor under one inconvenience not usual in detachments or separate portions of the Army. The block–house or citadel comprises only four small appartments, and is hardly sufficient for the accommodation of my recruits —the consequence is that I am obliged, together with my Lieutenant, to quarter in town, a distance of near three quarters of a mile. This of course puts it out of our power to attend so strictly to discipline as is requisite in a regular corps. If this post is to be occupied in future by the troops of the United States, an additional building must be erected —and perhaps no better time than the present spring will offer for the execution of this necessary measure. At all hazzards my men must go into Tents early the ensuing summer —otherwise, from their compact situation, they will be exposed to contagious disorders. Nothing more is requisite to urge [than] an immediate supply of Tents for a full Company."* [174]

On the April 4th he again wrote Samuel Hodgdon: "As my men are crowded into a very small building, disorder will inevitably prevail among them very soon, unless some more convenient quarters are provided for them. Tents would be very acceptable —and if you would forward them the first opportunity, you will much oblige me." [175]

On April 15, 1799 he followed up with: "I have heretofore written you respecting 20 vests, and the necessary quality of tents for the summer. I have enlisted 61 men, and the vests are very much wanted. —Our Blockhouse or Barrick is more like a loathsome prison than a wholesome habitation." [176]

By July 18th Capt. Stoddard was still pleading with Samuel Hodgdon: "Be so obliging as to inform me thro' what channel I must make application for clothing. Whether they be made immediately to you —to the department of war, or to Gen[l] Hamilton. I never have been regularly instructed; nor can I myself on this point by any enquiries I have made on the subject." [177]

One can only imagine how difficult it must have been to be asked to recruit, train, and retain men in such conditions. As Capt. Stoddard points out, desertions were a constant and plaguing problem. Whether this was due more to the influence from others (who were possibly against a Federal Army?) or to the conditions in which they were subjected is not known.

Based on letters sent to Hodgdon from other commanders at seaport fortifications during this time, the situation for them was very much the same. It is apparent that developing this new Army in terms of supply was going to be a very slow and painful process for its members. In fact, it never improved significantly during the remainder of Major Amos Stoddard's life. In the fall of 1812, leading up to the siege of Fort Meigs during the first 10 days of May of 1813, the military supply and logistics problems still had not significantly improved in the United States Army.[178]

By the late fall of 1799, Capt. Stoddard was reassigned to Fort Wolcott on Goat Island in Newport, Rhode Island. [179] On November 6, 1799, due to the absence of his direct commander, Major Daniel Jackson, Capt. Stoddard wrote from "New–port" to Major General Alexander Hamilton to request "a three week furlough" as his "presence at the department of war will be necessary" to provide "explanations of several items in my account…" [180] Before he took command at Newport he apparently traveled from Portland to New London, Connecticut for the purpose of surveying Fort Trumbull in New London and Fort Griswold in Groton, Connecticut.[181] Capt. Stoddard served at Newport until March 1802. There is relatively little information available to determine whether his situation dramatically improved at Newport or whether he continued to suffer supply shortages while managing in this new seaport fortification command.

Amos Stoddard was next assigned to Fort Constitution in Portsmouth, New Hampshire in March 1802.[182] Apparently on arriving at Fort Constitution, Capt. Stoddard found similar morale and desertion problems. The following advertisement was published in the May 8, 1802 edition of the *United States Oracle and Portsmouth Advertiser*:

> ## 20 Dollars Reward.
>
> BRADBURY KENNISTON, a Private in the Artillerists of the United States, was directed on the 1st instant to repair to the Post Office in Portsmouth, by land, after the letters and papers belonging to the Officers of this Garrison; and on the receipt of some letters and papers at the post–office, he deserted the service of the United States. Said KENNISTON was born in the town of Epsom in this state. – 24 years of age – 5 feet and 8 inches in height – black eyes – black short hair – and dark complexion; wore away a round hat – a regimental coat – short blue pantaloons and boots. Whoever will apprehend said KENNISTON, and return him to the subscriber, or secure him in any Goal, so that he may be obtained, shall receive a reward of TWENTY DOLLARS, and a reimbursement of all necessary expenses.
>
> AMOS STODDARD, Capt.
> Commanding
>
> Fort–Constitution
> May 3, 1802 [183]

On April 1, 1802 the command structure of the Artillerists and Engineers was changed, dividing engineers from artillerists, and the artillery became the Regiment of Artillerists.[184] Capt. Stoddard signed many of his letters and correspondence after this time, "Corps of Artillerists." In January 1812, when the 2nd and 3rd Regiments of Artillerists were formed, this original Regiment of Artillerists became known as the 1st Regiment of Artillerists.[185]

By January 6, 1803, Capt. Stoddard was now writing to the Department of War from Fort Fayette at Pittsburgh, Pennsylvania "in relation to D. Scott." [186] Therefore, he was apparently reassigned out west to Fort Fayette at the end of the 1802.

Once he arrived in Pittsburgh, Capt. Stoddard wrote to Col. Henry Burbeck on January 19, 1803:

> *"I believe I have been remiss in not informing you of my arrival at this post, and the state of my Company. But the truth is, this omission was occasioned by constant Garrison duty and a want of something of real consequence to communicate. I will observe, that the <u>appearance</u> and <u>behavior</u> of my men, were never so good as when on the late march, and since their arrival here.....you have, perhaps, seen by the public papers, how much we attracted the attention of the <u>sovereign people</u> on the road: They loaded us with a profusion of encomium; as much the effect of ignorance as of judgment —yet on the whole, they were not altogether wrong —for the soldiery appeared clean and expert —were very civil, especially to the Irish and German girls; and they kept themselves free from whiskey and plunder! The winter clothing of the men is finished —and all the summer articles are now in the hands of the Taylor. We now begin to puzzle ourselves about the place of our destination. People of great prominence tell me, that we are going to descend the Mississippi —others again will insist on it, that we are bound to Black Rock at the Out–let of Lake Erie. I have prepared for my fate, whatever it may be..."* [187]

Under what orders and purpose Capt. Stoddard was sent to Pittsburgh at the end of 1802 has not been determined. Apparently he did not know either. However, as we will see, his assignment is an indication that the wheels for exploration of the Louisiana Territory were already being set in motion at the end of 1802.

President Thomas Jefferson waited until January 18, 1803 to send a secret letter to Congress describing the mission of the Lewis & Clark expedition and requesting $2,500 "for the purpose of extending the external commerce of the United States." [188] In the meantime, Capt. Meriwether Lewis had already been to Philadelphia receiving instruction on botany and zoology and other sciences at the time the acquisition of the Louisiana Territory was being negotiated. [189] The agreement between France and the United States was only finalized and dated April 30th [190] and signed on May 2, 1803.[191] Yet, by this time, Capt. Stoddard's Company was already well on its way to Kaskaskia on the Mississippi River to unite with Capt. Russell Bissell's Company of infantry.[192]

On March 9th and 10th Capt. Stoddard received orders from the War Department through Adjutant General Thomas H. Cushing to first "descend the Ohio on the first day of April" to the Mississippi River, and next to "ascend the Mississippi to Kaskaskia." [193] During the month of March, between the 10th and the 30th, Capt. Stoddard sent at least four letters to Secretary of War Henry Dearborn from Fort Fayette at Pittsburgh. In these letters it is clear he is preparing to leave Pittsburgh and is gathering supplies for his mission.[194]

On July 2, 1803, Capt. Stoddard, Capt. Russell Bissell and Capt. Daniel Bissell received the following orders from Secretary Dearborn at the War Department:

> *"Sir,*
>
> *You will please to afford Capt Meriwither Lewis all the aid in your power in selecting and engaging suitable Men to accompany him on an expedition to the Westward. If any non–commissioned officer or private in your Company should be disposed to join Capt. Lewis, whose characters for sobriety, integrity and other necessary qualification render them suitable for such service, you will detatch them accordingly."* [195]

News of the signing of the agreement for the purchase of Louisiana, in the form of a letter received from Paris and written on May 13, 1803, had just reached the United States and was published in the *New–York Evening Post* on the first of July 1803 and was subsequently published in various newspapers.[196] The agreement was formally announced by President Jefferson on Independence Day.[197] However, President Jefferson had already given Capt. Meriwether Lewis lengthy instructions regarding the expedition on June 20th and Secretary Dearborn had already instructed Captains Stoddard and Bissell, who were pre–positioned at Kaskaskia, to assist Capt. Lewis with "all the aid in your power" on July 2, 1803.[198] Clearly, they were operating as an advance team for the expedition.

On February 19, 1803, Capt. Stoddard received orders at Pittsburgh from Secretary Dearborn to call on "Mr [Moses] Hook the Assistant Military Agent" for supplies and for him to make his "first stand at the place where Captain Bissells Company is posted at Kaskaskia, until you have decided on the most suitable scite for a Post near the mouth of the Illinois, and until you shall have made the necessary arrangements for the reception of your company." [199] By the term, "the reception of your company," it is supposed he is referring to Capt. Lewis and the Corps of Discovery.

It should be noted that William Clark was *not yet* even a designated member of the Corps of Discovery expedition team at this time. In fact, he *had not yet even been asked* to join. Capt. Lewis only wrote to William Clark on June 18, 1803 to invite him on the expedition, [200] but due to the slowness of the mail, he still had not received a reply from Clark by the time he arrived at Pittsburgh in mid–July. In the absence of a response from Clark, Capt. Lewis set his eye on Moses Hooke at Pittsburgh as an alternate should Clark reject the opportunity to join the expedition.[201] On July 26th he wrote to President Jefferson to introduce Hooke as a suitable substitute for Clark if necessary.[202]

At this point, it is worth contemplating and considering whether there was a concerted plan, devised as early as the end of 1802, and initiated through the War Department, to send Capt. Stoddard and a company of artillery (and a company of infantry) ahead of Capt. Meriwether Lewis to lay the ground and set in motion the necessary support elements and security detail for the expected expedition. It appears Capt. Stoddard was consistently ordered one step ahead of Capt. Lewis —first to Fort Fayette at Pittsburgh in January (Capt. Meriwether Lewis did not arrive at Fort Fayette until July 15th at which time Capt. Stoddard had already been ordered west and was on his way to Kaskaskia on the Mississippi River) and the second to Kaskaskia.[203] Lewis and Clark only arrived at Kaskaskia on November 28, 1803.[204]

On July 19th Secretary Dearborn again wrote to Capt. Stoddard:

"WAR DEPARTMENT July 19th 1803

AMOS STODDARD.

SIR: In consiquence of the recent cession of Louisiana to the United States, It will probably become necessary in the course of a few months to place an American Garrison in the Military Post on the Western Bank of the Mississippi now occupied by Spanish Troops —Your Company will probably be ordered to that Post, you will therefore discontinue any arrangements for establishing a post on the Eastern side of the River, and will unite yourself & Company with Capt Bissell at Kaskaskias. You will please to take the earliest opportunity of ascertaining the present state of the Post on the Louisiana side, without giving any uneasiness to the Spanish Officer. You may inform him of the Cession & the probability of our taking possession previous to the next winter. You will ascerttain the situartion of the Barracks &c. If there is not suffient accommodations for a Company, it may be prudent to provide temporary accommodations at Kaskaskias for such part at least of your Company as cannot be accommodated on the other side. You will give me the earliest information on the subject of this letter generally, noticing the state of the works and buildings on the Louisiana side, also the number of Inhabitants as nearly as you can ascertain, their local situation relative to the mouth of the Missouri, the quality of the land inhabited, What proportion of the people are from the United States, the situation of the lead mine, whether any considerable number of Indians inhabit the Country near the white settlements, what Nation is nearest, and the probable number of said Nation —

You and Capt Bissell will please to give me your opinion on the most eligible site for a permanent Garrison on the Louisiana side, taking into view with other considerations the Command of the mouth of the River Missouri, the Garrison to consist of one company. You will also note the number of Militia who have been or may be enrolled, and whether they are armed or not. You will likewise note the distance between the Post now occupied by Capt Bissell, and the Post now occupied by Spain, and also the distance of the Spanish Garrison from the mouth of the Missouri. I enclose you a Sketch of the treaty as published which you will communicate on both sides of the River." [205]

It appears Bissell and Stoddard joined forces at Kaskaskia within days of that letter being sent. On the 27th of July, Secretary of War Henry Dearborn again wrote to Captains Russell Bissell and Amos Stoddard:

"Your joint letter in relation to the most suitable site or sites for a Military Post in that quarter has been duly recd, by which it appears that you have been particularly attentive to the object: Your description of the several proposed sites, together with the adjacent Country on both sides of the Mississippi is highly interesting and pleasing —But the probable <u>immediate</u> change of circumstances relative to our possessions on the Mississippi, will make different arrangements in our Military positions necessary, and although the site you discribe on the eastern shore between the mouths of the Missouri and Illinois may ultimately be selected as the most eligible position for a permanent Military Post, it will be advisable at present to possess the site described near Kaskaskia Village. You will endeavor to obtain a lease of from fifty to one hundred acres of land for that purpose, and commence a post on the plan proposed to Capt Stoddard, of which he has a Sketch, the lease should be for two or three years —In the Months of November or December at farthest I presume we shall have possession of Louisiana, and Capt Stoddard's Company will of course take post at St Louis. In the mean time the proposed post for Capt Bissells Company should be establish'd with the necessary buildings, in order that Capt Stoddards Company may occupy the huts now occupied by Capt Bs Company when the cold weather commences until his Company shall be removed to St. Louis." [206]

Gass' Request, Ft. Kaskaskia, December 13, 1803
Private Patrick Gass confers with Capt. Meriwether Lewis as a local Creole looks on.
Lt. Zebulon Pike watches as Capt. Stoddard's artillerymen gather opposite the door.
Used with Permission of the Artist, Michael Haynes

An agreement between Secretary Dearborn and John Edgar (written by Amos Stoddard) for leasing the land and the construction of a garrison at Fort Kaskaskia was completed and dated September 4, 1803:

> "...*the following tract or parcel of land, situated, and lying on the east side of the Kaskaskias River, opposite to the village of Kaskaskias aforesaid, bounded and described as follows, viz. Beginning at said Kaskaskias River, at the dividing line between said Edgars and Peter Minard; thence in an easterly direction on said dividing line, fifty rods, across the spring run, so as to include the source of said spring,*"

And describing the required development of the land as:

> "...*the right of erecting a garrison on said premises, of procuring such quantity of stone, of making such quantity of brick and of cutting such quantity of timber and of taking such other materials as may be necessary to complete said garrison, to erect the necessary buildings in it, and to keep all and every part of them in repair; and also to cut on said premises such quantity of wood from time to time as may be wanted by the troops now stationed or to be stationed in or at said Garrison;*"

John Edgar's signature is witnessed by Captains Bissell and Stoddard. Thus was the arrangement for establishing Fort Kaskaskia on the east bank of the Mississippi River in the fall of 1803.[207]

Captain Meriwether Lewis and William Clark arrived at Fort Kaskaskia on November 28, 1803. A few days later, on December 1st, Capt. Lewis signed a receipt for powder from Capt. Stoddard:

> "*Received of Capt Amos Stoddard, 50 pounds of public powder, for the use of my command.*" And it was then added: "*Rec. twenty five pounds of powder in addition to the above, as also one 100# powder cask.*" [208]

Later, five men from Capt. Stoddard's Artillery Company and six men from Capt. Bissell's Infantry Company joined the expedition. Those from Stoddard's company included: John Dame, Alexander Hamilton Willard, John Robinson, Ebenezer Tuttle, and Isaac White. These men were allowed to take their military–issue Model 1795 muskets with them which helped alleviate both the personnel and equipment supply concerns of the expedition leaders.[209] Their recruitment by Lewis & Clark at Kaskaskia is depicted in a scene painted by Michael Haynes presented on the facing page.

Capt. Stoddard and the men of his Artillery Company (notwithstanding the five who volunteered for the expedition) played an important support role for the expedition as an advance team. Their crucial help and assistance to Capt. Lewis & Clark at the embryonic stage of their secret mission was instrumental to their ultimate success. The significance of their role in assisting the expedition has never before been fully recognized —as historians have previously focused more on where Meriwether Lewis and William Clark were and what *they* were doing. Little attention has been paid to the orders or activities of Capt. Stoddard or Capt. Bissell.

Regardless of all the possible motives for sending Capt. Amos Stoddard west at the end of 1802, he demonstrated that he was the right man with the right skill set and the right temperament for the assignment. It was natural that he was therefore chosen to accept the Upper Louisiana on behalf of the United States of America and to become the first civil commandant (and interim governor) of the Upper Louisiana. His orders and appointment came from both Henry Dearborn at the War Department in Washington, in orders dated November 7, 1803,[210] and in the form of his formal commission as the First Civil Commandant of the Upper Louisiana from Governor William C.C. Claiborne in New Orleans dated January 24, 1804.[211]

V. Duty in the Louisiana Territory — 1804 to 1807

At the beginning of 1804 life just started to get interesting for Capt. Amos Stoddard. Almost overnight he became a man of power and prestige. He was immediately thrown into a world filled with problems looking for solutions. It was within all of these difficult conditions that Amos Stoddard best demonstrated his honor and integrity, legal acumen, self–control, level–headedness, and his industry, enterprise and determination to succeed. As we shall learn, there were unscrupulous and self–serving men swirling about him (some even directing him) hoping to take advantage of his possible naiveté and good nature. In the end, and through it all, Amos Stoddard's honor and reputation stayed intact —while others' were tarnished.

One of those unscrupulous figures attempting to direct Capt. Stoddard was Brigadier General James Wilkinson, the senior officer of the United States Army, and one of the two commissioners of Louisiana.[212] Capt. Stoddard received a letter from General Wilkinson from his headquarters in New Orleans on January 23, 1804. The letter appeared to be an early attempt by the infamous general to exert control over Capt. Stoddard on the day before he was officially appointed the first civil commandant of Upper Louisiana, by saying, "it remains to me to give you some directions in your military capacity." We shall hear more of General James Wilkinson and of his attempt to discredit Capt. Stoddard and his acts of betrayal to his country later in this introduction.

The complete story of the transfer of the Louisiana to the United States is beyond the scope of this introduction. At different times, lands included in what was negotiated and known as "The Louisiana Purchase" were claimed by both Spain and France, and these lands were ceded between those two parties at different times for political and economic reasons. We shall use the subject of this introduction's own words, from his book, *Sketches, Historical and Descriptive, of Louisiana*, to summarize this complicated real estate transaction:

> "*On the third day of the preceding November [1763], France ceded to Spain all her territories on the west side of that river [Mississippi], including the island and city of New Orleans, which cession was accepted by the later on the thirteenth of the same month.*" [213] "*On the first of October 1800, she [Spain] entered into a conditional agreement to retrocede the colony [Louisiana] to the French republic, and this retrocession actually took place by treaty on the twenty first of March 1801. The French made preparation to take possession of Louisiana, and an army of twenty–five thousand was designed for that country; but the fleet and army were suddenly blockaded in one of the ports of Holland by an English squadron. This unexpected occurrence…induced the French republic to cede Louisiana to the United States by treaty bearing date of the thirtieth of April, 1803. The Spanish authorities in early December of the same year [1803] delivered possession of Lower Louisiana to M. Laussat, the French commissioner, and it was by him duly transferred on the 20th of the same month, to the commissioners of the United States, governor Claiborne and general Wilkinson.*" [214]

However, the formal transfer of the Upper Louisiana had never been completed. The French Republic had never formally taken possession of Upper Louisiana from Spain. Therefore, a creative solution was devised. As Capt. Amos Stoddard tells it in his book, *Sketches*, "the author of these sketches, was the constituted agent of the French republic in Upper Louisiana, and in her name received possession of that providence on the ninth day of March 1804, and the next day transferred it to the United States." [215]

Capt. Stoddard's Artillery Company ascended the Mississippi from Fort Kaskaskia and landed at Cahokia on the east bank of the river (directly across from St. Louis, present–day location of Cahokia Courthouse State Historic Site) and cantoned with Lewis and Clark before crossing over to the west bank of the Mississippi River on March 9th. Stoddard's Company of the Regiment of Artillerists marched into St. Louis under the command of 1st Lt. Stephen Worrall for the transfer ceremonies.[216] There, Capt. Amos Stoddard accepted transfer of Upper Louisiana from Spain on behalf of the French Republic. The Spanish flag was lowered, and the French flag rose. The French flag was allowed to fly until the next day, when Capt. Stoddard accepted transfer of Upper Louisiana on behalf of the United States from the French Republic. The French flag was lowered, and the Stars and Stripes rose. Amos Stoddard then took command of the territory of Upper Louisiana as the first civil commandant and governor. This transfer of the Upper Louisiana, from Spain to France on March 9, 1804, and from France to the United States on March 10, 1804, is known as "Three Flags Day" in St. Louis, Missouri.

A copy of the signature page of the Upper Louisiana transfer document, transferring Upper Louisiana from Spain to France on March 9, 1804, signed by Spain's Charles Don Carlos Dehault Delassus and received by Amos Stoddard, representing France, and witnessed by Capt. Meriwether Lewis, Antonio Soulard and Charles Gratiot, is provided on the following page.

Dn. Carlos Dehau...sus en calidad de Teniente de Gobernador de ella, por requirimiento que debidamente se me hizo por el citado Amos Stoddart, agente y comisionado de la Republica francesa le entrega la plena posesion, Soberania, y Gobierno de la mencionada Luisiana alta con todos los Puestos Militares Quarteles, y Fortificaciones que dependen, y yo el referido Amos Stoddart, como tal Comisionado reconozco haber recibido la dicha posesion en los mismos terminos que queda prevenido de que me doy por satisfecho y entregado en este dia, en cuyo testimonio el susodicho Señor Teniente de Gobernador y yo hemos firmado respectivamente estas presentes, Selladas con el Sello de nuestras Armas asistidos de los testigos abajo firmados de las quales se sacaran seis exemplares, tres de ellos en Ydioma Español, y los otros tres en el Ynglés

Dado en la Villa de Sn. Luis de Ylinois a 9 de Marzo de 1804

Amos Stoddard

Meriwether Lewis.
Capt. 1st. U.S. Regt. Infty.

Como Adjudt. del Sor. Mayer Gral.
Antonio Soulard

Carlos Dehault Delassus

Ch. Gratiot

Upper Louisiana Transfer Document, March 9, 1804.
Signed by Amos Stoddard, Charles Don Carlos Dehault Delassus, Meriwether Lewis,
Antonio Soulard and Charles Gratiot
Used with Permission. Louisiana Transfer Collection, Missouri Historical Museum,
St. Louis, Missouri

After the transfer ceremonies were complete on March 10th, Capt. Amos Stoddard, as first civil commandant, calling on the public–speaking skills he developed and perfected in his earlier Masonic addresses, spoke eloquently to the people as the newly install representative of the United States of America:

> *"Louisianians,*
>
> *…Thus you will perceive, that you are divested of the character of Subjects, and clothed with that of citizens —You now form an integral part of a great community; the powers of whose Government are circumscribed and defined by charter, and the liberty of the citizen extended and secured. Between this Government and its citizens, many reciprocal duties exist, and the prompt and regular performance of them is necessary to the safety and well fare of the whole. No one can plead exemption from these duties: They are equally obligatory on the rich and on the poor —on men in power as well as those not intrusted with it. They are not prescribed as whim and caprice may dictate; on the contrary, they result from the actual or implied compact between society and its members, and are founded not only in the sober lessons of experience but in the immutable nature of things…Governments differently constituted, where popular Elections are unknown, and where the exercise of power is confided to those of high birth and great wealth, the public defence is committed to men who make science of war an exclusive trade and profession; but in all free republics, where citizens are capacitated to Elect, and to be Elected, into offices of emolument and dignity, permanent armies of any considerable extent are justly deemed hostile to liberty; and therefore the Militia is considered as the palladium of their safety. Hence the origin of this maxim, that every soldier is a citizen, and every citizen a soldier…If in the course of former time, the people of different sides of the Mississippi, fostered national prejudices and antipathies against each other, suffer not these cankers of human happiness any longer to disturb your repose, or to awaken your resentments; draw the veil of oblivion over the past, and unite in pleasing anticipations of the future; embrace each other as brethren of the same mighty family, and think not that any member of it can derive happiness from the misery or degradation of another."* [217]

Later on this day, Capt. Stoddard wrote to Secretary Dearborn, "On the 9th Instant the Province was yielded to me in due form, as Agent of the French republic; and on *this day* I assumed the Country and Government in the name of the United States….I have not been able to discover any aversion to the new order of things; on the contrary a cordial acquiescence seems to prevail among all ranks of people." [218]

Amos Stoddard was kept busy in his role as both military and civilian administrator of Upper Louisiana over the next six months. In order to summarize his activities and challenges, his own words best tell the tale.

Capt. Stoddard wrote to Governor Claiborne in New Orleans on March 26th:

> *"I find that the civil administration in this quarter will draw after it considerable expense, and I have no further money in my hands to defray it…I experience infinite trouble from the Indians. They crowd here by the hundreds to see their new father, and to hear his words. The friendship under the former Government was purchased by presents; they expect the continuance of them; and it is apprehended that, if the customary presents be denied or suspended, they will commit depredations or murders on the Inhabitants…A multitude of people in this quarter, several years ago, sent their necessary writings to New Orleans to obtain Grants for their lands. As these Grants cost an exorbitant price they were not obtained, and the writings left behind. From the various revolutions which have happened in the offices at New Orleans, it is much to be feared that these original writings are lost. I have been pressed to write you on this subject."* [219]

On April 7th Secretary Dearborn wrote to ask seven question of Capt. Stoddard regarding the make–up and composition of the population as well as inquiring with regards to available men suitable for military service in his district. Capt. Stoddard replied with detailed responses to each question on June 3rd.[220] The Secretary closed his correspondence with the statement, "I herewith enclose you the Act of Congress for establishing a Government in Louisiana, by which it will be observed that all civil and religious rights are fully secured to its inhabitants, and no restriction which can effect such as hold slaves." [221] This ending had the effect of notifying Stoddard that his time as commandant of Upper Louisiana would be soon coming to an end, and that Upper Louisiana would in the future continue to be a slaveholding territory.

In the meantime, Capt. Lewis and Clark were busy preparing the Corps of Discovery for their departure up the Missouri River. On May 16, 1804, Capt. Lewis provided Capt. Amos Stoddard with power of attorney, by writing, "In virtue of the authority vested in me by the President of the United States, I do constitute and appoint you my sole Agent to do and perform all and singularly the duties hereafter expressed…" This authorization document was witnessed by two commissioned officers of Stoddard's Artillery Company, 1st Lt. Stephen Morrell and 1st Lt. Clarence Mulford. Later, on April 20, 1805, due to his possible long absence, Capt. Stoddard transferred this agency to Charles Gratiot, Esq.[222]

On May 19th Capt. Stoddard again wrote to Governor Claiborne in New Orleans:

> *"I am now to give you an account of such incidents, worthy of notice, as have occurred since my last.*
>
> *The people of this country have long been troubled with a party of 15 or 20 vagabond Creeks or Muskoe Indians. These Indians, in consequence of their crimes, not only abandoned, but have been disavowed, by their own nation*
>
> *In the month of Novr last some Creek chiefs held a council with the Commandant of New Madrid, and requested that these vagabonds might be killed. During the time of the council one of them stole a Rifle from a white man in the neighborhood. The chiefs pursued him —apprehended him, and bro't him back to New Madrid. They requested leave of the commandant to punish him —which they did by beating him to death with clubs —I mention these circumstances to show in what light these stragglers are viewed by their own nation.*
>
> *….A more than ordinary portion of tranquility prevails at this time in my District. Nothing seems to disturb the people, except the prospect of a connection between them and the Indiana territory."* [223]

Captain Stoddard then wrote to Secretary Dearborn on June 3rd with good news:

> *"I have the pleasure to inform you that Captain Lewis, with his party, began to ascend the Missouri from the village of St Charles on the 21st ultimo. I accompanied him to that village and he was also attended by most of the principal gentelmen in this place and vicinity. He began his expedition with a Barge of 18 oars, attended by two large perogues all of which were deeply laden, and well manned. I have heard from him about 60 miles on his route, and it appears that he proceeds about 15 miles per day —a celerity seldom witnessed on the Missouri; and this is the more extraordinary as the time required to ascertain the courses of the river and to make the other necessary observations must considerably retard his progress. His men possess great resolution, and they were in good health and spirits."* [224]

By mid–June he finally found time to respond to a letter that he had received in the middle of April from his mother, now Phebe Benham and residing in Middlebury, Connecticut at that time. An image of the damaged but preserved third page of the original letter, clear and legible, with his unique signature, appears on the following pages. The overall content of this letter is so insightful that only some trivial and personal details were omitted. His signature, with his finishing flourish, is also one of his best —perhaps due to a feeling of confidence and a sense of pride when writing to his mother.

"St Louis, (Upper Louisiana) June 16. 1804

My dear Mother,

I have duly received your letter of 15th of April last; and I am happy to hear, that you and yours enjoy good health…In consequence of some previous arrangements at the seat of Government, I took possession of Upper Louisiana, in the name of the French Republic, on the 9th day of March; and on the next day, I assumed the Country and Government in the name of the United States. The Spanish laws are still in force, and will continue in force till the first day of October next. In the meantime I have the honor to act as the Governor of the Province, and my time is wholly occupied in the administration of justice. The number of souls in my jurisdiction is about twelve Thousand. The country is beautiful beyond description. The lands contain marrow and fatness, and produce all the conveniences, and even many of the luxuries of life. Several large and rich compact villages are founded on the banks of the Mississippi, and other rivers; some of them are pretty ancient —for you must know that this Country was settled by the French as early as 1679. The compact part of St Louis contains upward of 200 houses, mostly very large, and built of stone; it is elevated and healthy, and the people are rich and hospitable: They live in a style equal to those in the large sea–port towns, and I find no want of education among them. In fine, you may rest assured that my situation is pleasant, and that I enjoy good health. The only circumstance I have to regret is the great expense I am at in living —for all kinds of West India, and other foreign produce is extremely dear. As I am entrusted with temporary office of Governor, I have been obliged to rent a large house in town. This however, is at the expense of the Government —but the daily expenses of my table are considerable. On my arrival here, the Spanish Governor made a public Dinner for me, particularly as I was the Agent and Commissioner to receive the Country. This soon followed by a public Dinner and Ball, made me by the inhabitants of the town. These acts of civility I was obliged to return, and my station required it. Accordingly I also gave a public Dinner and Ball at my own house, and the expense amounted to 622 Dollars and 75 cents. I am in hopes that the Government will remunerate me for this expense as also for the daily extra expenses at my table. Even if I be denied a compensation for these particular expenses, I shall not regret them for the pleasure I have given and received is adequate to them.

When I shall be in the States again, is quite uncertain. A Military man never knows what to depend on. He must always be ready to move when duty calls, and to consider his time and talents as the property of the public. I mean, however, to shape my course Eastward in the fall, if possible. At that time a party of Indian Chiefs from the interior of Upper Louisiana will set out on a visit to the President. They must be conducted by an Officer; and if I can obtain leave of absence, I will conduct them myself to the seat of Government.

Remember me to my brothers and Sisters, as well as to my other relations —particularly to Mr Smith and wife; and you may rest assured that I do not forget my aged mother.

Amos Stoddard, Capt
& First civil Comdt U. Louisiana.

Mrs Benham" [225]

station required it. Accordingly I also gave a public Dinner and Ball at my own house, and the expense amounted to 622 Dollars, and 75 cents. I am in hopes, however, that the Government will remunerate me for this expense, as also for the daily extra expenses of my table. Even if I be denied a compensation for these particular expenses, I shall not regret them: for the pleasure I have given and received is adequate to them.

When I shall be in the States again, is quite uncertain. A military man never knows what to depend on. He must always be ready to move when duty calls, and to consider his time and talents as the property of the public. I mean, however to stop _____ _____ in _____ _____ impossible. At that time a party of Indian Chiefs from the interior of Upper Louisiana will set out on a visit to the President. They must be conducted by an Officer; and if I can obtain leave of absence, I will conduct them myself to the seat of Government.

Remember me to my brothers and Sisters, as well as to my other relations – particularly to Mr. Smith and wife; and you may rest assured, that I do not forget my aged mother.

Amos Stoddard, Capt
& first civil Comm dt. U. Louisiana.

Mr. Benham.

Signature page of Capt. Amos Stoddard's letter to his mother
written June 16, 1804 while First Civil Commandant of Upper Louisiana
Used with Permission. Amos Stoddard Papers, Missouri Historical Museum,
St. Louis, Missouri

Meanwhile, back on March 1, 1804, Secretary Dearborn sent an order to Adjutant and Inspector General Thomas H. Cushing to command Major James Bruff to "repair to Upper Louisiana to take Command of that Department" and for Cushing to direct Stoddard to "send a suitable boat" to Fort Massac for Bruff to "convey him up the River" to St. Louis. [226] This was certainly an unexpected development. Captain Stoddard was just days away from taking possession of the Upper Louisiana at the time —and at the last possible moment Dearborn was proposing a change of command? This order must have been quite disheartening to Capt. Stoddard.

Major James Bruff, like Stoddard, was a veteran of the Revolutionary War but was only recently commissioned in the Army in November 1803.[227] The order to send Bruff to replace Capt. Stoddard was reinforced in a letter from Secretary Dearborn to Stoddard on May 4th, in which he says, "Major Bruff will probably arrive soon after this reaches you, he will have command of Upper Louisiana & its vicinity to whom you will communicate all instructions you have recᵈ from me, Genˡ Wilkinson or the commissioners at New Orleans —and you will afford Major Bruff every aid in your power on all matters appertaining to the interest of the Country or the good of the Service…" [228] However, later, when Secretary Dearborn had time to reflect more clearly on this order, he changed it on May 16th by saying, "In my letter of May 4th Insᵗ I observed that on the arrival of Majʳ Bruff, you would consider him as Commandant of Upper Louisiana & that you would deliver him all instructions you may have recᵈ as Commandant, but on reflection, it appears that as Civil Commandant you must continue until an appointment can be sent by Governor Claiborne to Majʳ Bruff, and of course you will perform the duties specially appertaining to a Civil Commandant until further orders, and Majʳ Bruff will have Command of the Troops & Garrisons in upper Louisiana & its vicinity —." [229]

But why the desire to make a change at the last minute? For the answer we must go back to the election of 1800. President-elect Jefferson directed his secretary, Meriwether Lewis, to draw-up a list of all military officers noting their political leanings —with the intention of purging the army of Federalists.[230] Capt. Stoddard's name appeared on this list with the cryptic note was that he was *"unknown to us."* So, at least at this time, Amos. Stoddard was not recognized as a Federalist nor seen as opposed to the new administration.

The truth is: Amos Stoddard *was* a Federalist. In fact, he had authored an anonymous political address in the *Kennebeck Intelligencer* under the pseudonym, "an Old Soldier," in January 1797 in which he leveled condemnation on James Madison, Albert Gallatin, and Robert Livingston —the Democratic-Republican opposition leaders. He also provided some political advice about Henry Dearborn, the incumbent federal representative, and counseled the people not to vote for him. Dearborn then lost his bid for reelection the next month. In this same article, Stoddard was especially harsh in his renunciation of Albert Gallatin: "the seditious Galitin! *(sic)* What shall I say? How shall I describe that compound of vice and depravity —that disciple of meanness, debauchery and idleness! He is a foreigner by birth and education. —and for some time after his arrival in this country, he wandered about the District of Maine, like Cain, a fugitive and vagabond, destitute of the means of honest subsistence, wholly supported by the bounty which an indignant foreigner naturally excites---Possessed, however, of a little smattering of English and French grammar, he applied to our University at Cambridge for leave to instruct the students in his native language; but he was treated with scorn, rejected as an imposture, considered as totally deficient in capacity of mind, —much more so for his midnight orgies, and other infamous vices to which he was addicted— the *ne plus ultras* of human depravity!" [231]

In September 1797, Amos Stoddard met with Henry Dearborn and they discussed the article of the "Old Soldier." Amos then disclosed to Dearborn *that he was, in fact, the author of the article*! A few days later he wrote a letter to Dearborn: "Revolving in my mind the subject of our conversation, which took place on the 7th Instant, related to the strictures of the old soldier…I am led, in justice to myself and to you…to ask your pardon for the injury they have occasioned to your character and feelings…" [232] However, he did not apologize for his views.

On May 11, 1804 the Secretary of the Treasury, Albert Gallatin wrote President Jefferson: "I dislike so much military commandants in Upper Louisiana, and, perhaps for that reason, think so probable that the whole system will be repealed. That the choice of proper persons has not appeared to me to be of first-rate importance." [233] Therefore, when it was realized by Gallatin that Capt. Stoddard, a Federalist, was appointed civil commandant of Upper Louisiana, he probably strenuously objected to his appointment.

In any case, it is a near certainty that Capt. Amos Stoddard's political leanings were probably unearthed and his acceptability as first civil commandant reconsidered. Henry Dearborn may have exposed him within the administration as being the author of the article attacking Madison, Gallatin, Livingston and himself.

Politics: this is likely why Captain Amos Stoddard ran afoul of the Jefferson administration and why he was nearly dismissed in March 1804 and ultimately pushed out of power at the end of September 1804.

There was also a kind of dysfunction that existed within the overall command structure at this time. Governor Claiborne was responsible for civil administration of Louisiana, while Secretary of War Dearborn, General Wilkinson, and Adjutant General Cushing represented the military administration. There was great deal of suspicion, mistrust, and dislike between these key members of the military and civil administration. Cushing was listed as *"violently opposed to the Administration"* but was loyal to General Wilkinson and was retained solely on ability. Secretary Dearborn never trusted General Wilkinson since the Revolutionary War. General Wilkinson didn't like or trust Governor Claiborne.[234]

It should be noted here that during the trial of Aaron Burr for treason in 1807, with General Wilkinson suspected as being a co–conspirator, Major James Bruff testified at the trial. On Tuesday, October 6, 1807 he stated that in the summer of 1805, Colonel Burr and General Wilkinson were together in St. Louis, and that, "Captain Stoddard also hinted to me, after his return from Fort Massac, that some great scheme was in agitation between Colonel Burr and General Wilkinson, but he did not say what." Therefore, suspicion and mistrust of General Wilkinson and Aaron Burr by Capt. Stoddard had certainly been raised by the time he left St. Louis for Washington to escort the Indian Chiefs in the fall of 1805. Major Bruff testified a great deal to the treasonous acts of General Wilkinson, and it is therefore apparent that he was not complicit with General Wilkinson. [235]

In any case, Major Bruff took over military command on July 1, 1804 [236] while Capt. Stoddard continued to exert control over civil administration and justice.

There was plenty of political maneuvering during this time. This vast, new territory represented a great opportunity —with significant potential for deceitful and corrupt men as well as those vying for power.[237] Governor William Henry Harrison of the adjacent Indiana Territory (consisting of the present–day states of Indiana, Illinois, and part of Ohio) was at this time attempting to exert *his* influence and trying to extend *his* power. As an example, Capt. Stoddard on June 3rd replied to a letter from Gov. Harrison from May 2nd regarding Harrison's request for intelligence and soliciting Stoddard's ideas in dividing the Upper Louisiana territory. Capt. Stoddard provided Gov. Harrison with his specific ideas to divide the territory into five districts and counties —including providing census statistics for each area and designating the boundaries. This came from information Stoddard gathered and sent at the request of Sec. Dearborn.[238] Previously, on March 31, 1804, President Jefferson had asked Gov. Harrison to make these recommendations to him.[239] Conveniently, Gov. Harrison used Capt. Stoddard's recommendations from the June 3rd letter nearly verbatim in a letter dated June 24, 1804 from Vincennes (capital of the Indiana Territory) to President Jefferson —without mentioning Stoddard's name or letter in his reply and recommendations.[240] [241] This information was then forwarded to Secretary Dearborn. On June 6th President Jefferson wrote to Dearborn, "The division of Louisiana into districts relating to the military as well as the civil administration, will you be so good as to consider those proposed by Governor Harrison." However, Sec. Dearborn had also received the census and demographic information provided to him by Capt. Stoddard's sent the same day Capt. Stoddard replied to Gov. Harrison's request.[242] President Jefferson then replied to Gov. Harrison on July 14, 1804 outlining the approved divisions —exactly as Gov. Harrison suggested and the same as provided by Capt. Stoddard in his June 3rd letters to Secretary Dearborn and Governor Harrison.[243]

It is interesting to note that these letters between Capt. Stoddard and Gov. Harrison were missing from Harrison's official papers and were not included in the book, *Governors Messages and Letters: Messages and Letters of William Henry Harrison,* published in 1922. Ultimately, Harrison was appointed as the governor of the District of Louisiana and replaced Capt. Stoddard on October 1, 1804.[244] Whether Capt. Amos Stoddard realized Harrison had used his recommendations and did not bother to provide him even a mention of credit is not known.

As a consolation for losing both his military and civil administration power, Capt. Stoddard was "constituted and appointed" Justice of the Peace by the newly installed Governor of the District of Louisiana, William Henry Harrison, on October 1, 1804.[245] This was a rather large fall from power. Capt. Stoddard was still a military officer but he was no longer commanding any troops —his artillery company had been turned over to Major Bruff. Further, it's hard to imagine how a military officer could be assigned by a civilian governor to a civil administration position. What exactly his duties and responsibilities were are unclear. He probably presided as a judge over trivial local judicial matters. As a lawyer, he was probably effective during the short period he likely served in this capacity.

However, Capt. Stoddard continued acting as agent for Capt. Meriwether Lewis. On October 29, 1804 he wrote to President Jefferson:

> *"St Louis 29th Octr 1804 —*
>
> *Sir,*
>
> *Captain Lewis, before he left this [place], engaged a trader on the River Demoine [Des Moines] to procure vocabularies of the Ayovais and Sioux languages. The trader has obtained that of the former, which I do myself the honor to enclose: That the latter will be furnished sometime next spring, when it will be transmitted to you agreeably to the request of Capt. Lewis.*
>
> *I am, Sir, with sentiments of high respect,*
> *Your very huml Servt,*
>
> *Amos Stoddard, Capt*
> *corps of Artillerists*
>
> *The President of*
> *The United States"* [246]

Capt. Stoddard followed up with a second letter to President Jefferson on behalf of Capt. Lewis with the vocabulary of the Sioux Indians provided by trader Mr. Crawford on March 24, 1805,[247] and facilitated the delivery of specimens from the Lewis and Clark expedition sent from Fort Mandan on April 7, 1805.[248] Shortly after this, on April 20, 1805, Capt. Stoddard assigned agency for Capt. Lewis to Charles Gratiot, Esq.[249]

While the weight of administration responsibility was lifted from Capt. Stoddard's shoulders, accusations, possibly stemming from jealousies or from more political posturing, soon began to surface.

First, in a lengthy letter to General Wilkinson on September 29, 1804, just two days before Harrison was to assume responsibility of civil administration as the new governor, Major Bruff expressed some complaints about Capt. Stoddard and suggested Capt. Stoddard had been "offended" by him during the transfer of his command.[250] General Wilkinson forwarded the letter to Secretary of War Dearborn. Perhaps this was done as an attempt to discredit Capt. Stoddard.[251] In any case, it does not appear that Major Bruff and Capt. Stoddard had a friendly relationship.

Before we go on, it is important to understand that one of the biggest problems in the transition of the Louisiana Territory to the United States was the determination of the validity of Spanish land grants. This rather convoluted situation would itself require a separate volume to explain —and still might not provide clarity. Therefore, only a cursory mention can be made of it.

One of the first persons to bring up the issue of fraudulent grants of land in Upper Louisiana was Capt. Amos Stoddard in a letter to the Secretary of War from Fort Kaskaskia on January 10, 1804.[252] Capt. Stoddard held a powerful position for just over six months, and part of his administrative role was to inventory and validate bona fide land grants and recognize and cancel fraudulent ones. The worst examples of human nature reached its peak during this time as unscrupulous men attempted to grab valuable lands in Upper Louisiana, primarily those with known mineral deposits, through fraudulent land grants at the time of the transition.

In late 1804, Major Seth Hunt of Northampton, Massachusetts, was appointed Commandant of the newly formed Ste. Genevieve district in Louisiana.[253] He soon ran afoul of General James Wilkinson in the late summer of 1805. General Wilkinson wrote to Major Hunt on August 22, 1805:

> *"I think proper to inform you, that it has become necessary I should confer with you, at this place, as I have done with other Commandants of the Territory on various topics relative to the State of your district, and also touching on information which you gave me respecting the mal–conduct of Capt Stoddard, which I am disposed to institute an inquiry into, in Such manner as may be most agreeable to you: you are therefore not to leave this Territory, before you have complied with this order..."* [254]

Major Hunt sent a snarly reply on August 31, 1805, writing:

> *"If I have declined answering your letter of the 18th of July, it was because I conceived it, from its style, not entitled to a reply —Since however you appear to desire an answer, you may rest assured that I will not leave Louisiana...With respect to Captain Stoddard, I have only to remark that I have no personal knowledge of his having been guilty of any misconduct either as a civil or military officer —You are already informed of the reports that I heard circulated to his disadvantage at St Louis, if they are true, they merit an inquiry which you will institute in any and "such manner as may be most agreeable to" yourself—"* [255]

The "mal–conduct" alluded to against Capt. Stoddard had to do with the Spanish land grants.[256] It is a well–known fact that Amos Stoddard received (or purchased) a large Spanish land grant around this time, and the validity of this land grant was later proved in the Supreme Court of the United States by Henry Stoddard, as previously mentioned.

On September 5, 1805, a court of inquiry was held at the town of St. Louis, *"at the request of Capt Amos Stoddard of the Reg of Artillerists,"* as announced in "General Orders, Head Quarters St Louis —Septr 3rd —1805."

It was then announced from "Head Quarters, Sepr 19th 1805," that:

> *"The General approves the opinion of the Court,"* that *"The Court after hearing and Maturely considering the Testimony adduced as aforesaid, as well as Support of, as in defense of the Charges alleged are of the opinion that the aforesaid charges are wholly unfounded, and that Captain Amos Stoddard, in his official transactions has conducted himself with discretion, ability, and honor and to the general Satisfaction of the People of Louisiana, and that he deserves the approbation of Government —"* [257]

General Wilkinson wrote yet another lengthy discourse to the Secretary of War on September 8th. In it, he laid out his case against Major Hunt and made accusations of misconduct against Capt. Stoddard, stating the facts of such misconduct as he perceived them. Perhaps he was attempting to undermine the outcome of the court of inquiry proceedings held three days earlier? [258]

Governor Wilkinson, on September 21, 1805, then included an enclosure to a letter he wrote to Secretary of War Dearborn, in which he stated, "You have under cover also, the Opinion of a court of enquiry, held at the request of Captn Stoddard, and shall be furnished the proceedings by the next mail, which will give you a glimpse of a Combination, that has occasioned much inquietude in this Territory, and is Still laboring to excite discontents, and to break this Community into intolerable factions —" He also in this letter requested a court of inquiry upon his own conduct —indicating that he somehow felt himself in somewhat of a compromised position in this matter.[259] However, General Wilkinson's court of inquiry (in fact, two of them) would come later.

Why General Wilkinson still seemed to be attempting to discredit Capt. Stoddard is not known. However, the following day, September 22nd, he wrote to Secretary Dearborn to give him an account of the impending visit to Washington of the "Missouri and Mississippi Indian Chiefs" and to say "Captain Stoddard will accompany the Indians, as he has long requested a furlough."[260] His demeanor towards Capt. Stoddard in this letter was far more congenial than in his more recent correspondences. However, this may have been the result of a letter he had previously received from the Secretary on August 5th in which Dearborn wrote:

> "As it is probable a number of Chiefs from the Missouri and Mississippi, will come on to the Seat of Government, you will please to make such arrangements, as to the numbers, conductors and interpreters, as good policy and economy combined, will dictate; and you will give the person, who may conduct them, such particular instructions as to the route and expenditures, as the case may require. I wish that Capt Stoddard may be the conductor, if you shall judge it expedient."[261]

Then, in a surprising reversal, General Wilkinson makes a referral of Capt. Stoddard on October 22nd 1805, when he wrote to President Jefferson:

> "The Bearer hereof Capt Amos Stoddard who conducts the Indian deputation on their visit to you, has charge of a few natural productions of this Territory…Permit me Sir to name Capt. Stoddard to you, as a Man of worth & Intelligence, He understands well the political History of this Territory, and no one is better acquainted with the view, Interests & merits, of the Individuals composing its population."[262]

In this referral, he certainly spoke the truth regarding Capt. Amos Stoddard. There were few at that time in Upper Louisiana who had a better understanding of the history of the territory than Amos Stoddard. Wilkinson himself also had much experience in this territory, but he was not very interested in its history. He only had his own self–interest —and to this end he had given his allegiance to and was on the payroll of the Spanish government. He soon would take his traitorous personal interest to a new level when he conspired with Aaron Burr and participated in an attempt to make the Orleans Territory and the Spanish controlled lands west of the Mississippi an independent and sovereign territory from the United States.[263]

Gov. Harrison also took time to support Capt. Stoddard with the Secretary of War by providing an acknowledgement of the Captain's performance as first civil commandant of Upper Louisiana in a letter to "Honble. Henry Dearborn, Esq., *Sec. of War,*" on October, 18, 1805, in which he wrote:

> "I beg bearer to repeat to you by Capn Stoddard what I have before communicated that his whole conduct whilst acting as Civil Commandant of Upper Louisiana was as far as I can judge extremely proper and upright and such as my opinion greatly contributed to destroy the prejudices which existed in this country prior to the cession against our country and our countrymen."[264]

Capt. Stoddard then commenced with the Indian deputation order. He was probably glad to be leaving Upper Louisiana and the men left in charge of it.

Governor Wilkinson wrote to the Secretary of War on October 22, 1805 to say:

> *"Sir/ The Kickapoos deputation did not arrive here until the evening of the 14ᵗʰ Instant, and we commenced our conference the next day and finished it on the 18ᵗʰ as you will perceived from Governor Harrison's [letter] of the 19ᵗʰ, which accompanies this —The Deputation destined to visit the President, will commence their journey this day under the conduct of Capt Stoddard, and will consist of twenty six persons from eleven Nations."*

Then it was added:

> *"N.B. since closing this letter, one of the Scioux Chiefs, has agreed to accompany the deputation. W"*

This brought the total to 27 persons from 11 nations.[265]

Captain Stoddard makes an interesting observation about Indians and their eating habits during this deputation in his book, *Sketches*, which is worth mentioning here. He stated:

> *"Nothing is more unfounded than the assertion, that the Indians in general are small eaters. This is probably the case with those who live in warm climates, where vegitables, and the spontaneous productions of the earth, are usually preferred to animal food. The Indians in all parts of Louisiana, as also those on the east side of the Mississippi, are known to be voracious eaters; and the truth can be illustrated by a thousand examples, one of which follows: When the author of these sketches conducted about thirty Missouri chiefs to the seat of government in 1805, as before stated, the first three hundred miles of the way was too thinly inhabited to furnish them with regular meals; so that it became necessary to purchase fresh beef for them, of which they devoured on an average, three hundred and fifty pounds per day, or nearly twelve pounds per man!"* [266]

Thus ended the year 1805 for Captain Amos Stoddard. When he wrote in the first paragraph of his autobiography in 1812, "I have never been depressed so low —raised so high, or whirled about with such a mixture of good and bad fortune…," he was likely speaking, at least in part, of his trials during this period from 1803 to 1806. He escorted the Indians and delivered them to the "Seat of Government" in Washington on December 22, 1805, thereby completing his mission.[267] He probably removed himself from responsibility of the Indian Chiefs as quickly as possible and took his furlough time, but not before presenting the Indian Chiefs to President Jefferson on January 4, 1806.[268]

In the fall of 1806, Capt. Amos Stoddard recruited a new company of men. The next we hear from the intrepid captain he is on his way to Newport Barracks in Kentucky and on to Fort Adams in the Mississippi Territory.

VI. Duty in the Mississippi Territory — 1807 to 1810

Capt. Amos Stoddard deserved the rest from his furlough. In a letter from Philadelphia dated September 29, 1806, Capt. Stoddard reported to Colonel Thomas H. Cushing in New Orleans:

> *"I was lately removed from Connecticut to this City, where I opened a rendezvous on the 15ᵗʰ Instant. As I am prepared to enlist as many men as will complete my Company by the 10ᵗʰ of Novr I have reason to expect that I shall pass over the mountains about that period. When once started, I shall hasten with all possible expedition to my Company —especially as I find you have some work with the [?]. The private Secretary of the Spanish Minister, some weeks ago, mentioned to a friend of mine, with whom he is intimate, that Louisiana would not be long in our possession. I suspected then, that he spoke the language of his master, and this suspicion has been fully confirmed by the subsequent aggressions in your quarter."* [269]

Stoddard wrote to Cushing again on November 1ˢᵗ from Carlisle, Pennsylvania, an Army training depot and gateway to the frontier at that time:

> *"I shall start for Pittsburgh in the course of about ten days with about 140 recruits. I am directed by Col. Burbeck to repair with them to Fort Adams. From the low state of the water in the Ohio, I am apprehensive, we shall probably be detained sometime, if not all winter, at Pittsburgh...I have made a proposition to Col. Burbeck to exchange Companies with Capt House —but have received no answer. I have two reasons to offer in favor of this exchange. The first is, that all my baggage and papers are at St Louis —and Col. Burbeck says, that the detachment cannot be detained at Massac till I can obtain them; and without them I shall be much distressed. The second is, that I have been three years engaged in compiling an account, historical and descriptive, of the upper Louisiana —and without a short residence in that territory, I cannot complete it...It would, however, be very disagreeable to me to be placed under the command of Major Bruff, who I understand, means to continue in service, not–withstanding his frequent promises to resign next spring. —"* [270]

Stoddard here is speaking of his book, *Sketches, Historical and Descriptive, of Louisiana*, published in September 1812, and reflects on his unhappy experience with Major Bruff in St. Louis during 1804 and 1805.

Capt. Stoddard once again wrote to Col. Cushing on November 8ᵗʰ to say:

> *"Tomorrow I start for Fort Adams with 133 men, viz. 69 Artillerists, and 64 Infantry. I shall proceed with as much expedition as possible, but I expect the Ohio is very low...I expect that the Company at the southwest point is destitute of a captain —for Colonel Burbeck informs me, that Capt [Lemuel] Gates [271] was designed for that post —but he died a few weeks since at this place. Transfer would answer the views I mentioned to you in my last —a direct communication exists between that place, and the various parts of Upper Louisiana, and this weekly. It is also very healthy —of such a place I really stand in need, as my frame is still shattered in consequence of the fever, under which I languished for more than seven months. I however, submit the whole to your consideration, with this remark, that I have no disposition to be gratified at the expense of my duty."* [272]

This is a very insightful communique. We learn from it that Capt. Stoddard was ill with fever for seven months during 1806 while he was on furlough —probably from February until September. We also learn he has recruited a new company of artillery as well as a company of infantry. At that time, captains in command of an Army company had the added responsibility to recruit men as well as outfit them and train them; Captain Stoddard has also asked to be transferred to Newport Barracks, Kentucky, "southwest point," along the Ohio River at present–day Newport, across the river from Cincinnati, in place of the deceased Capt. Gates. This request must have been granted, because Capt. Stoddard is known to have been in command there from approximately January 1807 until November 1807. His presence prior to February 8, 1807 is further evidenced in a letter written by James Taylor from "New Port, Kentucky," to the Secretary of State, in which he wrote, "Capt. Stoddard who now commands the Garrison here has a good many good artificers & others." [273]

Capt. Stoddard's time at Newport Barracks was indeed short, as he next is writing to Colonel Henry Burbeck (in Washington) from Fort Adams in the Mississippi Territory on November 18, 1807. The first part of his letter contains a report of the unfortunate death of Capt. John McClary on November 15th from illness. In the remainder of the letter, he reports high satisfaction with his command. He says, "The four Companies at this place are now healthy, and in appearance they are equal, if not superior, to any in service. I venture to say, that my own is superior to any in your Regiment —if not certainly the best in this quarter of the world of whatever Corps. —and I hope to deliver it over in good order to my successor." [274]

For the duration of Capt. Stoddard's command at Fort Adams (located 40 miles south of Natchez, Wilkerson County, Mississippi) the editor was able to draw upon information from the *Orderly Book of the Company of Captain Amos Stoddard* from the National Archives. The first entry in the orderly book is "Garrison Orders" dated "Fort Adams, November 9th, 1807" and reads, "For the future, Sergeant David Evans of Captain Stoddard's Company will perform the duty of Sergeant Major and consolidate the Provision Returns. (Signed) Amos Stoddard, Cap[t] Commanding" This orderly book, written by Sergeant Evans, provides clear and exceptionally good penmanship from a soldier who takes an obvious pride in his work as well as in his record book. While orderly books generally only provide a reprint copy of general orders received, dispositions of the proceedings of court martial and some garrison orders, they do offer a glimpse into the discipline of the troops, the movements of units and changes in command. Court martial proceedings are a nearly every day occurrence.[275]

An early entry is made under, "Orders, 16th November 1807":

> *"Captain Stoddard will parade Two Subalterns, Two Sergeants, Two Corporals and all the Music*
> *of Fort Adams, with fifty privates of the first Regiment, to attend the Funeral of Capt. McClary,*
> *who made his exit, last night at nine Oclock; This Detachment will pay the Funeral Honors due*
> *the Deceased. The funeral will take place this day at such an hour as the Commanding Officer*
> *of Fort Adams may think proper to direct; Captain Stoddard will give the necessary directions*
> *with respect to the Effects of the deceased, agreeably to the ninety fourth article of the first Section*
> *of the rules and Articles of War. (Signed), Jacob Kingsbury, Lt Col., 1st Regiment of Infantry,*
> *Commanding, Camp Columbian Spring."* [276]

As we shall learn later, not all officers were treated equally by their commanders when it comes to extending "Funeral Honors due the Deceased." Obviously it was important for Capt. Stoddard to personally ensure a proper show of respect and honor for this fine officer, whom he probably barely knew, and to provide him the dignity of a military final farewell.

Through to the end of January 1808, very little is recorded in the orderly book except matters of court martial for infractions ranging from "neglect of duty," to "desertion and losing sundry articles of public clothing" as well as "being drunk on post," and "speaking disrespectfully of his officer and disorderly conduct." Thirty to fifty lashes on the back was not an uncommon sentence.

It is noted that the garrison orders on January 26th are signed, "Amos Stoddard, Major, Commanding." [277] On November 24, 1807, Secretary of War Henry Dearborn submitted Capt. Amos Stoddard's name to President Thomas Jefferson for promotion to Major. Ironically, this promotion came as result of the resignation of Capt. Stoddard's nemesis, Major James Bruff, on June 30, 1807.[278] This promotion was approved and made effective, retroactively, to June 30, 1807. Major Stoddard must not have received word of his promotion until this time. However, "official" word must have taken longer. A page in the orderly book entered on March 1, 1808 provides official evidence with the handwritten "Lists of Promotions, and appointments in the Army of the United States" which shows Major Stoddard's promotion, and others, exactly as they were submitted by Secretary Dearborn to President Jefferson on November 24, 1807. [279]

As a demonstration that men found an outlet for their sporting nature while on garrison duty at Fort Adams and vicinity, Major Stoddard issued the following order on February 23rd: "For the future the odious and Cruel practice of Cock Fighting is prohibited within the limits of the public ground and all those invested with authority in the Soldiery are particularly enjoined to seeing that this order is carried out —" [280]

Romantic thoughts might easily pass through the mind of a lonely soldier on extended garrison duty in the Mississippi Territory. A barely legible entry in the orderly book, at the bottom of the page on April 20th, reads:"*Oh never, never, let a Virtuous mind despair; For constant Hearts are Love's peculiar care.*" [281] This is from a romantic British comedy, Cibber's *She Wou'd and She Wou'd Not*.[282]

It was during his time at Fort Adams that Major Stoddard first received word of his acceptance into the United States Military Philosophical Society (USMPS). He replied to this news with a letter to the founder of the society, William Popham, from Fort Adams on January 26, 1808,[283] thanking him for the privilege. The honor of being accepted into this society allowed Major Stoddard to connect with some of the greatest men of his time. Presidents John Adams, John Quincy Adams, Thomas Jefferson, and future presidents James Madison, and James Monroe were members, as were all of the leading men of the U.S. military establishment and its brain trust at the time.[284] Major Stoddard notes his membership in the Society on the title page of his book, *Sketches, Historical and Descriptive, of Louisiana*.[285] The motto of the Society, inscribed on an engraved diploma distributed to all Philosophical Society members, *Scientia Bello Pax*, translates to, "Science in war is the guarantee of peace" [286] (which sounds a lot like President Ronald Reagan's "Peace through Strength" of the 20th century).

Nothing significant is recorded in the orderly book from March through May. However, on June 17th the following garrison order is recorded:

> *"The Troops of this Garrison will be in readiness to move for Fort Dearborn at a moments warning; —Lieut Preble is to assume command of the company of Artillerists, to whom Lieut Reed will transfer all of the necessary books and papers, The soldiers are to take no useless baggage with them, —The Commanding officers of Companies will make out returns for tents. Tents will be distributed as follows, viz, To the Artillerists, 8 tents, To Captain Pikes Company 8 Tents, to Captain Swans Company 9 tents, and to late Captain Lockwoods Company 9 tents, —"* [287]

The next garrison order recorded in the orderly book is at Fort Dearborn on June 30, 1808. Fort Dearborn was located at present–day Chicago, Illinois, on the south bank of the Chicago River, near the present–day intersection of East Wacker Drive and North Michigan Avenue.

On July 3rd the garrison order entry of the day at Fort Dearborn was: "As tomorrow is imphatically the birthday of our Country, each Soldier will Receive one gill of extra whisky at 12 Oclock, After that day the troops will parade for roll call in their clean Summer uniforms with their arms in good order. —" [288]

It is unclear what situation prompted the quick removal from Fort Adams to Fort Dearborn, but nonetheless, they do not appear to be in danger or experiencing hardship during the summer months along Lake Michigan. A warning was issued in garrison orders on July 13th regarding complaints of the theft of vegetables from "citizens in this neighborhood…to prevent as much as possible such odious and disgraceful practices" and this appeared as the only major issue or concern recorded in July.[289]

Nothing more of significance is reported in the orderly book through August (other than the entry of numerous court martial proceedings —which consumed considerable time). However, on September 22, 1808, "Detachment Orders" are written: "The Troops at this Cantonment will hold themselves in readiness to march at the Shortest moment. (Signed) Amos Stoddard, Major, Commanding" This was the last entry made with Major Stoddard commanding. Immediately after this entry, "District Orders" are entered, with "Col. Thomas H. Cushing Commanding," beginning September 29, 1808, which stated: "The following dispositions of the companies of the first Regiment of Infantry within the Mississippi Territory is made in obedience to a Special Order of the Secretary of War." Cushing goes on to make the dispositions and orders, "these companies are to be marched to this cantonment tomorrow, and a Muster Role of each company made out, without Remarks, and to be presented to the Commanding officer." [290]

What exactly were Major Stoddard's orders, and where exactly did he go from Fort Dearborn, has not been emphatically determined. However, several clues to his whereabouts were found. In his book, *Sketches, Historical and Descriptive, of Louisiana*, Major Stoddard tells us, "The author of these sketches ascended the Red river in February 1809, at which time, owing to the swell of the Mississippi, the whole country was buried about 10 feet under water." [291] From this we can assume that he likely left Fort Dearborn, descended the Mississippi River, and arrived in the Red River area of the Mississippi Territory as early as the fall of 1808.

The second clue comes on September 22, 1809, when Capt. Meriwether Lewis wrote to him at Fort Adams from Fort Pickering, Chickasaw Bluffs (present–day Memphis, Tennessee), "I calculated on the pleasure of seeing you at Fort Adams as I passed, but am informed by Capt. Russell the commanding officer of this place that you are stationed on the West side of the Mississippi. —" [292] This would make Natchitoches, Mississippi Territory, northwest of Fort Adams, near the Red River and on the west side of the Mississippi River, as the most likely place for Major Stoddard to be during this time.

A third clue comes in a letter from John Sibley in Natchitoches to Amos Stoddard on April 2, 1812, in which he wrote, "Mr Mullanphy formerly of St Louis has a pretty large store in this town, [and] a few other stores are established since you were here..." [293]

Therefore, we can place Major Stoddard as being in the Red River and Natchitoches area and vicinity *at least* between February and October 1809.

Regardless of Major Stoddard's assignment or purpose for being in the Natchitoches and Red River area, it is certain that he made the best use of his time, in terms of satisfying his intellectual curiosity and accumulating knowledge, while exploring the region for his book *Sketches*. It is possible that he may have requested furlough for this pursuit during this time as no correspondence from him during these months has been found.

Before ending this section, it is appropriate to touch on the aforementioned letter Major Stoddard received from Capt. Meriwether Lewis on September 22, 1809.

From the beginning, when they first met at Kaskaskia in November 1803, Stoddard and Lewis (and Clark) became fast friends. Capt. Lewis trusted him enough to appoint him as his agent on May 16, 1804. When the Corps of Discovery expedition returned to St. Louis on September 23, 1806,[294] Amos Stoddard was busy escorting the Indian Chiefs to Washington to meet President Jefferson. Then he took furlough until September 1807. Stoddard's assignments in the Mississippi Territory during 1808 and 1809 again kept him and Lewis apart. While Capt. Lewis stated they had not kept in touch, he faults himself, saying, "I must acknowledge myself remiss in not writing you in answer to several friendly epistles which I have received from you since my return from the Pacific Ocean." [295] They are not known to have met again in person since that day on May 21, 1804 when Capt. Amos Stoddard traveled with Clark (presumably from Fort Dubois aboard his command boat) to St. Charles and saw the Corps of Discovery commence their mission up the Missouri River.[296]

The letter Major Stoddard received from Capt. Lewis was one of the last letters ever penned by the famous explorer and hero. He was distraught at the prospect of going to Washington to explain the "protest of some bills which I have lately drawn on public accounts form the principle inducement for my going forward at this time." He asks Major Stoddard, "I hope you will therefore pardon me for asking you to remit as soon as is convenient the sum of $200 which you inform me you hold for me." [297] While troubled by the accusations of financial malfeasance, and having at that time some obvious personal financial difficulties, Capt. Lewis nonetheless wrote with gentlemanly courtesy. Images of the pages of this important and historical letter are found on the facing and following pages.

Fort Pickering, Chickesaw Bluffs.

Dear Maj.   September 22d 1809. —

I must acknowledge myself remiss in not writing you in answer to several friendly epistles which I have recieved from you since my return from the Pacific Ocean. continued occupation in the immediate discharge of the duties of a public station will I trust in some measure plead my apology. —

I am now on my way to the City of Washington and had comtemplated taking Fort Adams and Reliance in my rout, but my indisposition has induced me to change my rout and shall now pass through Tennessee and Virginia. the protest of some bills which I have latily

---

Letter sent from Capt. Meriwether Lewis at Chickasaw Bluffs
to Major Amos Stoddard at Fort Adams on September 22, 1809
Used with Permission. Amos Stoddard Papers, Missouri Historical Museum,
St. Louis, Missouri

drawn on public account form the prin=
=cipal inducement for my going forward
at this moment. an explaination is all that
is necessary I am sensible to put all
matters right. — in the mean time the
protest of a draught however just, has
drawn down uppon me at one moment
all my private debts which have excessively
embarrassed me. I hope you will there=
=fore pardon me for asking you to re=
=mit as soon as is convenient the sum of
$200. which you have informed me
you hold for me. — I calculated on
having the pleasure to see you at Fort
Adams as I passed, but am informed by
Capt. Russel the commanding officer of this
place that you are stationed on the West
side of the Mississippi. —

Letter sent from Capt. Meriwether Lewis at Chickasaw Bluffs to Major Amos Stoddard
Used with Permission. Amos Stoddard Papers, Missouri Historical Museum,
St. Louis, Missouri

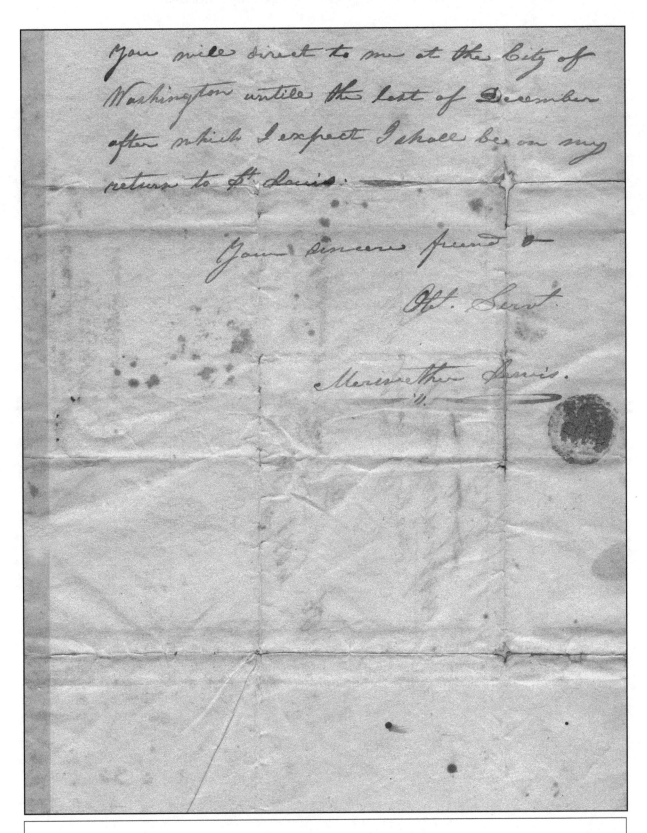

You will direct to me at the City of Washington untill the last of December after which I expect I shall bee on my return to St. Louis. ————

Your sincere friend &
Obt. Servt.

Meriwether Lewis.

Letter sent from Capt. Meriwether Lewis at Chickasaw Bluffs to Major Amos Stoddard
Used with Permission. Amos Stoddard Papers, Missouri Historical Museum,
St. Louis, Missouri

While the death of Capt. Meriwether Lewis on October 11, 1809 is still a matter of controversy, Major Amos Stoddard received the following letter from John Brahan on October 18, 1809. This letter from Brahan contains nearly the same words and language Brahan wrote in a letter to Thomas Jefferson on the same day.[298] The letter to Major Stoddard is as follows:

"NASHVILLE, TENNESSEE, 18th October, 1809

DEAR SIR: I am sorry to inform you of the death of Governor Meriwether Lewis, which took place on the Morning of 11th Instance at the home of a Mr. Grender about seventy–five mile from here on the Natchez Road, it is reported that he arrived there the evening before —the man of the house was from home —the Governor went to bed in a room alone. About three o'clock the woman of the house, who slept in a house near the other, heard two pistols fire —she awoke the servants, and they rushed into the Room, and found the unfortunate Governor weltering in his blood; he had shot himself in the head & just below his breast —he died in about three hours; in a few hours Major Neely Agent to the Chickasaws came up, who had remained behind to hunt two horses which they had been lost the night before —he had him interred and took into his care and possession two trunks, said to contain his valuable papers, amongst which is said to be his Journal to the pacific ocean, & perhaps some vouchers which he was taking on for settlement —Majr Neely has his pistols, Rifle, Watch, &c. —his servant, John Parney, will proceed on early in the morning with letters to Mr. Jefferson from Major Neely communicating to him the particulars of the unhappy affair —I lament extremely the unfortunate fate of this worthy Character.

With great esteem, I remain your friend also,

JOHN BRAHAM (sic)

P.S. My Kindest respects to Captain House and to Lieutenant Kingsby.   *J.B.*

To Major Amos Stoddard
U.S. Artillerist,
Washington City." [299]

After the disturbing news that his friend Capt. Lewis had passed, we next find Major Stoddard in command at Fort Columbus, on Governor's Island in New York Harbor, at the end of December 1809, reporting to his friend and mentor, Colonel Burbeck, and where he mostly stays until spring 1812.

VII.   Duty at Fort Columbus — 1810 to September 1812

Major Stoddard took command at Fort Columbus on Governor's Island in New York Harbor sometime in mid–December 1809. In a letter to Col. Burbeck from Fort Columbus on December 28, 1809 he wrote the following:

> *"Sir,*
> *I have just received your favor of the 24th Instant. —Perhaps I did not express myself so clearly as*
> *I ought in my former letter. The fact is that, on my arrival here, I examined the orderly books, and*
> *found an excellent system of police established. I therefore issued an order putting it into opperation,*
> *and confirming it."* [300]

Besides confirming that he had only recently arrived at Fort Columbus, Major Stoddard provides an example of what may have been one of the first cases of using the management technique "Best Practices" in his military command.

Once Major Stoddard returns to seaport garrison duty at Fort Columbus, his life, for the most part, was relatively quiet, peaceful and stable. Command on Governor's Island in New York Harbor provided a place of respectable prominence, convenient mail service, and close proximity to metropolitan centers, books and to his friends and family in Connecticut and Massachusetts.

One of the first things Major Stoddard did after he arrived in New York was to join the New York Historical Society. He became a member on April 10, 1810.[301] This probably allowed him access to libraries, books, and reference materials as well as enjoy the acquaintance of men of distinction. He notes his membership in this Society on the title page of his book, *Sketches, Historical and Descriptive, of Louisiana*.[302]

Major Stoddard came under a different military command in 1809 through 1812. James Madison defeated Charles Pinckney to become the fourth president of the United States and the new commander–in–chief.[303] Madison then selected former doctor William Eustis as his secretary of war in March 1809, replacing Henry Dearborn.[304] While General James Wilkinson was still senior general of the U.S. Army, Colonel Henry Burbeck,[305] the chief of artillery, became Major Stoddard's direct commander in 1810 at Fort Columbus.

In a letter to Col. Burbeck on June 12, 1810, Secretary of War William Eustis ordered Burbeck to "take your quarters at Fort Columbus and assume the command of the works and the troops in the Harbor & City." [306] In this regard, Major Stoddard may not have been first in command at Fort Columbus while Col. Henry Burbeck was present, but he certainly was first in command in his absence.[307]

Major Stoddard mentions "Doctor Eustis" in his autobiography, and it is clear that he did not hold William Eustis in high esteem. Yet there is no instance in which he shows any disrespect towards the Secretary of War. With Col. Burbeck reporting directly to the war secretary, and running back and forth between Fort Columbus and Washington and other seaport posts, Major Stoddard probably had little direct contact or communication with Secretary Eustis —and he may have preferred it that way.[308]

In his autobiography manuscript, Amos provides a nearly full page description of the plight of soldiers, especially officers, at the end of the Revolutionary War, and some intrigues that took place at that time. To better understand his commentary and the political conditions he now experienced in 1809, as well as to explain the animus by which many regarded Secretary of War William Eustis, and his successor, John Armstrong, it is necessary to provide some background at this time. However, in order to do so we have to revisit the end of the American Revolution, to a near mutiny of the Army that occurred at Newburgh, New York, on the Hudson River, north of West Point, the site of General Washington's Headquarters, which became known as the "Newburgh Conspiracy."

Towards the end of the war an "address and petition of the officers of the Army of the United States" was written to the Continental Congress in December 1782 and delivered to Congress on January 6, 1783. The petition is signed, by among others, "on the part of the general hospital, W. Eustis, hospital surgeon." [309] This address and petition outlined the issues and grievances of the officers of the Army by men who were worried about their fate.

In early March, fearing that Congress would not address their issues before disbanding the Army, two anonymous and unsigned letters were distributed at the Headquarters of the Army camp at Newburgh. These letters constituted an attempt to blackmail Congress for back pay and pensions, with a veiled threat of the mutiny of the Army if their grievances were not addressed. The key events that took place over the next three days are summarized as follows:

- A notice of a meeting of the general and field officers, to be held the following day, March 11 at 11am, was first distributed in the Army camp at Newburgh on March 10th followed by the circulation of an unsigned letter addressed to the officers of the Army the same day. This first anonymous letter took the form of a grievance petition;

- General Washington then issued general orders on the morning of March 11th commanding a meeting of the officers to be held on March 15, 1783; [310]

- A second unsigned letter was then circulated on March 12th. This letter was in the form of a rebuttal to General Washington's general orders rescheduling the meeting of the officers.

The conditions and circumstances that led to the events at Newburgh in the middle of March 1783 are many and complex. The issues were as old as the war itself: Lack of financial resources; regional and individual resentments and jealousies; and politics.

There was, without a doubt, primarily an economic component to most of the soldiers' grievances — including those of the officers. The soldiers had not been consistently paid throughout the war as they were promised and many desperately needed the compensation they were due in order to restart their civilian life. In a testimonial, Private Joseph Plumb Martin wrote his opinion on the subject in his memoirs:

> "I received one months pay in specie while on the march to Virginia, in the year 1781, and except that, I never received any pay worth the name while I belonged to the army. Had I been paid as I was promised to be at my engaging in the service, I needed not to have suffered as I did, nor would I have done it; there was enough in the country and money would have procured it if I had had it. It is provoking to think of it. The country was rigorous in exacting my compliance to my engagements to a punctilio, but equally careless in performing her contracts with me, and why so? One reason was because she had all the power in her own hands and I had none. Such things ought not to be." [311]

There was also a political component to the affair. As the war neared its end, many powerful people started to compete for influence and control. There was a nationalist group in favor of a strong federal government, which became known as the Federalist Party, started by Alexander Hamilton —and a powerful central government required revenue derived from the states. Then there were those "anti–nationalists" who desired that the individual states should continue to largely operate autonomously and not be required to fund a large federal government. They were to become known as the Democratic–Republican Party started by Thomas Jefferson and James Madison. These men also feared a standing federal army and promoted returning to the security and defense practice of using militias controlled by the states.

Many states were in desperate financial straits, and they could hardly afford to support a new central government. Without a remedy to the future finances of the country, there was no possibility of reaching an agreement for funding the back pay and pensions of the soldiers.

Some nationalists in Congress, such as Alexander Hamilton, used the Army's grievances to further push their position concerning the issue of public credit and funding for the central government, citing the Army's restlessness on the issue of back pay and pensions and predicting dire results if Congress refused their satisfaction.[312][313] There was no shortage of unhappy, dissatisfied and nearly destitute lower ranking officers in the Army who served the needs of the nationalists in this clash. Regardless of their individual motivations, they were easily manipulated.

The actions of the conspiracy were set in motion on March 8th upon the arrival of General Walter Stewart, who rode into camp at Newburgh from Philadelphia with news of the most recent proceedings in Congress, and soon after his arrival went to see General Gates, his former superior. Within hours, rumors began circulating around the camp that Congress was going to disband the Army without addressing the soldiers' issues of back pay and pensions. This was the spark that ignited the proverbial fire and triggered the notice on March 10th for a meeting of the officers on the 11th and the distribution of the anonymous letters that followed on March 10th and 12th.[314]

General Washington was made aware of the notice calling for a meeting of the officers, and the first "anonymous letter" circulating at the camp, on the same day. The first anonymous letter was addressed as follows:

> *"To the Officers of the Army.*
> *Gentlemen, —A fellow soldier, whose interest and affections bind him strongly to you, whose past sufferings have been as great, and whose future fortune may be as desperate as yours —would beg leave to address you…"* [315]

The next day, March 11th, General Washington issued his own order for a meeting of the officers on March 15th to be presided over by Major General Horatio Gates:

"GENERAL ORDERS
Head–Quarters, Newburgh, Tuesday, March 11, 1783

The Commander in Chief, having heard that a general meeting of the officers of the army was proposed to be held this day at the new building, in an anonymous paper which was circulated yesterday by some unknown person, conceives, although he is fully persuaded that the good sense of the officers would induce them to pay very little attention to such an irregular invitation, his duty, as well as the reputation and true interest of the army, requires his disapprobation of such disorderly proceedings. At the same time he requests the general and field–officers with one officer from each company, and a proper representation from the staff of the army, will assemble at 12 o'clock on Saturday next, at the new building, to hear the report of the committee of the army to Congress. After mature deliberation, they will devise what further measures ought to be adopted as most rational and best calculated to attain the just and important object in view. The senior officer in rank, present, will be pleased to preside, and report the result of the deliberations to the Commander in Chief." [316]

General Washington likely suspected that General Gates was a knowing participant in the calling of the meeting and of the mysterious, unsigned letter. His Excellency's order had the effect of canceling the illegal meeting proposed for that very day, and placing himself, and not others, firmly in charge of the situation at a meeting of the officers scheduled for March 15, 1783.

A second "anonymous letter" was then circulated the next day, on March 12th. In the letter, there was actually an attempt to claim that General Washington *agreed* with the content and tone of the first letter, and had *merely* rescheduled the meeting of the officers. It read, in part:

"To the Officers of the Army.

Gentlemen, The author of a late address, anxious to deserve, though he should fail to engage your esteem; and determined, at every risque, to unfold your duty, and discharge his own, would beg leave to solicit the further indulgence of a few moments' attention…The General Orders of yesterday which the weak may mistake for disapprobation, and the designing dare to represent as such, wear in my opinion a very different complexion, and carries with it a very opposite tendency. Till now, the Commander in Chief has regarded the steps you have taken for redress with good wishes alone: his ostensible silence has authorized your meetings, and his private opinion has sanctified your claims. Had he disliked the object in view, would not the same sense of duty, which forbade you from meeting on the third day of the week, have forbidden you from meeting on the seventh? Is not the same subject held up for your discussion, and has it not passed the seal of office, and taken on the solemnity of an order? This will give system to your proceedings, and stability to your resolves. It will ripen speculation into fact; and, while it adds to the unanimity, it cannot possibly lessen the independency of your sentiments." [317]

On March 15, 1783, General Washington, in what is called his "Newburgh Address," spoke to the officers. A portion of his statement reads as follows:

> "*Gentlemen, —by an anonymous summons, an attempt has been made to convene you together. How inconsistent with the rules of propriety, how unmilitary and how subversive of all order and discipline, let the good sense of the army decide…This dreadful alternative of either deserting our country in the extremest hour of her distress, or turning our arms against it, which is the apparent object, unless Congress can be compelled into instant compliance, has something so shocking in it, that humanity revolts at the idea. My God! what can this writer have in view, by recommending such measures? Can he be a friend to the army? Can he be a friend to this country? Rather is he not an insidious foe?…let me conjure you, in the name of our common country, as you value your own sacred honor, as you respect the rights of humanity, and as you regard the military and national character of America, to express your utmost horror and detestation of the man, who wishes, under any specious pretences, to overturn the liberties of our country; and who wickedly attempts to open the flood–gates of civil discord, and deluge our rising empire in blood.*" [318] [319]

When General Washington finished his prepared comments, he removed from his breast pocket a letter that he had received from Joseph Jones, a member of the Continental Congress from Virginia, which he desired to read to the officers as a way of demonstrating the goodwill of Congress in addressing their concerns. After reading the first sentence, he paused for a moment, began fumbling in his jacket pocket to retrieve a pair of spectacles, and put them on. Then, he looked up, and in an apologetic tone, said, "Gentlemen, you must pardon me. I have grown gray in your service, and now find myself growing blind." [320] This was the first time General Washington had ever appeared in public wearing eyeglasses.

General Washington continued to read the letter —but it was unnecessary. His point had been made: while they had suffered in the pursuit of liberty, so had he. His audience was stunned and silent. Some wept. General Washington immediately left after finishing. He had effectively shamed the Army officers into setting aside their grievances, and had defused the potential for insurrection.

Motions for resolution were offered to the officers by General Gates, and seconded by General Putnam, which passed unanimously among the officers, and which read, in part:

> "*Resolved, unanimously, that the officers of the American army view with abhorrence, and reject with disdain, the infamous propositions contained in a late anonymous address to the officers of the army, and resent with indignation, the secret attempts of some unknown person to collect the officers together, in a manner totally subversive, of all discipline and good order.*" [321]

Doctor Eustis, a participant in this scandalous affair, was chosen by President James Madison in March 1809 to the position of secretary of war, a position he was highly unqualified to hold. Dr. Eustis was a close personal friend of Aaron Burr, the divisive vice president under Thomas Jefferson, who killed Alexander Hamilton in a duel in 1804.[322] Aaron Burr had been the one who introduced the widowed Dolly Todd to Congressman James Madison of Virginia.[323] Burr was later tried for treason in a conspiracy plot to undermine the United States government in May 1807 but was acquitted. This plot included the participation of General James Wilkinson among other men of great prominence.[324] General Wilkinson was later tried at a court martial at Fredericktown, Maryland, in 1811, where, ironically, Major Amos Stoddard served as a member of his trial. [325] [326] Wilkinson was acquitted in December 1811.[327] He was tried a second time in 1815 and acquitted as well.[328]

Oddly enough, former Vice President Aaron Burr, the grandson of Rev. Jonathan Edwards, was a distant relative of Major Amos Stoddard. Whether Major Stoddard knew this or not is not known.

President James Madison, with the war going badly, lost confidence in Secretary William Eustis. Eustis resigned on December 3, 1812 [329] and Madison replaced him temporarily with Secretary of State James Monroe. On January 13, 1813, Brigadier General John Armstrong, Jr. was appointed secretary of war [330] — *yet another member of the central Newburgh conspirators!* As Secretary of War, Armstrong was so convinced that the British would not attack Washington during the War of 1812 that he took no actions to defend the capital. The British then marched into Washington on August 24, 1814 and burned down the White House. For this military blunder, Secretary Armstrong was forced by President Madison to resign in September 1814.[331]

Neither Eustis nor Armstrong was particularly effective in the important position to which they were appointed. Dr. Eustis was a particularly poor choice with the possibility of a renewed war with England looming on the horizon. He was a political appointee. At least John Armstrong, a former brigadier general, had previous military experience.

William Eustis later admitted to Dr. James Thatcher that "he was in the secret" [332] while Armstrong later admitted writing the "anonymous letters" of the Newburgh conspiracy. Gen. Joseph Gardner Swift in his memoirs says that Armstrong told him in December 1813, as they discoursed on the "Newburgh Letters," that, "had he been one year older he would not have written them; they have been a mill–stone hung about his neck through his life. He corroborated Dr. Eustis' [333] by saying that Colonel [Timothy] Pickering was on the committee that appointed him [General Armstrong] to write, and that Dr. Townsend had also been on that committee." [334] Therefore, Major Amos Stoddard, in his autobiography, was absolutely correct in his assessment of these men and their direct involvement in attempting to blackmail Congress and undermine General George Washington in the spring of 1783. Yet he followed their orders as a loyal and dedicated soldier and officer.

Before we continue the saga of Major Amos Stoddard, it is important to emphasize that since 1798 many men of questionable character had risen to power in government and in the Army, while other men of strong patriotic values and high morals languished in their political and military careers. It was previously mentioned that there were "unscrupulous and self–serving men swirling about" Amos Stoddard. In this, the editor refers primarily to the accused conspirators, Aaron Burr and James Wilkinson, and the supporters, contributors and collaborators of their schemes; and secondarily, to those men of questionable loyalty and honor from the end of the American Revolution. While Burr and Wilkinson were acquitted of their accused crimes, and while Eustis, Armstrong, and Pickering were never brought up on charges for their involvement in the Newburgh Conspiracy, all these men were tainted from these scandals. Yet they all succeed to positions of power. Thus was the political environment in which Amos Stoddard found himself during his post–revolutionary military life and career.

Major Stoddard, in a letter to Henry Burbeck on February 15, 1810, provides some intelligence to his old friend and shares his thoughts on the quality of the officer corps of the Army:

> *"[General] Wilkinson is at present at Natchez; he is expected here [Fort Adams] the last of the month on his way to New Orleans; it is rumored that he does not intend visiting Washington at present…Capt Cross was on his trial at the date of the letter, and will be acquitted. Lieut Newman, and Capt Armistead of the 2d Regiment of Infantry are awaiting their trials. It appears that Lt Col. Freeman is about to be arrested again, and the writer is of the opinion, that the event will prove serious to him —much more than his former trial. General Hampton is rigid in his duty, and a number of officers under him are in limbo. Perhaps all is right, as at least one half of us must to the <u>right about</u> before the United States will have a good corps of officers."* [335]

During 1810, Major Stoddard was writing Col. Burbeck frequently —an indication Col. Burbeck was either in Washington or traveling to other fortifications and posts. On March 8th Major Stoddard wrote Col Burbeck a lengthy letter on his progress at Fort Columbus.[336] As previously mentioned, Col. Burbeck was ordered by the Secretary of War on June 12, 1810 to take command and to take quarters at Fort Columbus.[337] However, that order does not seem to have been enforced or was later reversed. Except for the period he served on a court martial trial, Major Stoddard is clearly in command at Fort Columbus during 1810 until the spring of 1812. In February alone there are eight known letters which he sent to Col. Burbeck from Fort Columbus.[338] This rate of correspondence continues into 1811 and through April 1812. As Fort Columbus was a garrison post assignment, most of this correspondence would have related to routine matters and is therefore not detailed for this introduction.

However, there were a couple of interesting developments which occurred during this period that merit mentioning. One is the important opportunity this posting allowed for Major Stoddard to work on his book, *Sketches, Historical and Descriptive, of Louisiana.*

Stoddard spent nearly a decade compiling information during his assignments out west and in writing his book. He must have conceived the idea of the book almost immediately after arriving at Kaskaskia in the spring of 1803. In his letter to Col. Thomas H. Cushing on November 1, 1806, while on his way to Pittsburgh, he stated he had already spent three years compiling information for it.[339] On January 10, 1811, Thomas Jefferson (or his secretary, at least) wrote to Major Stoddard from Monticello:

> *"Th. Jefferson presents his compliments to Majr Stoddert and his thanks for forwarding the inclosed paper, which he now returns with his signature. altho generally declining to subscribe for new books, he has done it with pleasure in this instance, & hopes that Major Stoddert's subscriptions in this state may make it convenient for him to name some person in Richmond who may be authorised to receive the price of the work. he salutes him with esteem & respect."* [340]

Therefore, Major Stoddard, in early 1811, had apparently nearly completed his book and was already soliciting subscriptions. Thomas Jefferson must have followed through on his promise to subscribe and purchase the book —a copy of the book can today be found in the archives of the Thomas Jefferson Library at Monticello.[341]

On April 2, 1812, Major Stoddard received a letter from John Sibley from Natchitoches, Mississippi Territory (whom he probably befriended during his time there in 1808–9) in which Sibley wrote, "By the last Mail I had the pleasure to receive your letter of the 10th of Jany, for which I am obliged to you: It gives me great pleasure to hear of your extraordinary good health, Justly attributable to good living & a climate that agrees with your Constitution —you Say nothing about the publication of your Book, your last letter says it is in the press. —" [342] Therefore, we can surmise that Major Stoddard put his garrison command duty time to good use in completing his book and getting it to the printer sometime in 1811. The publishing year of the book is 1812.

It should be mentioned that Major Stoddard's book, *Sketches, Historical and Descriptive, of Louisiana*, is nearly 500 pages in length. It was his magnum opus. It fulfilled his pursuit of knowledge, love of writing, and intellectual curiosity. In it, he demonstrates his vast knowledge of the world and the Louisiana territory, geography and history, as well as many sciences, including but not limited to: geology, botany, meteorology, metrology, and mathematics. His vocabulary is extensive, his grammar exceptional, and his spelling nearly flawless. How many among us today can write 500 pages in longhand with minimal corrections —and without the use of spellcheck or an Online dictionary and a thesaurus? His highly descriptive narrative of the Creole people of Louisiana, as an example, reflects his natural ability of observation. Since a journal for note–taking has never been found, it is likely this book is written largely from memory —and from his own words we know he is known to have possessed a powerful memory.

In his book, Major Stoddard was also one of the first men of his age to write openly and publish his thoughts on the dehumanizing practice of slavery. In it he wrote:

"It is an invidious task for a man, born and educated where slavery is unknown, to indulge any strictures on the municipal policy of respectable states and territories, or to arraign at the bar of public justice the flagitious conduct of their citizens; yet considerations of a higher nature than those resulting from local prejudices and habits, suggest the propriety of a few remarks. When we see the feelings of humanity outraged, the most odious tyranny exercised in a land of freedom, and hunger and nakedness prevail among plenty, who but must lament the infraction of those universal moral obligations, which subsist between different nations, societies, and individuals, and which are inscribed on the heart of every man, and mistaken by none!...It is a stain on the character of civilized nations, that slavery was ever authorized among them; and how a Christian people can reconcile it to their consciences, no one can determine, except maybe on account of interest. Here then we find a motive for all our actions, much more powerful than the dictates of morality or religion. While we keep so many of our fellow creatures in bondage, let us cease to talk about liberty and the rights man; let us not claim what we deny to others." [343]

Major Amos Stoddard was far more than just a soldier, a lawyer, a writer, a military officer or a war hero. He was an honest, moral, highly intelligent and scholarly man of adventure He had many gifts, but his greatest gift was his constant pursuit of knowledge and his willingness to share it with his fellow man.

The other significant occurrence during Major Stoddard's duty in New York at Fort Columbus was that he was called to serve as a member of the court martial trial of General James Wilkinson held in Fredericktown, Maryland in the months of September through December 1811.[344][345] On October 20th Major Stoddard wrote to Col. Burbeck from "Frederick Town," "It appears to me, that we have nearly completed this trial —we seem waiting only for the Judge Advocate's pleasure —what he has to detain us, I know not —but presence that, in two weeks, we shall adjourn…" [346][347] Again on November 10th he wrote Col. Burbeck, "The Court has adjourned to receive the General's defense —so that we expect to wind up our business this day fortnight…I shall be at my post as soon as possible, and God knows, that I very much regret the obligation I was under to leave it." [348] Apparently, Major Stoddard wasn't happy to be serving at the trial. His last correspondence to Col. Burbeck from "Frederick Town" was on December 24th, in which he reports, "We shall begin this day to decide on the charges —and if wading through a thousand difficulties, and escaping from perplexities innumerable, and sharing a great deal of labor, do not entitle us to some honor, we shall at least expect to avoid censure." [349]

General Wilkinson was finally acquitted on Christmas Eve, December 24, 1811.[350] However, they did not entirely escape "censure." General Joseph Gardner Swift, a member of the trial, wrote in his memoirs, "The members of the court soon dispersed, and on the 26th December I paid my respects to the Secretary of War, Washington, and found myself not so graciously received as was the wont of that gentleman who had favored me with his intimacy. I also found in this place of large gossip, especially so in the time of the session of Congress, that the acquittal of General Wilkinson was received with disappointment by the executive, and it was rumored that some of the charges had been made by an underling of the War Department adverse to the impartiality of some of the older officers on the court, but Mr. Madison would not consent to any such mode of impugning the right of opinion, and thus the charges were suppressed." [351]

By January 5, 1812, Major Stoddard is back at Fort Columbus.[352] On January 27th Stoddard wrote to Secretary of War Eustis from Fort Columbus that he will commence work for a new boundary for West Point as soon as he is released from court martial duty, "I will make it my business, Sir, to have the report transmitted as soon as practical." [353]

Again, a flurry of correspondence between Major Stoddard and Col. Burbeck takes place. Nine letters are sent by Major Stoddard to Col. Burbeck in March and eight in April.[354] In one exchange, Major Stoddard appears to be watching his mentor's back. On February 10th he wrote:

> *"There is a story circulating in the City, (where it came from I know not) that you declared last summer your determination not to oppose the British in case they should attack this harbor, or something to this effect. I simply mention this circumstance to put you on your guard —especially as it is said, that the declaration has been or soon will be reported to one of the heads of departments, —not to the Sect of war."* He goes on to add: *"if the british strike, they will not take the trouble to give us any warning —I even doubt whether they will give us time to rally the militia —think of this. —Everything shall be done, which depends on me."* [355]

Another new military assignment was presented to Major Stoddard in the spring of 1812 —and Stoddard was an experienced, smart and logical choice for it. It also helps explains the gap in correspondence with Col. Burbeck from the first of May until the end of August 1812.[356]

In the fall of 1811, Secretary of War Eustis was presented with a set of recommendations for the improvement of the military establishment of the United States by a board of officers. They made specific recommendations related to the artillery. However, the initiative for writing an artillery training manual appears to have come from Col. Henry Burbeck, commanding the Regiment of Artillerists, and a veteran of the Continental Artillery in the American Revolution. Col. Burbeck apparently appointed Major Stoddard to edit, correct and revise the manual *"Manoeuvres"* of General Tadeusz Kosciusko, an engineer credited with building the fortifications at West Point (and elsewhere) during the American Revolution.[357] On December 24, 1811, writing from the court martial trial of General Wilkinson at Fredericktown, Maryland, Major Stoddard inquired of Col. Burbeck, "What has become of our Artillery Exercise? I understand Col. Smyth is preparing one for the Infantry. Can a man of nine months service actual service only, do this?" [358] Alexander Smyth was commissioned a colonel in July 1808 and served as inspector general for Secretary of War Eustis. He was promoted to brigadier general in 1812 before being forced out of the Army due to incompetence.[359]

On February 14, 1812, Major Stoddard proposed to Secretary of War William Eustis that, "if the simple exercise was prefixed to these manoeuvers, the system would not, in my opinion, be susceptible of much improvement." [360] [361] Eustis approved of this suggestion, and Stoddard moved quickly. He purchased the copyright (on behalf of the Government) for Kosciuszko's manual from Col. Jonathan Williams of the United States Military Philosophical Society (USMPS), of which he was a member, added gun drills for both field and garrison ordnance, as well as other new material, and edited and corrected the original text and sent everything to the printer in May 1812 —paying the $607 printing expense out of his own pocket to save time.[362] [363] Stoddard's *Exercise for Garrison and Field Ordinance Together with Maneuvers* [364] was the first official manual of drill and tactics for the United States artillery and remained in use until well after the War of 1812.[365]

On June 18, 1812, a Declaration of War against Great Britain was signed by President James Madison. [366] By July 9, 1812, Major Stoddard was still in Washington, writing to Dr. Phillip Turner and offering some career advice.[367] On July 16, 1812 he accepted an appointment from Secretary of War Eustis as Deputy Quartermaster.[368] He would now stay in Washington and be working in the War Department with Col. Dedius Wadsworth, Commissary General of Ordnance.[369]

On July 17th the British captured Fort Mackinac (on Mackinac Island) in the Michigan Territory. On August 23, Major Stoddard was sharing his thoughts about the loss with Col. Burbeck:

> *"I very much suspect that [Lieut. Porter] Hanks was <u>surprised</u> —indeed it has been said so in the papers. It appears to me, that 80 men in that Garrison, with the artillery they had, could have defended themselves agt the Indians —the Indians would not have stormed it —and the 40 regulars were not able to carry it alone. I have always been of opinion that this place would be attacked —you remember I urged you to have another company sent there —but you thought one sufficient. On my first arrival here, I told the Sect that Makanak would fall —but he did not believe it. We shall next hear, that poor [Captain Nathan] Heald is a prisoner or massacred —you may rest assured, that Chicago will also fall."* [370]

The Major was exactly right on all counts. Lt. Porter Hanks had been surprised by the attack on the morning of July 17th —but Hank's didn't put up a fight either —not a shot was fired.[371] He was also right about Fort Dearborn at Chicago.

However, Fort Detroit fell first. William Hull surrendered the garrison on July 16th. Hull was later tried for treason and cowardice [372] but was acquitted of the charge of treason and found guilty of cowardice and sentenced to death by firing squad. He was granted a reprieve by President Madison due to his Revolutionary War service.[373]

Fort Dearborn in Chicago was then evacuated on August 15th for fear of being unable to supply it. Captain Nathan Heald tried to escape and flee to Fort Wayne [374] with his 54 U.S. regulars, 12 militia, 9 women and 18 children, but they were attacked and massacred by the Indians less than 2 miles from the fort. Capt. Heald and his wife along with 28 regulars, seven woman and six children were taken prisoner. The rest were killed —some viciously.[375]

The start of the war looked bleak. Fort Mackinac, Fort Detroit, and Fort Dearborn had been lost in the first 60 days. As Major Stoddard pointed out, "the consequences of these misfortunes are that the Indians will be encouraged…" [376] The Indians to whom he refers were the indigenous tribes which formed a tribal confederacy, led by Tecumseh, who sided with the British during this war.

Major Stoddard again wrote to Col. Burbeck from Washington on August 29th:

> *"The Secretary wants a description of the fortification at Makinak, and of the one at Detroit, and he has requested me to ask it of you. He wishes to know whether they are simple stockades or regular works —whether built of Earth, or more solid materials —whether they have ditches & whether they could not have resisted a storm, especially if attempted by Indians. As you are well acquainted with these fortifications, you can easily give him the outlines, and dimensions."* [377]

It seems odd that the Secretary of War would be asking these questions after the forts were lost. Perhaps that is what is being inferred. He goes on to write:

> *"The Sect told me last evening, that Genl Hull and his army were undoubtedly prisoners of war—and that Detroit was in the hands of the English. This is commencing the war with a witness. The suspicion is, that the Militia took to their heels at the moment when firmness was required—and that the General was left to defend himself with about 400 regulars—but could not these have defended themselves for some time in this Garrison, supported by 34 pieces of artillery? There is a mystery in this business, which will no doubt be unraveled in a few days. Chicago and Fort Wayne must unquestionably fall—and perhaps the troops massacred. Poor Heald! Poor Rhea!"* [378]

Major Stoddard refers to Captain Nathan Heald in command of Fort Dearborn at Chicago, which had already been abandoned, and Captain James Rhea in command at Fort Wayne. Captain Rhea, however, disgraced himself at Fort Wayne, apparently being drunk and in his quarters during the Indian attack on that compound.[379] He was later forced to resign from the military for his conduct.[380] The Indian attack on Fort Wayne did not succeed. However, Major Stoddard had identified the main question regarding the quick surrender of Fort Detroit: whether or not the fort could have been held during an attack.

The War of 1812 was now entering a new phase, with the Americans desperately trying to forward position supplies and attempting to take some initiative. At a time when Amos Stoddard probably wished for less chaos and more stability in his life, and when he likely preferred intellectual pursuits to adventure, he was tossed about in a major war effort. As he wrote to his mother in June 1804, "A Military man never knows what to depend on. He must always be ready to move when duty calls, and to consider his time and talents as the property of the public." And so, duty called.

VIII. War of 1812 — September 1812 through April 1813

The war was going very badly at this point. Major Stoddard is working in the pinnacle of military power —at the War Department in Washington. It was probably Col. Wadsworth who ordered Major Stoddard to Pittsburgh at the beginning of September 1812.[381] On September 10th Secretary of War Eustis wrote to William Henry Harrison, the governor of the Indiana Territory and head of the Indiana Territory militia:

> *"Sir:*
>
> *Your letters of August 28th and 29th have been received. You will perceive by my communications of August 22d and 28th that you have anticipated the wishes of the President. In addition to the Instructions to Mr. Buford Deputy Commissary and to the assistant Deputy Quarter Master at Newport to furnish whatever you require, the assistant D. Q. Master at Pittsburgh has been directed to forward with all possible expedition, arms, ammunition equipment, tents, and other camp equipage. Arrangements have been made for increasing those supplies and Major Stoddard of the Artillery is now at Pittsburgh, to give additional energy to those measures, to prepare artillery & other necessary munitions for that service, & correspond with the Commanding General relative to the same. You must be sensible that to make carriages & get up a Train of Artillery will require time."* [382]

On September 17th Secretary Eustis again wrote to William Henry Harrison to inform him he had been appointed the command of the Northwestern Army by President Madison. He goes on to say, "Every exertion is making to give you a Train of Artillery from Pittsburgh —to effect which you must be sensible requires time. Major Stoddard the Senior Officer of Artillery at that place will advise you of his arrangements and progress & receive your instructions. Captain Gratiot of the Engineers will report himself to you from Pittsburgh. He will receive your Orders & join you with the first pieces of Artillery which can be prepared or receive such Orders as you may direct." [383]

"Captain Gratiot of the Engineers" refers to Charles Gratiot Jr., son of the fur trader in St. Louis who so much assisted Capt. Amos Stoddard back in 1804, and who so graciously wrote to thank Capt. Stoddard as a member of the local committee of St. Louis upon Stoddard's departure as first commandant and interim governor. His son Charles was appointed as a cadet to West Point by President Thomas Jefferson in 1804. He graduated in the fourth class of West Point in 1806 and was commissioned into the Corps of Engineers.[384] Capt. Gratiot would later play a key role in designing and engineering Fort Meigs in spite of the illness he suffered there.

The biggest problem Major Stoddard was experiencing at Pittsburgh was in procuring wood for the artillery gun carriages.[385] Major Amos Stoddard wrote to Col. Henry Burbeck from Pittsburgh on September 21, 1812:

"Pittsburgh 21. Septr 1812

Dear Colonel,

I duly received your favor enclosing me the Draft of an 18pd Carriage. I have got a hard task before me. After causing a man to ride about the Country for three days, some old oak Gunnels of Kentucky boats were discovered, which were of a size suitable for [conversion] to 18 pounder carriages. These I have procured and am now at work on them. Perhaps I shall be able to make 3 or 4 carriages from them. It is very difficult to obtain workmen —the late fire in this place has caused them all to be engaged. Besides, ammunition wagons, travelling forge, fixed ammunition, and implements of every kind have to be made —the whole are now underway —You will therefore judge of my perplexity — and if everything is not ready so soon as may be expected, I am in hopes to escape blame. In addition to the artillery, I have to furnish the militia and Volunteers (nearly 6000) which occupies most of my time. I have already furnished about 4000 —and the other 2000 must be furnished on the 2d of next month....Septr 22d. Since writing the above I have received your favor of the 15th. I at the same time recd one from the Secy —you appear to expect more from me than can be performed by ten men, under like circumstances." [386]

Major Stoddard wrote to the Secretary of War on September 16th, 22nd and 24th and informed him that he will attempt to outfit the militia gathered at Meadville (PA) and Cleveland as far as is practical, and warns of the disorganization of the militias ("the greatest confusion and insubordination prevails") and that equipment shortages abound. He also stated, "I have scoured the country for 30 miles around for wheelwrights and blacksmiths. The result is not favorable." [387]

Secretary of War Eustis, on September 26th, updated Harrison on the progress of supplies and artillery:

"I have the honor to inclose for your information Lists of Ordnance and Military Stores which have been ordered from Philadelphia and this place to Pittsburgh since the 1st Instant in addition to those at that place and coming in under contracts from that vicinity. The cannons, ammunition, shoes, blankets, and part of the other Stores are on the way, and most of them will probably reach that place before the 5th of October. Major Stoddard the Department Quarter Master will continue to forward supplies to you and will advise you of all his issues to the Troops, as well as those sent forward to the Army, and keep you informed of all the resources at Pittsburgh." [388]

On October 20th Major Stoddard reports to Captain Piatt, the deputy quarter master general, from Pittsburgh regarding the state of the artillery destined for Ohio, consisting of five 18 pound guns, eight 12 pound guns, and six 6 pound guns, and three howitzers. He adds, "The carriages and ammunition are not yet completed —but I presume they will arrive at the rapids of the Miamis [Fort Meigs] as soon as the guns." On the 21st, he updated the War Department about progress of repairing and shipping artillery, and also mentions the confusion in the local militias he has observed, by adding, "From what I can learn the men manifest a strong spirit of insubordination, disorder, and even mutiny." He also mentions that Brigadier General Harrison is clamoring for supplies of every description and that he is endeavoring to oblige him. [389]

It should be noted here that in a letter he sent to Lieut. Bryson, assistant deputy quarter master at Newport, Kentucky on November 15, 1812, Major Stoddard signed the letter, "Amos Stoddard, Maj., Dep^y Quarter Master." [390] This is the only correspondence noting his role as deputy quarter master that was uncovered. Previously, on September 18th, he signed his correspondence to Capt. James R. Butler of the Pittsburgh Blues,[391] "Amos Stoddard, maj., 1 Reg^t Artillerists," and on the 2nd of December, he again ended his correspondence to Col. Cushing, "Amos Stoddard, maj., 1st Reg^t Art^y." This trifle is noted primarily as a matter of record. It seems that the department or role he was representing depended on who he was writing to and for what purpose he was writing. His position and role once he arrived in Pittsburgh does not appear to have been well defined.

Major Stoddard and Lieutenant Hezekiah Johnson must have been feeling the pressure to get the supplies to General Harrison. Capt. Johnson wrote General Harrison a rather straightforward reply in response to the General's complaints about himself and Major Stoddard —complete with itemized supply lists of the shipments sent.[392] General Harrison then wrote to the Secretary of War on November 17th to say that he had received Lieutenant Johnson's letter, and that, "It is in reply to a complaint I made equally of Major Stoddard and Lt. Byron and himself as to the State of supplies under their care, and directing them to send me weekly statements of everything received, forwarded, and on hand. From both the other officers, I received polite and satisfactory answers. Mr. Johnson alone has thought not only to be very insolent upon the occasion, but instead of the documents required to send me those of which copies are herewith enclosed." [393] This is clearly an indication that General Harrison desired to be intimately involved in all supply–related matters at this time. This point becomes important later with regard to General Harrison's letter to Secretary of War Armstrong of May 13, 1813, in which he infers the supply responsibility was delegated to others and pleads command ignorance —which is entirely inconsistent with his present demand for constant updates and reports.

On November 18th, Major Stoddard informed Secretary Eustis of supply and artillery preparations and that he is now being assisted by Captains Charles Gratiot and Joseph Wheaton, and says, "I hope it will be believed, that everything has been done by me, which it was in the power of *one man* to do." He also informed Secretary Eustis that he regrets being ordered to join the Northwest Army, which means serving with the militia, whom he regards as incompetent.[394][395]

Major Stoddard then wrote to the War Department on November 24th to say he was pleased to enclose a detailed return of ordnance stores forwarded to Brigadier General Harrison, and that he also declines to get involved in a heated dispute between General Harrison and Lieutenant Johnson, writing, "He [General Harrison] seems not, however, to be very popular among the people in this quarter —but I never deemed it necessary to enquire into the cause." [396]

William Henry Harrison and Amos Stoddard had known each other since 1804 —even before Harrison replaced him as the governor of Upper Louisiana on October 1, 1804. At that time, Harrison appointed then Capt. Stoddard, "Justice of the Peace." This seems to have been a rather demeaning and almost insulting appointment. However, Stoddard never discloses any negative personal feelings toward those people he reported to directly or indirectly. His personal opinion regarding William Henry Harrison, James Wilkinson, Henry Dearborn, William Eustis or John Armstrong is not divulged. While at the same time his respect and affections for military men he reports to and trusts, such as Henry Burbeck and Thomas Cushing, are clear from his correspondence. The rest, he simply treated respectfully and professionally.

About this same time, on November 18th, Major Stoddard wrote a very telling letter to Brigadier General Thomas H. Cushing. The following is the entire transcript:

> *"I have received orders to join the North–western army —and therefore find myself in a curious predicament —I left the whole of my baggage in my chamber, except a few articles of summer clothing which are now of little use to me. I have directed a letter to Col. Wadsworth or in his absence to his clerk, to pack up my baggage and to hire a small wagon, or horse cart, and send it to me as soon as possible. The fact is, that I cannot possibly move without it —I have not funds to procure new clothing —and if I had, it is not to be procured in this place —at least uniform clothing. Should Col. Wadsworth be absent, will you have the goodness to break open the letter I have sent him, and ask Capt Lee, or some other friend, to pack up my baggage in the manner mentioned in the letter? Mr Barlow from this place, nephew of Joel Barlow, will arrive in Washington on the Monday after this letter —and will aid in the business, if necessary —he will call at your office.*
>
> *I very much dislike joining the militia army of the north west —because I suspect it will meet with nothing but defeat and disgrace: —Witness Hull —witness Van Rensselaer, and witness Genl Hopkins. I am perfectly satisfied, that the militia, I mean those from Pennsylvania, will never cross Detroit river. This sentiment was general before they left here —and they have omitted no opportunity of expressing it on the route to Genl Harrison. I should have supposed that the inefficacy of militia was clearly seen before this. My best respect to Ms Cushing —and please to accept for yourself the sentiment of esteem with which I am, Sir, your Huml Servt.*
>
> *P.S. Please & let me hear from you by the next express mail, which I believe leaves your City on Sunday –*
>
> *P.S. The militia are already returning home in great numbers —by desertion. The three large Companies of Volunteers for a year, which went from this quarter to Buffalo, are reduced to 8 and 12 men each. The deserters are daily passing here to their homes by fives and tens, with public arms and other public property in their hands. When they marched out, and on their return, they committed greater waste and devastation, on the private property of people, added to insults, than the most savage enemy would have done. Vaux populi, vaux Deii."* [397]

Vaux Populi, Vox Dei, is Latin for, *"The Voice of the People is the Voice of God."*

Major Stoddard wrote another lengthy letter to General Thomas Cushing from Pittsburgh on the 12th of December, in which he stated, in part, the following:

"…I shall be able to join Genl Harrison at [Sandusky] —tho' my progress will not be rapid, as I have some Ordnance Stores to take with me, which arrived here from New York after the departure of my wagons. Some of the articles, such as quick match, postfires, tubes, and fuses, will probably be wanted, and must go dry. To facilitate this progress and safety, they will be sent out in a covered sled, drawn by public horses now on hand. I have advised Lt Johnson to forward all his supplies in this way during the winter. Wagons cannot now move —and the Ohio [River] is too much filled with ice to admit the passage of boats.

The business at Black Rock [Buffalo, NY] has put things in a flame. Cowardice! Cowardice! is the universal cry. I am extremely mortified at our disasters —and feel most terribly the dishonor cast on our arms. I know it will be attempted to throw the blame on the militia, and perhaps it may be done with propriety, as a large proportion of them refused to enter Canada —but this will not satisfy the public mind —truth has a poor chance in a contest with prejudice. The whole transaction has been detailed to me by a Gentleman of intelligence and veracity —and if he is not mistaken, it appears to be of a singular and [notorious] nature. He solemnly swears (and he was an eye witness) that, after the failure, Genl Porter assembled about 600 of the New York militia, and made a long speech to them —in which he denounced a certain great character "as a coward and poltroon" —that such was the detestation against the same character, that he was dismissed from his quarters —and that he tried in vain to obtain other lodging in the vicinity of the army. It does not become me to dwell on topics of this nature —you will, no doubt, have a more correct statement than I can give you —my object is merely to explain the sense, and express the feelings of the people in this quarter. The disasters at Detroit seem wholly to be merged in those lately experienced at Black Rock. I have seen the order of battle; —some party of which are according to my apprehension, repugnant to the wages of modern war. The artillery, instead of forming batteries of position, is mostly paced on the flanks of Battalions and Regiments —in this situation it seldom fails to embarrass the movements of the troops…I mentioned in a former letter, that Desertions from the militia prevailed to an alarming extent. I fitted out a fine Company of Volunteer Cavalry under Captain [Alney McLean?] —the men received two months advance pay, and sixteen Dollars each on account of clothing, besides equipment of every kind. This Company joined Genl Harrison —and not a man now remains with the army, except the Captain —one of the subalterns disgraced himself, and was obliged to resign —and the others deserted. Desertions are much more frequent from the Volunteers than from the Drafted Militia. Our Government must dispense with the services of such men, or its treasury will be exhausted to no purpose." [398] [399]

The episode of Black Rock is best described in a letter, *Isaac A. Coles to a Young Friend in Virginia*, found in the Thomas Jefferson Papers Collection.[400] In essence, it involves an attempt to invade Canada from Buffalo, New York. It should be noted that Major Amos Stoddard proposed a detailed plan for the invasion of Canada from Detroit, Niagara, and Plattsburgh (NY) to Secretary of War Eustis back on August 20, 1812 while still working in the War Department in Washington. He felt Ogdensburg, New York was a well–situated location for a battery placement to prevent British boat traffic along the St. Lawrence River. It sounds like he proposed to attack the British rear and cut its lines of communication and supply.[401] Military historians may want to examine the details of Stoddard's proposal in his letter to the Secretary of War to determine if his tactics and plans would have been effective and could have met with success at that time.

It wasn't the first time during the war that Major Stoddard volunteered tactical ideas. He later wrote to General (Elijah) Wadsworth:

> *"Pittsburgh 28ᵗʰ September 1812*
>
> *Sir,*
>
> *I shall in a few days dispatch to you some powder, flints &c —I am fearful you will be in want of them. News has reached us that 200 English and a large number of Indians left Detroit to attack Fort Wayne, and Fort Harrison on the Wabash —and that Malden is almost destitute of Troops. If this story is true, you have a fine opportunity of falling in behind the enemy, and perhaps taking of Detroit and Malden [present–day Amherstburg, Ontario, Canada]. I merely suggest these hints for your consideration —and am, Sir, your Huml Servt.*
>
> > *Amos Stoddard, maj.*
> > *corps of Artillerists*
>
> *Genl Wadsworth"* [402]

General Elijah Hill Wadsworth was a 65–year–old commander of a 3000 man Ohio militia force based at Camp Avery on the east shore of the Huron River near present–day Sandusky, OH. Major Stoddard then received a reply from General Wadsworth on October 4ᵗʰ informing him that he had received the supplies ("but not a flint have we in camp") and that his situation was apparently deficient enough not to be able to make any attacks in his current condition.[403] The apparent sound military advice went unheeded. General Wadsworth appears to have had significant numerical superiority. Capture of those forts, it would seem, offered the potential for resupply.

Amos tells us in his autobiography, "Old Generals are seldom successful —and perhaps this want of success may in part be imputed to timidity and irresolution." General George S. Patton, Jr. would later prove to be an example of the exception to this observation. However, perhaps his sentiment applies in this case. Regardless, it must have been demoralizing for Major Stoddard to hear news of defeats while seeing opportunities for success.

It was only after the first of the year 1813 before Major Stoddard started for Cleveland and ultimately the rapids on the Maumee River (sometimes referred to as the Miami). He passed through Boardman, Ohio on January 8th (as previously reflected in a letter from his brother Eliakim to his mother[404]) and on January 14th he wrote to recently promoted Brigadier General Henry Burbeck from Cleveland:

> *"Cleveland, Ohio, 14th Jany 1813*
>
> *Dr General,*
>
> *I am this far, (in company with Captain [Eleazor Darby] Wood), on my way to Genl Harrison, who is yet at Upper Sandusky. I have wallowed in the mud and water from Pittsburgh to this place. The roads, however, are getting good —The snow is now three feet deep —and teams are hourly starting for the army —I shall pursue them as soon as I can get my horses shod.*
>
> *What Genl Harrison will be able to do this winter is mere conjecture with me —but, from what I see here, I apprehend, that army supplies will be scarce —I believe the Country produces supplies of every kind in abundance —but they are much scattered —and those employed to collect them appear to be more dilatory than the nature of the service will admit. —I have nothing new to communicate —of course I shall be brief —If you take the trouble of writing me, send your letter under cover to Genl Harrison, of whose family I am about to become a member. My respects to all the officers with you, and I am, Sir, your very Huml Servt.*
>
> *Amos Stoddard"* [405]

Upper Sandusky, located on the Sandusky River, about 60 miles south of Lake Erie and about 70 miles southeast from the rapids on the Maumee River, was established as the principal depot for the Army. The Sandusky River and the Maumee River are about 36 miles apart, and the land that lay between them and extended to Lake Erie was almost entirely a marsh or swamp, known in those days as Black Swamp.[406] This area was later drained and converted to farmland. Traversing this area was extremely difficult at that time unless it was frozen over in winter.

On the 18th of January, General Winchester, (previously in command of the Northwest Army, but replaced by General Harrison, and now second–in–command), commanding the left wing of the Army, comprising approximately 1,000 regulars and volunteers, mostly from Kentucky, decided to attack the British at Frenchtown Township on the River Raisin in the Michigan Territory south of Detroit. His orders had been to go to Fort Wayne and to strengthen its defenses, and then rejoin General Harrison and the right wing of the Army at the rapids of the Maumee River. Instead, General Winchester arrived at the rapids and decided to advance to Frenchtown on the River Raisin There ensued a minor skirmish with a picket guard of the British forces on the 18th. Winchester won the day —but paid a heavy price four days later. The British and the Indians counter–attacked at the break of day on the 22nd and routed the Americans. Many of those taken captive were later killed in a savage and barbaric manner.[407]

The news of Winchester's folly at Frenchtown sent shockwaves throughout the Army and throughout the country. It was even referred to in Eliakim Stoddard's letter to his mother on March 28, 1813.[408] General Harrison initially applauded the victory of the 18th and was in the process of reinforcing General Winchester.[409] [410] However, Capt. E.D. Wood said General Harrison was astonished at the imprudence of General Winchester, and stated that, "Nor was it a difficult matter to for a man entirely destitute of theory of the art of war, to foresee the terrible consequences which were certain to mark the result of *a scheme, no less rash in its conception, than hazardous in its execution.*" [411] The letters of General Harrison between January 20th and January 23rd contradict this testimony of Capt. Wood.

Now that the left wing of the Army had been decimated or captured, General Harrison had his forces fall back to 15 miles below the rapids on the Maumee River. General Harrison nervously waited for reinforcements and supplies. They began working on a fortification on the east bank of the Maumee River that was named Fort Meigs (initially, Camp Meigs) after the Governor of Ohio by General Harrison.[412] Gov. Meigs and Harrison went back a long way —to the District of Louisiana where Harrison had appointed Meigs commandant of the St. Charles district in 1804.[413]

Major Stoddard joined General Harrison sometime between the middle of January and the first of February. According to the letter sent to his mother by his brother, Amos was near the Maumee River and rapids on January 18th and could hear the cannon engaged in the action taking place at Frenchtown.[414] It is certainly possible that Major Stoddard, along with Captains Charles Gratiot and E.D. Wood, transferred the responsibility for the train of artillery and supplies to Captain Daniel Cushing and the 2nd Regiment of Artillery while these three officers forged ahead in haste to catch General Harrison and the right wing of the Army.

It is also possible that they traveled with the 2nd Regiment of Artillery, escorted by regular army and militia reinforcements, with a train of artillery, ammunition and supplies. The orderly book of Captain Daniel Cushing's Company of the 2nd Regiments of Artillery, and the personal diary of Capt. Daniel Cushing, does not mention Major Stoddard by name during their journey. There is only one reference during the trek across Black Swamp country to the rapids of the Maumee River in January which could indicate the presence of Major Stoddard:

> *"January 22nd: This morning fine weather, clear, pleasant. Left Sandusky plains last evening, crossed small prairie and left that in our rear…Marched this day eight miles with a great deal of difficulty —sleds broke, chains broke. Crossed the upper end of a large prairie, myself in front, the Major and Quarter Master in the rear. Night coming on I called a halt, laid out the ground to camp on and fixed our tents. The Petersburg volunteers were late coming up as they fetched our rear."*

Although Major Stoddard is not mentioned by name, it could be reasonably assumed that "the Major" may be our subject —although there was also a Major Robert Orr in command of a detachment of the Pennsylvania militia on the same march. However, why would Capt. Cushing mention the presence of a militia officer? The "Petersburg volunteers" were a Virginia militia brigade under the command of Brigadier General Joel Leftwich.

In any case, by February 1st Major Stoddard and Capt. Cushing and his company of 2nd U.S. Regiment of Artillerists, along with the accompanying militia units, arrived (or were already present) at the encampment on the Maumee River, below the rapids, with artillery, ammunition and supplies.[415 416]

Around the middle of February it was directed by General Harrison to lay out a fortification for 2,000 men.[417] The camp was about 2,500 yards in circumference, complete with eight blockhouses and four large batteries, and picketed with timber, 15 feet long, from 10 to 12 inches in diameter, and set three feet in the ground according to the instructions of the engineer, Capt. Charles Gratiot. The fort was later completed by Capt. E.D. Wood due to the illness of Gratiot.

A great deal of immense labor and fatigue were required to be undertaken to complete the fortification by excavating ditches, cutting and hauling trees, and clearing away the woods and bush about the camp so as to provide an open field of view and fire. To make matters worse, the ground was completely frozen and it was nearly impossible to dig. The Army, however, was tolerably healthy and well provisioned.[418]

On February 24th a diabolical plan was hatched to set fire to the Queen Charlotte, a 17–gun British warship tied to the wharf at Malden (Amherstburg, Ontario, Canada). Capt. Angus Lewis Langham, in command of 100 men of the 17th Regiment, was assigned this clandestine attack.[419] General Harrison describes the mission in a letter to Secretary of War Armstrong on February 24th as follows:

> *"The destruction of the enemy's naval force in Lake Erie has never ceased to occupy my attention and after having examined in my mind every prospect which occurred to myself or those whom I consulted there appears to me to be no other practicable but that of crossing over Lake Erie from the mouth of the Sandusky Bay along the chain of Islands which extend at small intervals from that bay to within eighteen miles of Malden. The intention is to put between one hundred and fifty and two hundred men in sleds to pass to the northernmost island in one night and on the succeeding one to reach the vessels one hour before day. The Detachment is selected and the combustible matter preparing."* [420]

Major Stoddard of the artillery, and Capt. Wood, an engineer, devised the combustible to be used in the attack but did not participate further in the folly.

The men set off to Put–in–Bay (South Bass Island near Sandusky, OH). Only then did they realize the ice on Lake Erie and would not support a man. Crossing would be extremely hazardous. The wind was from the south and the warming would continue to melt the ice. The impossibility of the task was concluded at a council of the officers and guides on the night of March 3rd and again the next morning. It was unanimously decided to abandon the mission and return. They made their way to the mouth of the Maumee River and returned to Camp Meigs on the 6th of March.[421]

General Harrison, shortly after this disappointment, returned to Chillicothe (the capital of Ohio at that time). He left in charge Brigadier General Joel Leftwich of the Virginia militia. According to Capt. E.D. Wood:

> *"The conduct of General Leftwich on this occasion was highly reprehensible indeed, for notwithstanding he had received express directions to prosecute the lines of defense with all possible vigor, and to place the camp in the best possible situation to sustain a siege, which it was almost certain sooner or later it would have to undergo, and evidences of it became more apparent every day; yet this phlegmatic, stupid old granny, so soon as General Harrison left camp, stopped the progress of the works entirely, assigning as a reason that he couldn't make the militia do anything, and therefore they might as well be in their tents, as to be kept out in the mud and water, and accordingly were gratified."* [422]

On March 17th (St. Patrick's Day), Lt. Joseph H. Larwill of Capt. Daniel Cushing's Company of the 2nd U.S. Artillery Regiment stepped into the tent of Captain Joseph Wheaton, the deputy quarter master, where he found Major Stoddard and Capt. South (although Larwill recorded in his journal on March 4th that, "13 or 14 men of the Pennsylvania Line deserted us, as did Capt. South of the Indians with several of his men").[423] Larwill wrote in his journal that he, "Spent the evening together and took tea, then returned to my quarters," returning to the tent which he shared with Capt. Cushing. He mentions that the officers he had conversation with that evening, some of whom had service experience from the Revolutionary War, reported, "this was the most disagreeable encampment they ever saw." Major Amos Stoddard and Capt. Daniel Cushing were nearly the same age, Cushing being almost exactly two years younger. The both served in the American Revolution. Undoubtedly this was the sentiment expressed by both Major Stoddard and Capt. Cushing.[424] Lt. Larwill goes on to say:

"I am much surprised that the troops keep as healthy as they do, having to suffer on account of fuel being difficult to obtain and nothing to lay on but the ground which is not only damp, but wet. Some indeed have puncheons [split log mattress] to lay on which affords some little relief from the damp. You cannot go into any tent in camp without feeling for the suffering of the occupants. You then begin to lose sight of your own situation, seeing many worse than your own. Scarcely any of the troops have more than one blanket to lay on, which is too little at the inclement season of the year and situation of our encampment. Nothing transpires worthy of note this day. In camp we are entirely shut out from any communication whatever. This night it rained considerable, makes our encampment still worse." [425]

By the 18th of March, the spring rains came in a torrent. According to Captain Cushing:

"The whole country is inundated with water and broken ice. Our camp is overwhelmed with mud and water; my eyes never saw such a place for mankind to live in —not a markee or tent in the whole encampment but what has more or less mud and water in it, and what makes it much worse is for the want of wood. The timber is all cut off for a long distance from camp and there are no teams to haul any for the men; not a bushel of forage in this place; what teams we have cannot work, for they have nothing to eat. Our men are very sickly; no wonder lying in mud and water and without fire; not less than two or three men die every day, and I expect the deaths to increase unless the weather changes very soon." [426]

To make matters worse, the militia began to burn the supply of timbers brought into camp for fencing and blockhouses for firewood. In fact, when Capt. Wood returned to camp on 20th of March, he was mortified to find the men employed in pulling the pickets out of the ground and conveying them off for fuel. This officer was entrusted and responsible for the engineering works of the fort, but he had great difficulty getting the militia to stop their destruction —let alone to get them to act to repair the damage they had already caused to their mutual safety and security. [427]

The fears and prophesy of Major Amos Stoddard regarding this army of militia were being realized. One can only imagine the thoughts going through his head as he watched the mayhem and wanton lunacy that surrounded him —and yet he could do nothing about it. While it is understandable that the men were wet and cold, the timbers were needed for their protection and survival.

Major Stoddard was no longer a young man. He had turned 50 the previous October. When he accepted the appointment as deputy quarter master, he probably recognized he was no longer fit for strenuous frontier duty. He was described as being portly [428] at that time —even corpulent [429]—although no collaborating evidence of this has been found. A desk job at the Department of War in Washington probably suited him best. And then war was declared on Great Britain. He likely went to Pittsburgh thinking it was going to be a forward supply depot assignment and nothing more. But Harrison started clamoring the War Department for engineers and for men with experience in artillery. [430] He probably recognized he was susceptible to being pushed to the front lines. Always the patriot, he did as he was ordered, he did his duty, and he did his best. He probably hoped he would survive his circumstance. His biggest concern was the lack of dependable men in these state militias and the absence of command leadership.

At the end of March, three citizens came to the camp to inform the command that British General Henry Proctor had issued a proclamation directing all the militia in the vicinity of Malden and upon the Detroit River to assemble at Sandwich (present–day Windsor, Ontario) on the 7th of April for the purpose of an expedition against Camp Meigs. One of the men who arrived, a man by the name of Bucknel, a respectable citizen of Detroit, said he had heard British Major Adam Muir give details of the attack: the principal plan was that the Indians would disembark on the east bank of the Maumee River above Camp Meigs and envelop the rear, cut off all communications and resupply, and eliminate any escape route into Black Swamp country and to safety. The regular troops would then be deployed on the opposite side of the river to prepare the batteries and mount the cannon and bombard the camp. After the first couple of hours, the Americans would be forced to flee the camp and run right into the hands of the Indians and their tomahawks. Major Muir's opinion was that they would be able "to smoke the Yankees out" in the course of the first day's cannonade.[431]

Meanwhile, when the Virginia and Pennsylvania militias' enlistment periods expired at the first of April, they departed camp. This was not unlike the militia men who abandoned General Washington at Valley Forge when their enlistment ended at the end of December 1777.

Brigadier General Joel Leftwich and his Virginia militia left Camp Meigs first on the 2nd of April followed by the Brigadier General Robert Crooks and most of the Pennsylvanians on the 6th. They would not wait for the Kentucky militia (who were on their way) to arrive to replace them —even though the fort was under threat of British and Indian attack at any time.[432] Capt. Woods wrote of the Virginians: "The 2nd of April arrived, and away went every Virginian belonging to the drafted militia, without the least concern as to what became of those they left behind, or caring whether the enemy or ourselves were in possession of the camp, so long as they could escape from the defense of it." About 150 patriotic militiamen from Pennsylvania were, with some difficulty, prevailed upon to remain an additional 15 to 20 days. Command of the fort now fell to Major Stoddard, the senior officer, who went right to work.[433][434]

The garrison orders from the orderly book of Capt. Daniel Cushing's Company of the 2nd U.S. Artillery Regiment, on April 2, 1813, were as follows:

> *"Garrison Orders*
>
> *Fort Meigs 2nd April 1813*
>
> *Major Stoddard as Senior officer assumes the command of the troops in this Garrison— All orders & requisitions now in force will continue to govern untill altered or modifyed by the commanding Officer.*
>
> *Lieut. O'Fallon will receive reports and make the details, and he is to be respected accordingly— the Guards will be turned off from the grand parade by the several adjutants in rotation.*
>
> *There will be four guards. The Boat guard will be composed of a noncommissioned officer and six privates and be fixed at the boat landing— The Magazine guard will be composed of one Noncommissioned officer & nine privates, which will keep two centinels at the Magazine and over the Hospital Stores— Guard No. 1 will consist of one Commissioned officer and two Noncommissioned officers and thirty-two privates— Guard No. 2 will consist of One commissioned officer and 2 noncommissioned officers and 32 privates— The Sentinels will be placed under the officer of the day & usual orders distributed by him*
>
> *The Sentinels are prohibited from the use of fire while on their posts They will constantly walk on their posts & are on no account to sit down*
>
> *No noncommissioned officer or soldier will leave the Garrison after retreat beating except to repair to the sinks or in pursuit of wood & water— they are prohibited from passing the chain of Sentinels with theirs arms either by day or night or of crossing the river without permission of the Commanding officer & they are prohibited from firing arms in or about the camp without the like permission*
>
> *The field officers in Camp will attentively perform the duties of officer of the day"* [435]

It is clear that on April 2nd things began to turn around. Finally, there was someone in charge and organizing the men. Major Stoddard had years of experience managing military garrisons on the frontier and molding raw recruits into a disciplined corps of men. He knew how to mount, assemble and sight the guns for seaport defense. He put all his knowledge and skill to good use —realizing it would not be long before General Harrison would return and he would become subordinate once again.

On the 9th of April, Lt. Col. Stephen Ball arrived with 220 Dragoons, or mounted infantry.[436] Their timing could not have been better. They jumped right in and helped in the completion of the fortification works —and the enemy did not yet make their appearance to interfere in the progress.[437][438]

More garrison orders from Major Stoddard were entered on April 9th, primarily dealing with alarms, work parties outside of camp, cavalry readiness and preparedness, policing and the safety and security of the men and camp, and health and sanitation.[439]

General Harrison returned to Camp Meigs on April 12th with Colonel John L. Miller of the 19th U.S. Infantry Regiment and 100 regulars and 100 militia.[440][441] Harrison then took over command. He issued the following statement which was entered into the orderly book on that day:

> *"Head quarters N.. W.. Army*
> *Camp Meigs 12. April 1813*
>
> *The commanding General has received from Major Stoddard a report of good conduct of the troops in this Camp since they have been placed under his command which gives him great satisfaction— He requests the Major the Officers, noncommissioned officers & privates of his late command to accept his thanks for their past conduct as well as for the disposition which they at present manifest for the performance of their duty—our situation indeed requires the greatest exertion upon the part of every Individual attached to the army— Threatened with a siege by the enemy with our works in an unfinished State every man must devote all his thoughts & all his strength towards their completion— Their own safety their honor & the Interest of their country demands this from them— The General confidently expects it as a result of their own reflections and of those principally which glow in the breast of every true American."* [442]

On or about April 15th General Harrison wrote to Secretary of War Armstrong:

> *"I found on my arrival here that Genl Leftwitch had done little or nothing towards completing the defenses of the post. Major Stoddard had however employed himself very actively after the command devolved on him and since my arrival the whole of the troops have been engaged in finishing the old works and erecting new ones. Amongst the latter are an earthen Parapet (nearly complete) round the whole Camp and several new Sod Batteries in addition to those which were laid down in the plan which I had the honor to forward. A Grand Traverse across the whole Camp and a few additional counter Guards will render all the efforts of the enemy unavailing."* [443]

General Harrison seems to be insinuating here that since his arrival all this work had been started and completed. It is obvious that Major Stoddard, while only in command for 10 days, had accomplished more in the defenses of Fort Meigs than at any other time —prior or later. His experience in rebuilding Fort Columbus' seaport defense fortifications likely served him well in this untenable situation.

General orders from Harrison were entered into the orderly book on April 16th that stated:

> *"The orders issued by Major Stoddart on the 9th Inst are to be considered and observed as the standing regulations of this Camp until otherwise directed…Col. Miller is to command that part of the lines occupied by the regular Troops— Major Ball the River or front line as far as it is occupied by the Dragoons— Major Nelson (or the Kentucky officer who relives him) the rear line from the termination of the line of the regular Troops to the commencement of that of the Ohio Militia— the left flank of the Camp will be commanded by the Senior officer of the Ohio Militia & all the Batteries by Major Stoddard—"* [444]

Colonel John L. Miller, who commanded the 19th U.S. Infantry, was elected Governor of Missouri in 1828 and would later serve in Congress.[445]

As a general siege was soon expected, the men worked to shore up the defenses and to bring in wood for fuel and timber for repairing breaches. Two or three wells were dug. Everything was done that could be done to sustain an extended siege.[446]

On the 20th of April, the Pennsylvania volunteers who remained behind departed. There were about 1,200 to 1,300 men left, evenly divided between militia and regulars, with only about 850 fit for duty.[447] A party of men crossed the river for the purpose of clearing brush. The party included General Harrison and Major Stoddard who surveyed the ground. Capt. David Holt of the 17th Infantry Regiment arrived that evening with the 35 regulars in his company and an additional 150 Kentucky militia. Holt's men were attached to the artillery.[448]

On the 25th of April, a combined British and Indian force, consisting of 800 militia, 500 regulars, and 1,500 Indians under Tecumseh, under the overall command of British General Henry Proctor, arrived at the mouth of the Maumee River on Lake Erie. On the 26th an advance party of British and Indian scouts arrived across the river from Fort Meigs to observe and reconnoiter. On the 27th the British arrived downriver with their gunboats at the site of old Fort Miami and began unloading Indians on the south (or east) bank of the river just below Fort Meigs. The fort responded by firing a few shots into their ranks sending them fleeing into the woods. Capt. Cushing noted in his diary, "This is the first time I have discharged a piece at an enemy in thirty years." [449] On the 28th the fort's guns were again fired to disrupt the placement of the British work parties constructing artillery batteries across the river.[450]

As soon as the British batteries and guns were nearly ready, the American commanders realized they would be greatly annoyed by the enemy's artillery fire inside their fort. A plan for further internal entrenchment of the fort was conceived. A "grand traverse," or trench, of 20 feet depth, was dug through the middle of the entire camp running parallel to the river, with an earthen wall facing the enemy. Behind this wall, and in this avenue, the men could shield themselves from the expected cannon fire from the British. To conceal their business, the camp's tents afforded an obstruction to the British. Capt. E.D. Woods provides us his impression upon the completion of the grand traverse:

> *"This particular piece of work was completed early on the morning of the 1st of May, just as it was discovered that the enemy had finished three of his principle batteries had got his guns in, was then loading and bringing them to battery; when orders were directly given for all the tents in front to be instantly struck and carried to the rear of the transverse. This was done in almost a moment, and that beautiful prospect of beating up our quarters, which just in an instant before presented itself to the view of the eager and skillful artillerists, had now entirely fled, and in its place suddenly appeared an immense shield of earth, obscuring from his sight every tent, every horse (of which there were 200) and every creature belonging to the camp. How disappointed must have been the indefatigable and skillful engineer on discovering the futility of all his works, and what a gloomy and hopeless prospect presented itself to the ardent and scientific artillerist!*
>
> *Those canvas houses, which in a great measure had covered the growth of the transverse, by keeping from the view of the enemy the operations about it, were now with their inhabitants in them, entirely protected in their turn." [451]*

What is not entirely understandable is why General Harrison would simply watch the British construct their offensive gun batteries across the river and allow them to work unmolested. Perhaps the reason came after the siege ended, when he wrote the following to the Secretary of War on May 13th:

"I have not yet been honored with your command upon the subject of assembling the Troops, the direction of their march etc nor do I know whether it is expected that I should give directions with regard to providing of Artillery, ordinance Stores etc. From a letter written by Major [Isaac] Craig at Pittsburgh to Major [Amos] Stoddard it would seem that that order had been given to the D^y Commander of Ordinance there to make the proper provisions. I can now state to you a circumstance which prudence forbid me to mention in any former letter—at the commencement of the siege we had but 360, 18 Pd. shot and less than that for the 12 pounders, the whole quantity of the former sent on from Pittsburgh was 500. We were therefore obliged to be extremely sparing of our fire from the 18 pounders or I do believe from the effect which they produced on the Enemies Batteries we could have completely silenced them before they were spiked. Their 12 pounders provided us with shot of that description but they had no eighteens their large guns all being twenty fours." [452]*

So, the reason is answered: there was insufficient artillery ammunition, or shot, on hand at the fort.

It seems completely unreasonable that an experienced officer and artillerist like Major Stoddard would not have frequently brought to the attention of General Harrison the shot ammunition supply shortage issue. Cannons without shot and powder are rather useless.

As has been previously demonstrated, General Harrison was constantly meddling with the operations of the Quarter Master Department, lodging complaints, requesting reports, even making accusations of impropriety.[453][454] He no doubt counter–commanded supply orders as demonstrated below. As Major Stoddard said about Hull's surrender at Detroit in 1812, "There is a mystery in this business…"

In a letter to Secretary of War Armstrong on May 18th, General Harrison spins an explanation, of sorts, regarding cannon and ammunition, which goes as follows:

"In the course of last winter I directed Major [Amos] Stoddard to prepare an estimate of the Ordnance, ordnance stores and ammunition which would be wanted for the ensuing campaign. His estimate was made out and forwarded to Capt [Hezekiah] Johnson at Pittsburgh who delivered it to the Dy Commissary of Ordnance there. As I had not information at the time of the determination of the government to obtain naval superiority on Lake Erie, I directed the cannon (5–18 Pounders) to be sent in the early spring to Cincinnati, that it might be taken by the route of the Miami of the Ohio and that of the Lake to Fort Meigs. I was accidentally informed some time since that five cannon of that description had arrived at New port, but that it was not known whether they were intended for the North Western Army or to descend the Mississippi. Three days ago I received information from the Dy Commissary of Ordnance [Abram R.] Woolley that they were those which I required." [455]

In essence, the fort only had the same amount of ammunition Major Stoddard had labored to bring with him all the way from Pittsburgh —and they had received no additional supplies of ammunition since. Regardless of the circumstances and fault, the consequence was that the Artillery had a very limited supply of ammunition with which to defend the fort let alone launch offense operations which could have prevented the enemy from securing a beachhead. This allowed General Proctor and the British to establish a base across the river and a build their batteries within sight of the men in the fortress. It would not have gone unnoticed by the British that the fort did not have a proper supply of ammunition with which to impede their work.

IX. The Siege of Fort Meigs — May 1813

Amos Stoddard had been in a siege before —but he had never experienced being besieged. At Yorktown, he had been manning an artillery battery and firing on an enemy with its back to the sea and no chance of escape. Capitulation to an honorable Army like the Continental Army of 1781 was a quite different thing then surrendering to the ruthless British Major General Henry Proctor and Tecumseh and his band of savages. Surrender was not an option in the minds of the Americans at Fort Meigs when the British opened fire from their boats a mile and a half downstream on the Maumee River.

The British started their fire at 2 o'clock on the morning of May 1, 1813 from their boats downriver.[456] At 8 o'clock, the British ships hoisted a red flag as a signal for their batteries which commenced firing with 24, 12, and 6 pounders and 8 inch mortars. At 11 o'clock that night, the firing ceased. They fired 240 shot and shells this day —causing very little damage. Two were killed and four wounded.[457][458] However, one of the wounded was our hero, Major Amos Stoddard.[459]

Major Stoddard received a wound in his thigh from an incoming shell bursting over the Grand Battery. This exploding shell probably came from a mortar. Even though the Fort was not rapidly returning fire, Major Stoddard was out in front directing the inexperienced artillery crews. It was likely the first time some of these men had ever been in battle or had even ever manned an artillery piece.[460]

As the siege continued, one would imagine Major Stoddard was moved to a safe, dry place. One would at least think that, as a senior officer, he would have received some preferential treatment. Unfortunately, there is no record of where Major Stoddard was taken for recuperation. To remain exposed out in the cold in a wet, dirty trench with a leg wound was a death sentence.

On May 5th the Kentucky militia led by General Green Clay arrived upriver from Fort Meigs with 1200 men. General Harrison sent word by courier for the force to be divided, with 800 landing on the north (or west) side of the river (the British–held side), attacking the British batteries and spiking their guns (by hammering a steel spike in the touch hole, making the cannon inoperable), blowing up their magazines, and then immediately re–crossing the river and fighting their way into camp. The other 400 would land on the south (or east) side of the river and fight the Indians while making their way into camp. Colonel William Dudley, commander of Dudley's Regiment of Kentucky Volunteers, was assigned the task of attacking the British batteries.

Everything went as planned. They caught the British soldiers manning the pieces by surprise, and they immediately fled. Col. Dudley was in complete control of British artillery batteries. He had nothing further to do but spike the guns, blow up the ammunition supply, and cross back over the river to the fort to safety.

But Dudley either did not know how to obey orders, or how to profit from his success. He stayed on the ground up to thirty minutes in idle or vain curiosity. Part of his distraction was a skirmish that took place between some of his men and Indians firing from a copse of woods. This drew their attention to fighting Indians rather than completing their mission and escaping.[461] They only spiked some of the guns, and left the magazines intact, before the British and Indians had time to collect their forces from their nearby encampment upriver and return to repossess their guns. Of the 800 sent on the mission, only 100 were able to affect a retreat and escape; 60–70 were killed; and the rest were taken prisoner. Captain Dudley was later found on the field of battle, scalped and with his chest cut opened and his heart removed. Many of the prisoners were savagely massacred before Indian Chief Tecumseh stepped in and put a stop to the slaughter.[462]

A second attack was then ordered by General Harrison to silence the guns that the British had erected on the south (or east) bank of the river, 300 yards downstream from the fort on the third morning of fighting. This attack was led by Col. John Miller of the U.S. 19th Regiment of Infantry with a force of 350 made up of both regulars and militia. While successful in this operation, their losses amounted to 30 dead and 90 wounded.[463]

General Harrison wrote the Secretary of War on May 5th to inform him of the losses suffered by the Kentucky militia, saying, "I'm sorry to inform you of another disaster to the Kentucky troops not indeed bearing any comparison to that of the River Raisin in point of killed or wounded but exceeding that in the number of captured." [464] He later, on May 9th, goes on to paint the loss to Secretary of War Armstrong in the most positive light, declaring "I am sorry to inform you that the loss of the Kentucky Troops in killed and missing is much greater than I first believed...However much this unnecessary waste of lives may be lamented it will give you great pleasure to learn that the two actions on this side of the River on the 5th were infinitely more important and Honorable to our army than I at first conceived." [465]

Major Stoddard was likely starting to feel the infection from his wound getting worse, but was probably awake and lucid on May 5th, and was probably generally aware of what happened to the Kentucky militia men. Regardless of his current condition, he was probably glad he wasn't a prisoner or victim of Indian savagery. He may have had thoughts that he might yet survive this siege and live to see his family again —and may have begun contemplating his future.

The British were quiet for the next several days. There was actually an exchange of prisoners conducted on the 7th of May.[466] By the 9th of May the siege had ended.[467]

In general orders issued on May 9th General Harrison wrote:

> "The information received by the General and the movements of the enemy indicates their having abandoned the siege of this Post— the General congratulates his Troops on having completely foiled these foes and put a stop to their career of victory which has hitherto attended their Arms...An unfortunate Wound at the commencement of the Siege deprived the General after that time of the able services of Major Stoddard of the Artillery whose zeal and talents had been eminently useful." [468]

The following testimony as to the events of May 9th is from the Journal of Capt. E.D. Wood:

"The day was extremely wet and cold, and having no comfortable place for our sick and wounded, both seemed to suffer much. But everything was done for them that possibly could be, and no means were spared to make them as comfortable as the nature of their situation would admit. The wounded had hitherto been lying in the trenches, on rails in many places, from the bleeding of the wounded, had the appearance of puddles of blood.…..Having many sick and wounded, as was naturally to be expected after a close siege of nine days (five days batteries open), and our forces greatly impaired besides by the sorties from the right and left, on the 5th, it now became an object of the greatest importance to make such provisions, and to take such measures as might tend speedily to a restoration of health and vigor in the army. The block–houses about the lines were immediately cleared of the guns and stores and converted into temporary hospitals; tents were pitched with arbors about them, and such general arrangements were made to soften and alleviate their distresses as their situation and the nature of circumstances would admit. They, however, were but sadly provided with the little necessaries and comforts which belong, and afford so much relief, to the brave soldier who had recently lost an arm or a leg, or had his side pierced with a bayonet while gallantly mounting the ramparts of his country's enemy.

There was no head to the Hospital Department, which was extremely deficient in almost every respect. Those to whom the important duties of that department had been committed, were but a young, inexperienced set of men, with nothing but the title of Surgeon to recommend them, or to give them a claim to employment, and the principle part of whom had been picked up here and there among the militia, wherever a person could be found with a lancet in his pocket, or who had by some means or other obtained the title of doctor. Such were the persons whose duty it became, to say whether the limb of a gallant officer or young soldier should be lopped off, or preserved. There had previously been a man of skill and talents at the head of the Hospital Department, but one alike destitute of honor and reputation, and whose departure from the army was followed with disgrace. What was to be expected from that department, thus managed and wretchedly supplied? What prospects had the wounded; dying for a gill of gin or a spoonful of vinegar? Neither were to be had!" [469]

Thus we can understand the conditions under which our brave hero clung to life and the treatment (or lack of treatment) he received.

By May 9th Major Stoddard was probably beginning to show the initial symptoms of bacterial infection from tetanus, then known as lockjaw. He would have had a fever and begun sweating —with an accelerated heartbeat and high blood pressure. He may have started to experience muscle spasms. He was probably aware the siege was over, and that the British were preparing to leave, yet he was probably also aware, based on his medical knowledge and long command experience, that he was not going to survive. A bacterial infection was his Achilles heel.

Whether Major Stoddard was able to speak and convey any instructions or final wish to anyone is unknown. Eventually, his neck muscles would have become stiff and it would have become difficult to even swallow let alone talk. His face muscles likely began to spasm, and his jaw muscles would have tightened to the point of being unable to open his mouth —hence the term, "lockjaw." His mind probably wandered as he lay dying. He may have had a vision and heard the voice of his long deceased father, saying "You will soon be sick of it," and thought of his mother, his family and friends; and worried about his books and his papers —the source and evidence of his knowledge which he so much valued in life. All he had to distract and comfort himself from the pain was his powerful mind and memories.

On Tuesday night, May 11, 1813, at 11 o'clock, Major Amos Stoddard passed away and thus his suffering ended.[470]

General Harrison reported the Major's demise as almost a passing afterthought in a letter he wrote to Secretary of War John Armstrong on the 13th of May, which reads as follows:

> *"I am sorry to mention to you that Major Stoddard died the night before I left the Rapids of a Lockjaw produced by a slight wound from the fragment of a shell which struck him on the thigh. Several have died in this way from their great unavoidable exposure to cold —but the Sergeons assured me and my own observations sanctioned the opinion that perhaps there never was so many instances of desperate wounds likely to do well."* [471]

General Harrison added a final comment on Major Stoddard's loss in a letter to the Secretary on the 18th of May, "Major Stoddard's death will make it necessary that another field officer of Artillery should be sent on to this army." [472]

Capt. Daniel Cushing, in his diary, tells us Major Stoddard was buried on Wednesday, May 12th, the day General Harrison unceremoniously left camp. He reports:

> *"I had the remains of Major Stoddard buried in front of the grand battery on the spot where he received the wound that caused his death."* [473]

Perhaps this was his last wish. At least he was surrounded by fellow soldiers and friends.

Our intrepid hero, with the wandering soul, a man of immense talent, worthy of his name, dedicated and honorable to his country until his last breath, is no more.

Amos Stoddard's legacy was his life, his book, *Sketches*, the manner in which he conducted himself, the respect he showed to others, and the duty and service he gave to his country. We now have his life's story as told by him to consider. If only he would have lived to complete it. There is no good substitute for his memory, thoughts and words. This introduction does not assume to speak for him. It merely attempts to provide as many of the facts as could be ascertained and reasonably presented within this space —and let the reader draw his or her own conclusion.

The Autobiography Manuscript of Major Amos Stoddard

Dear Sir,[1]

You are the most importunate[2] and teasing friend I ever had. If you think the events of my life in any degree amusing or interesting, you will find yourself mistaken. I have never been depressed so low —raised so high, or whirled about with such a mixture of good and bad fortune, as to excite curiosity, or to afford what you are pleased to call lessons of instruction. Notwithstanding this I will fulfill what I owe to friendship, and commit to your care a short but faithful narrative of my life.

My English ancestors, at least some of them, were puritans. I have traced them back to 1490.[3] At that time one of them lived in the Hamlet of Mottingham, in Kent, about seven miles from London Bridge —where he owned from 300 to 400 acres of land.[4] One of his descendants, Anthony Stoddard,[5] migrated to Boston,[6] where he died about the year 1676,[7] and left behind him six sons and six Daughters.[8] His house was a few years ago standing in State Street —and I believe a new public building, perhaps a bank, has been erected on its ruins[9] He was considered in his day as one of the leading congregationalists of Boston,[10] and his descendants have uniformly, I believe, been educated in the same principles of religion.

His eldest son, Solomon Stoddard,[11] was educated at Harvard University —and at first devoted himself to the sea —but providence intended him for other pursuits. He soon quit the habit of a sailor and turned his attention to divinity. The inhabitants of [the] respectable town of Northampton on Connecticut River prevailed [upon] him to become their minister. He preached in this place nearly 60 years —and was upwards of 80 when he died.[12] During the latter part of his ministry he had a colleague, the Rev.d Mr J. Edwards[13] who married his Grand Daughter,[14] and [was the] late President of Princeton College.[15] Solomon Stoddard was certainly one of the greatest divines of his day —and altho' his writings are tinctured with the spirit of sectarism, so prevalent at that time in New England —yet he is said to have been a man of considerable wit and humor —and many anecdotes are still told of him, which were doubtless intended to discontinuance bigotry and superstition. His funeral Sermon was preached in Boston by one of his contemporaries, the celebrated Dr Coleman;[16] —and from the character given him in this sermon, one might be almost led to believe, that he was divinely inspired —and his eloquence much above any then known. Until near his death, he made an annual visit to his native city.[17] The people flocked in crowds to hear him preach —and those, who were unable to get into the house of worship, built stages around the walls —so that every window was filled with the listening multitude. When young, I prided myself on my ancestry —and used to exclaim to my schoolfellows, "Don't you know, that I have the blood of the Stoddard's in me!"

When we attentively compare the apparent superstition, so prevalent in the early part of the last century, with the skepticism and laxity of manners of the present day, we are at no loss to decide where the preference lies. If the religion of New England was once, in some measure, obscured by prejudice and fanaticism —and if its professors were more intolerant than its dictates required, still its operation on society was much less prejudicial than the licentiousness of the present century. Mankind appears to be doomed to one extreme or the other; both are injurious —but licentiousness to society is more pernicious than the sullen gloom of religious bigotry.

Solomon Stoddard left a number of children.[18] One of his younger sons rose to considerable eminence in the civil gov.[t] —He commanded the militia of his county, and headed them in several rencountres with the Indians.[19] He was also a Judge —and many years Speaker of the house of Representatives. He was urged to take on himself the command of the expedition to Cape Breton in 1745 —but he declined it on account of his health —and General Pepperell[20] succeeded in the enterprise as the head of the New England militia. My kinsman, however, was willing to aid his Country in another way —his financial abilities were much relied on — and he adopted a singular expedient to obtain the means of carrying the expedition into effect. On his motion the Legislature of Massachusetts passed a law authorizing an emission of paper money, which was declared a tender in all cases, except taxes, —and instead of drawing interest, it was declared to lose[21] 4 per centum annually till the principle was extinguished. The consequence was, that it was constantly in circulation, passing rapidly from one hand to another, and finally was reduced to nothing, and no one felt the loss! He has a son[22] now living at Northampton, and occupies the mansion[23] of his Grandfather Solomon.

Anthony, the eldest son of Solomon, was my great Grandfather.[24] After taking the usual degrees at Harvard University, he studied divinity with his father, and was settled at Woodbury in Connecticut during the latter part of the 17th century. He lived to about the same age [as] his father, and was engaged in the ministry about the same number of years. I know not that he ever published any thing more than an Election Sermon[25] —but he was considered as an able man, and possessed a prodigious influence among the people. Some years before his death, the Rev[d]. M[r] Benedict[26] was settled with him as a colleague in the ministry —and what is very remarkable, these two divines preached the gospel in the same parish during part of three centuries![27] This circumstance was noticed by M[r] Benedict himself in his century sermon preached in the beginning of 1800. — M[r] Benedict is yet living —but approaching to 80.[28]

I know very little of my Grand father, Israel Stoddard, except that he was a farmer by profession, and died young.[29]

My father, Anthony Stoddard[30] was born about the year 1737 —He was also bred a farmer —and married Phebe Read,[31] whose father[32] was a captain of the provincial troops in the war of 1758.[33] I was the first fruit of that marriage —and was born at Woodbury on the 26 Oct[r] 1762. I was so cross as to vex and even to tire the patience of my mother —and so extremely small as to weigh but six pounds at seven weeks old —and hence an old Aunt of mine,[34] still living, used to say to her —"Let him die; He is not worth raising!" Thus you perceive that my stars at my birth were unpropitious; —nothing but parental care preserved me.

When I was about six or eight months old, my father removed to Lanesborough in Massachusetts, where he purchased a farm. If in my childhood I possessed any valuable qualities, they were a strong memory, and an aptness at acquiring whatever I aimed at. Thus at the age of 8, I was able to read scriptures with fluency, and with a passable pronunciation, and my memory seized and retained whatever I read. The battles of the Jews made strong impressions on my mind, and I used to recite from memory the whole of the books of Samuel, Kings and Chronicles.[35] The prayers I heard at School in the daytime, I frequently repeated to my mother in the evening —and I was more than once called on to recite the Sermons I had heard, and always succeeded —once indeed in presence of the Parson who had his notes before him. In learning to write and the use of figures, I was much less tractable. My inclinations, always leading me to books, were not so easily diverted to studies of another kind. If my memory was tenacious, I wanted ideas —if my ear was pleased with reading or hearing an eloquent sermon, or every other composition, my mind was too weak to profit by it —and I remember to have read many poetic effusions which filled me with warmth and animation, tho' I did not comprehend their meaning. Perhaps this is the case of all children —and I mention these trifles to show, that the lapse of 40 years has not erased them from my mind.

As I was of a weakly habit, my father kept me pretty much at school till I was 12 years of age —and after that period seldom less than six months in the year. During the summer season I assisted my father in carrying on his farm —and the season of labor was a season of impatience to me. At the age of 13 the praise of my school master, accidentally bestowed, excited all at once my ambition, and to write a good hand, and to acquire my arithmetic, was my sole object. I succeeded, and was soon at the head of the first class in every branch taught in the school. —Perhaps no one experienced the rod or ferula[36] more frequently than I did —and it was always for lying; my anxiety to screen a friend, when called before the master to testify, was sure to precipitate me into difficulty.

Portrait of Major General Baron de Steuben by Ralph Earl
Credit: Yale University Art Gallery

During the period of my school days, the war of our revolution commenced. The enthusiasm among the people at that time was great, and often led them into excesses —particularly in persecuting those whom they deemed Tories. My father was a strenuous Whig —he was in the war of 1758[37] —was in the battle of Bennington,[38] and among the militia at the capture of Burgoine.[39] The aspect of the times drew my attention from my studies. The sounds of the alarm Guns, particularly of military music, led me to regret, that I was not a man —and at the same time induced me to throw aside my books, my writing and figures. The boys of my neighborhood formed themselves into a company —and nothing pleased them more than to be instructed in the exercise of their wooden muskets, and to be taught some simple evolutions. Of this Company I was chosen a fifer —and altho' Yankee Doodle was the only tune I pretended to play —yet with the dignity of my station I was extremely proud. Two or three years passed away in these amusements —and during this time I paid little or no attention to my grammar or other books.

My father saw and lamented the turn of my mind. He was obliged to applaud the motive —but he thought my pursuits unnecessary —and often reprimanded me for neglecting my school. From a conviction, that my frame was too weak for labor, he aimed to prepare me for some other pursuit, and entertained a secret desire of making me a divine or physician. But my wayward inclinations soon blasted all his prospects. I ventured at last to tell him, that I wished to become a Soldier —and I shall never forget his reply, "Amos, one regular would drive a thousand of you." He at last reluctantly consented, with this remark, "you will soon be sick of it."

The town, in which I lived, was at that time called on for its quota of recruits —and a good bounty was offered. I accepted it; —and in the early part of 1779, I joined the army at West Point in the highlands, in which I was engaged to serve 9 months. On our arrival the recruits were drawn up to be inspected by the Baron De Steuben.[40] Fearing that my undersize would induce him to reject me, I gradually gathered the dirt under my heals —and when he arrived opposite to me in the line he asked me several questions —and finally said, "perhaps you may do" —and at the same time putting the hilt of his sword under my chin saying, "you must learn to hold up your head!" The hun eye and fierce countenance of the Baron, together with the large star glittering on his breast,[41] in some measure terrified me, and caused a trembling in my limbs.

We were soon distributed among the old troops, and it was my fate to join the 12th Massachusetts Regt of Infantry.[42] The change of Diet, and the sleeping in tents on the cold ground, soon caused the dysentery, the usual disease in camps, and my frame sunk under it. In this situation my father paid me a visit. He furnished me with money and necessaries, and these probably prolonged my life. It was sometime before my name was struck from the Sick reports —and even when in health the fatigues were too severe for me. I was almost daily sent with others to the mountains after pickets. One of these was usually borne on the shoulders of 6 or 8 men —and from the undulations of the ground the weight was seldom equal —so that I was frequently nearly crushed under it.[43] I waited with impatience for my turn to mount guard, as the fatigue was less severe, and I felt anxious to become acquainted this kind of duty.

After performing duty about five months in the Infantry, I resolved with a number of others about my age, to Enlist for the war —but we were determined to join another corps, in which the duty was more congenial to our strength. We observed, that the Artillery, encamped on West point, were exempt from the general fatigue and guard duty —and that their duty was confined to their own corps. Fourteen of us, therefore, enlisted for the war in the Company commanded by Captain Henry Burbeck,[44] in which we experienced as much enjoyment as usually falls to the lot of Soldiers. Our Captain was sure not to employ us unnecessarily —and our other officers were not more inclined to severity than their duty required. In the spring of 1780, I was of a detachment, stationed a short time on Constitution Island —was afterwards ordered to Stony Point,[45] where an attack was daily expected —and where I saw General Arnold pass in his Barge, and go on board an armed vessel on Haverstraw bay.[46] About fifteen or twenty minutes afterwards, some Dragoons arrived on the opposite [side] of the river in pursuit of him.

During the hard winter of 1780, I was one among those who suffered from the weather. About the last of Dec[r] 1779, I returned from furlough, and took up my lodgings in a tent. To this Tent we had a small chimney —a very little fire would create such warmth as to throw us into perspiration —and when destitute of fire, as we often were, we were obliged to sit with our blankets round us to keep us warm. All the wood we burned, we procured on the mountains and carried it more than a mile on our backs —and this was the more troublesome, as the snow was very deep. During this period, our provisions became scarce. No bread or flour was issued to us for 15 successive days —salted meat was all we had to eat, except once or twice, when we were so lucky as to obtain a few peas. In this distressed state I remember to have been one of the two Sentinels who stood at the quarters of Gen[l] McDougal in Fort Clinton.[47] The servants frequently threw from the kitchen the pairings of Betes, Potatoes and other vegetables, as also scraps of meat —and I and my companion used to scramble for this offal.[48] Sometimes the Servants deposited the waste of the kitchen on the opposite side of a gate or fence at the corner of the house, and we took care to secure and eat every piece of bread, meat, or vegetable, within the reach of our bayonets. In fine, the soldiers at that time considered it as fortunate to be on duty as Sentinel at those quarters, as they were sure to obtain some offal from the kitchen to mitigate the hunger. Besides, we had very few clothes to guard us from the weather. Four of us lived in one tent. We placed in the ground 4 [notched logs] on each side of the tent, with cross pieces, —on which we laid some round poles lengthwise — and on these poles we slept, two on each side, with nothing under or over us, but one blanket each. This is but a faint trait of the suffering of our revolutionary soldiers —and yet their Country has suffered them to want amid peace and plenty, and in a thousand instances verified the old observation, "that republics are ungrateful."

Just before, that General Arnold made his escape, and the unfortunate Major Andre was apprehended, the army crossed King's ferry,[49] so called, at Stony Point,[50] and marched into New Jersey, and opened the Campaign. I soon after joined my Company at Orangetown[51] where Major Andre was a prisoner. His fate made a strong impression on my mind. The gibbet[52] on which he suffered was about a quarter of a mile from his quarters. He marched in the interval between two large plattoons, I think sixteen deep, with an officer on each side of him with locked arms, and a select number of musicians playing an appropriate march in common time. He took the measured step, and kept it till he arrived at the Gibbet. I was so lucky as to obtain a station by the side of the horse, harnessed to a Cart, in which his coffin was placed. What he said on his first arrival, I did not hear —but as soon as the warrant for his execution was read, he sprung briskly into the cart —took off his hat and stock,[53] and laid them on his coffin —presented the hangman (who was a soldier disfigured with lampblack[54]) with a purse of 8 or 10 Dollars —put the rope around his own neck, after the noose was made with the knot under his ear. —He then drew from his pocket 2 white handkerchiefs —one of which he tied over his face, and the other he gave to the hangman to pinion his arms behind him. When this was done, he said, "Gentlemen, if you are ready, I am —but take notice, that I die as a soldier" —and the cart was instantly drawn from under him. Thus perished Major Andre without a struggle.[55] While he was fixing the knot under his ear, I observed a slight trembling in his fingers —but in no other instance did he manifest the least agitation —which induced the bigoted and narrow–minded General Stark[56] to exclaim, "that he died like a hardened wretch." When I was in England in 1792, I accidentally mentioned the above circumstances to some few gentlemen at a dinner party —they were reported to a brother of Major Andre, who paid me a visit on the occasion —requested me to repeat the story —which very much excited his sensibilities. The King erected a monument to his memory in Westminster Abby —it is represented as soliciting General Washington to let him die the death of a Soldier, and not to condemn him to the Gibbet. This monument exhibits taste, and the figure of Washington a good share of dignity. But I was mortified to find, that one shoulder and arm of this figure had been wantonly broken —and still more mortified at the discovery, that this shameful outrage was perpetrated by Americans —perhaps by some disappointed refugees.~

Immediately after the death of Andre, our army, which was pretty large, suffered extremely from the want of provisions. The brigade[57] to which I was attached, was five days without any —and our marches at the commencement of summer served to increase our hunger. The season was not sufficiently advanced to afford vegetables —but the soldiers devoured all the Sorril they could find, as also the green apples, which were at that time a little larger than musket balls. Necessity at last urged me to an act, which I have ever [since] regretted —tho' I then conceived it justifiable, and even praise worthy. The army had opened a new station of no great distance from the outpost of the enemy above Hackensack.[58] We were informed, that we were in the midst of a Country occupied almost exclusively by tories —and our appetites suggested the means of gratification. Six of us sallied from our camp in the evening, and we traveled about three miles towards the enemy. We discovered a house in a field, and by means of the light in it, two men sitting in the Door with muskets in their hands. That they were tories we had no doubt —but we had no other arms than our artillery sabers. In reconnoitering them, a cow and a calf presented themselves in the field —we endeavored to secure the latter but we were unable to do it. The Cow at length was within our grasp, and we deliberated about killing her. I was strongly opposed to the measure —but as my companions were otherwise inclined, I agreed to Stand Sentinel for them. The poor Cow was soon breathless, and one thigh nearly skinned, when we discovered some people lurking around us, which induced us to make a precipitate retreat, leaving all our beef behind. This event served but to stimulate our exertions. The next evening twelve of us took the same route; —and we agreed, as we were all armed with sabers, to pursue our game openly, and not in a clandestine manner. We entered the house, near which we had killed the cow the preceding night —and how great was my astonishment! how acute my feelings! I stood motionless, and in a manner transfixed to the floor. The poor old man told us, that he had no provisions on hand —that the British had driven away almost everything he had —that somebody the night before had killed his only cow —on the milk of which he depended for the support of his children —that he was aware of the sufferings of the Soldiers —and that had he been owner of two cows, he would willingly have given them one. I made my escape from the house as soon as possible —and cursed the moment when I was made accessory to the misery of an honest Whig family.

We pursued our route, and the adventure just mentioned taught us to be more circumspect in our conduct. After traveling about two miles, we came to the walls of a large house, which had been burned —the family was sheltered under some boards placed against the side —the owner was walking to and fro with his musket on his shoulder. We asked him the reason for his conduct? "The tories have robbed me of my property, and burned my house over my head: I hear that the soldiers are killing cattle about the Country, and I am determined to defend what few I have left —I may as well die in protecting them as by famine". We informed him of our starving condition, and that we were in search of a tory from whose stock we were resolved to obtain something to appease our hunger. "A Tory!" said he with emphasis —"there is one by the name of Drishilt, living across those woods, who has an abundance of stock of all kinds —he was one of those who drove my cattle to New York, and I wish you would take every things he has." We prevailed on the man to be our conductor. We found the yard of Drishilt to be well supplied with cattle, hogs, and sheep. We soon secured a fine fat steer—and in opening the barn to obtain some sheep, one of the large doors fell on one of the men, and nearly crushed him to death. While we were endeavoring to liberate him, the objects of our desires made their escape. We acted openly, and made considerable noise —but nobody appeared to dispute our right. We led the steer to the field where we had butchered the Cow the night before —provided the head and skin to our conductor, and luckily arrived in camp while it was still extremely dark. How we escaped detection, is a wonder to me, as we had to pass within a few yards of the Sentinels —but I suspect they saw us and winked at our transgression.

No sooner were we safe in our Tents than I selected about Ten pounds of the best beef for my captain, and deposited it in the Tent of his Servant, charging him not to disclose the author of the donation. The easy and incurious temper of Captain Burbeck led me to suspect, that he would not make any enquiries on the subject, and so it happened. While the beef was baking in a pot of one of the cook houses in the rear of the Tents, I observed a number of officers approaching Captain Burbeck's quarters, and vociferating, "Harry, you have got something to eat". So true it is, that they were attracted from the extreme part of the brigade by the sensibility of the nose.

These circumstances are in every respect trifling except as they serve to show the hardships of the American Soldiery. They were indeed, during some of the inclement seasons, as naked as they were hungry. I have seen whole regiments in the most wretched condition; the men obliged to wrap round them fragments of blankets to shelter them from the cold; their feet covered with rags instead of shoes, and heads either with the same instead of hats, or wholly naked. Those privations were more severely felt when the men were on duty, or on long marches. Witness those who gallantly attacked the enemy at Trenton and Princeton in the month of winter. The roads over which they travelled were spotted with blood —and the cantonment at Valley forge exhibited miseries beyond the power of description. Yet the exertions of Washington at this fearful period were crowned with success. The advantages gained by him in the encounters just mentioned, conducted by skill and supported by courage, animated the spirit of Americans; and the cause before conceived to be desperate was now viewed in a more promising light. Hope nearly extinguished, like an electric shock, agitated the whole mass of society, and the stupor of sullen dejection vanished like an erratic meteor.

At the close of the Campaign of 1780, the army, without laurels, retired to winter quarters; —and that part to which I was attached cantoned at New Winsor just above the highlands. Here we were inoculated for the Small pox, —and soon after my recovery from this disorder, in February 1781, I was detached to the Southward. The detachment of Infantry consisted of three Regiments commanded by Colonels Vose,[59] Gemot,[60] and Barber[61] —and the detachment of Artillery was commanded by Captain Savage[62] —the whole under the orders of the Marquis de la Fayette.[63] The report was, that we were about to make a sudden attack on Staten Island —and as the soldiery expected soon to rejoin their Companies they left all their best clothing behind them, and took with them such articles only as were calculated to accommodate them for a few weeks; nor were we undeceived till we entered the watercraft prepared for us at Trenton. We soon arrived at the head of Elk,[64] where we again embarked, and descended the Chesapeake to Annapolis. Here our little fleet of sloops and schooners was suddenly shut up in the harbor by two British ships of 20 Guns each. We repaired the battery on the point, and mounted some brass [cannon] —with which we frequently fired on the enemy, tho' the distance was too great for execution. The first Cannon I ever fired was at this place.[65]

To be kept pent up at Annapolis was by no means agreeable to the views of the Marquis —and a movement of the army by land would have exposed the town and transports to destruction. The mad project was therefore formed of attacking the two armed ships. A brig[66] of 10 Guns, belonging to some of the merchants, was at anchor in the harbor —and she was supplied with two 18 pounders, which were mounted forward, one on each side of the bowsprit. Several of the stoutest and strongest sloops were selected from the fleet, their decks strengthened by uprights or supporters below, —and two heavy pieces of ordinance mounted on the bows of each. The object was to board the enemy's ships —and for this purpose our Flotilla was filled with men. Early in the morning the signal was given to tow out of the harbor —for the wind was too light to fill our sails. The enemy immediately slipped their Cables and lay by for us. The sloop, on board of which I was stationed, as she was the lightest, so she was towed with more expedition than the others, and was able to commence the action. She "let slip the dogs of war" [67] from two 24 pounders; —and these so terrified the enemy that they immediately now did sail, and made the best of their way down the Chesapeake, much to the satisfaction of our fresh water heroes. During the following night the Troops embarked, and our Flotilla returned up the Chesapeake before a strong wind, and soon arrived again at the head of Elk.

From some cause or other, perhaps in consequence of new orders,[68] the troops after two or three days commenced their march overland to Virginia. The morning after we crossed the Susquehanna[69] an afflicting scene took place. Nearly opposite to that river, on ascending the Chesapeake as before stated, the owner of one or more flour mills, with two of his sons, went on board of the armed brig during a calm, supposing it to be a british Vessel of war —and congratulated the Marquis on his arrival —told him that he had several hundred barrels of flour on board of a Vessel near by, which he wished to dispose of for hard money —and alleged that he had frequently supplied the troops of his majesty with provisions —and then uttered many bad things against the Americans and their cause. A bargain was soon struck, and the flour was shortly after along side, when the Marquis caused the man to be seized. He was kept under guard till the army encamped in the vicinity of his own dwelling, where a Drum head Court martial[70] convened for his trial; when the general beat next morning, he was suspended by the neck to a limb of a tree; the army marched around him, and left his body to be taken down by his friends. I have often thought this precipitate if not an unwarrantable measure —but in times of war the execution of military power is sometimes necessary —and to check treason, examples of terror must be made.

By the time we reached Baltimore,[71] our shoes, and even clothing, were mostly worn out. We marched thro' that City on a fine day —and the houses were crowded with Ladies to behold the Spectacle. They probably noticed our wants —for the next day shoes were distributed to the troops, and they were said to be a donation from the Ladies of Baltimore. We gave them many blessings and remembered them in all the vicissitudes of the Campaign. In crossing the rope ferry at Patapsco,[72] a few miles to the southward of Baltimore, we met with a terrible misfortune: The artillery passed over in the first flat, and the weight of the load caused her to take in a considerable quantity of water. Part of Vose's Regiment composed the next load, about 150 men, and the flat filled in the center of the river. The scene was afflictive. The Soldiers were so much encumbered with their arms and accoutrements, their knapsacks and other baggage, that they were not in a situation to swim. They had immediate assistance from one or two boats —but nine of them perished. What is very remarkable, several woman and children were in the flat, and all of them saved. Near this place several deserters were shot.

We arrived at Alexandria[73] on the 4th of May —and not long after at Richmond.[74] Here commenced the most remarkable events of the campaign. The british burned Manchester[75] on the opposite side of the river.[76] They then crossed over below us; —and as our force was too weak to make head against them, we commenced a rapid retreat, and carefully avoided a battle. No doubt the Marquis was acquainted with the plan concerted between General Washington and the French. One of them no doubt was to draw the English as much into the interior as possible. It belongs to history to detail the events of a campaign, at the close of which we captured a british army, and by this means put an end to the war. It is therefore sufficient to remark that, from about the first of June to the siege of Yorktown in October, our troops were continually on the march. They were seldom encamped two days at any one place. We were rapidly pursued by the british Infantry and horse; —and to avoid the pursuit, we were obliged to maneuver under cover of the night —frequently to march directly into the woods, while the enemy, ignorant of this circumstance, followed the road, and sometimes passed us 40 or 50 miles before they discovered their mistake. Twice they were enabled to throw a large body in our front, which rendered it difficult for us to escape them. Once we secretly left our encampment soon after dark, and made a rapid march of more than 20 miles to attack a detached body —but they took to their heels at the dawn of day on our approach. At another time as we were fording a river, I think in Culpepper,[77] about 600 of the british horse made their appearance in our rear, and each horseman had an Infantry Soldier behind him. We immediately formed for action —but as they did not seem inclined to attack us, we continued our march. Less than an hour afterwards we were informed, that a british column was in our front, and while the Marquis was deliberating on what measures to take, exposed as he was in front and rear, its horse in sight. Luckily there was another road for us to take. A brigade of Militia, commanded by Genl Nelson,[78] was placed in front, the artillery in the center, and the three old Regiments in the rear. The front of the british repeatedly attacked our rear; and had not a most violent rain commenced, a brisk skirmish would probably have ensued. This, and the extreme darkness of the night, favored our escape. The mud became deep —and the Militia, a set of pale livered beings[79] raised in the lower part of Virginia, and unaccustomed to fatigue or discipline, found it difficult to move with any degree of celerity.[80] The streams of lightening enabled us to discover, that they were thinly scattered along the road for a great distance —and their tardy progress put the troops in the rear out of all patience. Col. Vose several times rode among them, and told them, that they would be cut in pieces by the british Cavalry, if they did not quicken their march. Soon after one of these declarations, the lightening shivered a dry pine tree near us —which frightened our artillery horses; one of them broke his tackling, and ran forward among the Militia. As the darkness rendered every thing invisible, the noise of the chains on the horse, and the words, "the British Cavalry are among you," created an instant alarm among the Militia; a large proportion of them dropped their arms and knapsacks —and all fled to the woods. Towards morning we encamped about three miles from this place; and the next day, when the Sun of mid summer darted his rays with violence, the militia came by fifties and hundreds from the woods —most of them without baggage or arms, and many of them without hats. Our rear Guard however, loaded their waggons with the spoil, and delivered it to those, who did not blush to claim it. Such were the Militias of the lower counties of Virginia. Those bred in the interior among the mountains, were of an opposite character. They were robust and active, entertaining and brave, mostly dressed in the garb of hunters, and excellent riflemen.

Somewhere near the blueridge,[81] General Wayne[82] joined us with a small detachment. This circumstance caused the British to fall back toward the sea coast. We pursued them at a respectful distance till we passed some distance below Richmond, where we encamped for a few days —about one mile from James' River.[83] The Marquis took up his quarters at a house on the bank of that river, and the British concerted a plan to surprise him. Two Gun Boats, filled with men, were discovered by his guard within gun shot at the dawn of day. Our Artillery, (four six pounders) were instantly put in motion, and we reached the bank of the river below the Gun Boats —Here we briskly cannonaded them. —and as I at that time acted as a non–Commissioned Officer, I had the direction of a Piece.[84] Major Read[85] of the Congress Regiment was with us. He offered a piece of gold of 8 dollars as a reward to the first, who should hit either of the boats. The distance was about 600 yards. A ball, which I fired a' ricochet, happened to carry away one of the masts. I received the money —and afterwards divided it among my companions —a precious treasure at the time when we stood in need of everything. No sooner were the Boats beyond our reach than we hastened down the river to head them again, and this we did at the elegant seat of the late Colonel Bird[86] —but they were under such quick way as to afford us no fair opportunity of a second trial. ~

About this time[87] part of the british army was encamped at Petersburgh[88] on the south side of the Appomattox —and the Marquis resolved to beat up their quarters. For this purpose he sent two Regiments to guard the fords above and below that place; Another Regiment, and our field Artillery, marched directly for Baker's hill on the north bank of the River opposite the town.[89] This detachment of the british Army was commanded by Gen¹ Phillips,[90] and the infamous Arnold[91] acted under him. We completely surprised them. Our first salutation was the discharge of several six pounders from a considerable elevation; the shot racked their line of tents, and levelled many of them with their ground. The british soldiery precipitated into a woods beyond our reach, where they formed. They were unable to annoy us with their three and four pound shot —nor was it practicable for them to cross the river and attack us, except under a gawling fire. When we first rose the hill, the Marquis steadily watched the quarters of Arnold with his glass —He soon discovered him mounting his horse. We instantly levelled our pieces at him —but the distance was great, and altho' we covered him with dust, yet we had the mortification to see him join the Troops in the woods apparently unhurt. After amusing ourselves about two hours in firing at the Cavalry horses in a field, at a number of beef cattle in another enclosure, and at the tents, we precipitately retired. We saw several men fall —and two in particular, at whom we levelled three pieces, after they had exposed themselves, and by their signs bid defiance. The mansion on Bakers hill[92] was deserted and it was said to belong to a refugee. An office adjoining contained several hundred volumes of choice books —and I was sorry to see these plundered by the Soldiery —and more so by some officers, who I am convinced, were never benefited by their contents.

But the smartest encounter we had during the summer of this Campaign was at James Town.[93] The 4th of July was celebrated by us as usual, on which we had a sham fight, and the day was closed with a <u>feu de joy</u>.[94] That evening we marched for Jamestown, a distance of 72 miles, and arrived near the enemy on the 6th.[95] General Wayne was detached with two or three small Regiments, and six field pieces, to reconnoiter the british; —and his temerity or ardor precipitated him beyond them, and also beyond a morass, over which a very narrow road led to the town. Finding the british in his rear, he commenced retrograde movement; —and to make our escape it was necessary to charge and break a strong column. This we did with considerable loss. The firing lasted about an hour, during which time that part of our army in our rear hastened to our relief —but arrived only in time to witness our dispersed situation, and to cover our retreat. The number of killed and wounded I do not recollect —but I believe it consisted of nearly one fourth of those in the action. Our artillery did great execution —I that day witnessed the advantage of oblique firing,[96] and instances of it occurred from the frequent change of our position. We lost four of our pieces. Two were saved by the skill and activity of Captain Savage, who commanded them. To one of these I was attached; and altho' few of the Artillerists left the field with us, none were killed: some were wounded and others overpowered by the heat. These took shelter in some copse of wood, and afterwards joined us. The british neglected to pursue us, and to that negligence many of us owed our safety.

It has been said that the Marquis discovered very little skill or foresight in this affair. —It was understood at the time, that he was deceived by false information —he was led to believe, that most of the british army has crossed the river, and that he should be able to make prisoners of about 400 men, who still remained in the town. Some indeed have said, that he did not contemplate an encampment, and that it was wholly owing to the rashness of General Wayne. At any rate, the Marquis joined us soon after the action commenced, and was extremely active in rallying and forming the fugitives, and in bringing away the wounded.~

Those, who have never been in an action, cannot well conceive the sensations, which such a scene is calculated to inspire. Never before this did I witness one —and never shall I forget the operations of my mind on that occasion —particularly at the commencement. I was not then 19 years of age —but I am inclined to believe, that youth is the season for courage, and that men become more timid as they increase in years. Old Generals are seldom successful —and perhaps this want of success may in part be imputed to timidity and irresolution.

From this period to the siege of Yorktown, nothing of importance occurred —and indeed we stood in need of some repose. During the whole season till that siege commenced, we were almost wholly destitute of tents. Our blankets, spread in the form of a waggon cover, defended us from the rains and dews. This privation, however, served to increase our activity. Scarcely ever more than 10 minutes intervened between the order to march, and the actual movement —nor were we encumbered with waggons. No troops were ever more healthful, and this is the more to be wondered at, as our provisions were usually scanty and bad, and most of the men were destitute of clothing. My whole stock consisted of one blanket, one hat, two shirts, and two pair of thin trousers. For more than four months I had no shoes on my feet. My companions were generally in the same condition —and it was fortunate for us, that the roads were sandy. A constant change of place no doubt contributed to health —but it is hard to believe, that even this salutary occurrence was sufficient to balance the evils of privations.

Sometime in September the British army became concentrated at Yorktown under Lord Cornwallis — and the Marquis at the same time encamped his Brigade at Williamsburgh.[97] He adopted several stratagems to gain information. Among others he caused a cunning and intelligent Soldier to desert over to the enemy, who enlisted into one of the british Regiments, found means to possess himself of the information required of him, and then make his escape and rejoined our service. While at the place, frequent rumors of an attack were circulated, and indeed it was expected —especially as it was well known to the British, that an army was on its march from the northward to cooperate with the French Fleet, which arrived about this time in the Chesapeake, and obstructed all communication with York River. At length, to arms! was suddenly cried from one end of the line to the other —the pack Guns were fired, and everything announced a battle —the troops paraded, and all were ready for the contest, when a large cavalcade was discovered in our rear, coming round to our right —and who should appear but our beloved Washington, who had just arrived,[98] and lost no time in viewing and receiving the salutations of the Troops. We were soon after joined by the combined army of the United States and France, and preparations were made to commence our operations at Yorktown.

The distance from Williamsburgh to Yorktown is eleven miles —but such was our caution, that the army, altho' it marched before sunrise, did not arrive within two miles of the enemy before near night. We encamped in a field and the next morning I beheld a sublime spectacle. The Artillery, to which I was attached, was in front of the army. On rising a small hill, the eye swept over at least ten thousand men in our rear, and the rays of the Sun, darting from their burnished arms, added much to the sublimity of the scene. From this hill, the british troops and works first appeared in sight, and they were sufficiently near to salute us with a few Cannon shot.

During the whole of this memorable siege, I was either on the works, or engaged in preparing and filling shells. We were very deficient in artillerists, and we looked to the Infantry for almost constant aid. I was usually stationed at the mortars and Howitzers —and from directions given to me by Gen¹ Nelson,[99] dropped several shells on the bank of Earth over the subterranean quarters of Lord Cornwallis. After the commencement of our fire, that of the british in a great measure ceased, tho' now and then their shot and shell would disturb us, as also their musquet balls. I was over thrown from the platform by a shot, entered the embrazure,[100] took a piece from the muzzle of a Howitzer I had just fired, glanced near my head, and killed several of the Virginia Militia, huddled together under a low pine in our rear. The streams of shot and shell from the works of the combined army was incessant —and in the night there were intermixed with fire balls and carcases,[101] intended to consume the stockades and abbatis,[102] which rendered the approach to the main works of the enemy extremely difficult. A more beautiful or interesting night scene cannot well be conceived.

Sometime in September the British army became concentrated at York town under Lord Cornwallis — and the Marquis, at this juncture, encamped his Brigade at Williamsburgh. He adopted several stratagems to gain information. Among others he caused a cunning and intelligent soldier to desert over to the enemy, who enlisted into one of the british Regiments, found means to possess himself of the information required of him, and then made his escape, and rejoined our service. While at this place, frequent rumors of an attack were circulated, and indeed it was expected especially as it was well known to the British, that an army was on its march from the northward to cooperate with the French Fleet, which arrived about this time in the Chesapeake, and obstructed all communication with York River. At length, to arms! was suddenly cried from one end of the line to the other — the park Guns were fired, and every thing announced a battle — the troops paraded, and all were ready for the contest, when a large cavalcade was discovered in our rear, coming round to our right — and who should appear but our beloved Washington, who had just arrived, and lost no time in viewing and receiving the salutations of the troops. We were soon after joined from the north by the combined army of the United States and France, and preparations were made to commence our operations at Yorktown.

The distance from Williamsburgh to York town is eleven miles — but such was our caution, that the army, altho' it marched before sunrise, did not arrive within two miles of the enemy before near night. We encamped in a field and the next morning I beheld a sublime spectacle. The artillery, to which I was attached, was in front of the army. On rising a small hill, the eye swept over at least ten thousand men in our rear, and the rays of the sun, darting from their burnished arms, added much to the sublimity of the scene. From this hill, the british troops and works first appeared in sight, and they were sufficiently near to salute us with a few cannon shot. During the whole of this memorable siege, I was either on the works, or engaged in preparing and filling shells. We were very deficient in artillerists, and we looked to the infantry for almost

---

Page 20 of the Original Autobiography Manuscript

This page describes the arrival of "our beloved Washington" near Williamsburg
prior to commencing operations at Yorktown.

*Used with Permission. Amos Stoddard Papers, Missouri Historical Museum,
St. Louis, Missouri*

constant aid. (21.) I was usually stationed at the mortars and Howitzers — and, by _____ of Genl. Nelson, droped several shells on the bank of earth over the subterraneous quarter of Lord Cornwallis. After the commencement of our fire, that of the british in a great measure ceased, tho' now and then their shot and shell would disturb us, as also their musquet balls. I was once thrown from the platform by a shot, which entered the embrazure, took a piece from the muzzle of a Howitzer I had just fired, and glanced near my head, and killed several of the Virginia militia, huddled together under a low pine in our rear. The streams of shot and shell from the works of the combined army were incessant — and it in the night there were intermixed with fire balls and carcases, intended to consume the stockades and abbatis, which rendered the approach to the main works of the enemy extremely difficult. A more beautiful or interesting night scene cannot well be conceived. —

What a proud day to the united States was that on which a british army marched out of their works, and grounded their arms! On that day, the french army was drawn up on the right side, and the American army on the left side, of the road leading from the town to the Country, facing each other. General Washington took his station a little to the right of our pieces, which were attached to the Infantry, forming the right of the army. The french General, with some of our own, were opposite to him, and on the left of the french line. At length the drums announced the approach of the british Army, preceded by General O'Hara, who, as soon as he arrived within 50 or 60 yards, took off his hat, and exposed a head extremely bald. He instantly rode up to General Lincoln, who was placed among the french Generals — both rode across the way, where General O'Hara was introduced to the Commander in chief, and at the same time presented his sword — which was instantly returned with some expressions of civility and politeness, which were not heard, except by those of the suite. He there took his station by the side of General Lincoln, where he remained till the british troops marched tho' our line to the plain, deposited their arms, and returned by the _____ to their old quarters, when he

22

(22)

took his leave and followed them ~~back into the~~ back to their old quarters.

The feelings of the ~~British~~ English and Hessian troops were manifestly different from each other on this occasion. The former observed no regularity in their movements; the intervals between the plattoons were by no means uniform; their steps did not appear to be measured by the music; the officers held down their heads, their countenances were sullen, and they marched with their arms akimbo: Whereas the latter discovered no mortification in their features, and they exhibited the same cleanliness and order as on a day of Review or Inspection. The contrast, indeed, was striking, and the cause needs no explanation.

The day after the surrender, I was one of thirteen, commanded by Lieut. Price of the artillery, who entered the town. We struck the British flag, and hoisted our own — took an account of their ordnance, as also of all the stores belonging to that department. I well remember to have numbered 169 iron, and 75 brass pieces of all discriptions. ~~I open~~ On opening a box in the Laboratory, a blue suit of clothes was found. It was the uniform of a hessian serjeant. The coat was covered with lace of an inferior kind. Lt. Price observed that I was destitute of clothing, and at the same time afflicted with the fever and ague, and therefore gave me the articles I had found. I soon ripped the lace from the coat — and before I left the Laboratory ~~was~~ was covered with a warm winter suit. The nights were frosty during the siege — and the cold rains fell in abundance — yet I had not so much as a vest to put on — and when not actively engaged at the pieces, I was obliged to put my blanket round me. This was the case with nearly all of us.

Late in the season we started for the northward — and the detachment to which I belonged ~~was~~ wintered at Burlington in New Jersey. I was one of the Guard dispatched to Lancaster after Captain Asgill,

---

Page 22 of the Original Autobiography Manuscript
This page describes striking of the British flag and the rising of the Star and Stripes
Used with Permission. Amos Stoddard Papers, Missouri Historical Museum,
St. Louis, Missouri

What a proud day to the United States was that on which a british army marched out of its works, and grounded their arms! On that day, the French Army was drawn up on the right side, and the American Army on the left side, of the road leading from the town to the Country, facing each other. General Washington with his suite took his station a little to the right of our pieces, which were attached to the Infantry, forming the right of the army. The French Generals,[103] with some of our own, were opposite to him, and on the left of the French line. At length the Drums announced the approach of the british Army, proceeded by General O'Hara,[104] who, as soon as he arrived within 50 or 60 yards, took off his hat, and exposed a head extremely bald. He instantly rode up to General Lincoln,[105] who was placed among the French Generals —both rode cross the way, where General O'Hara was introduced to the Commander in chief, and at the same time presented his Sword —which was instantly returned, with some expressions of civility and politeness, which were not heard, except by those of the suite. He then took his station by the side of General Lincoln, where he remained till the British troops marched thro' our lines to the plain, deposited their arms, and returned by the same route, where he took his leave and followed them back to their old quarters.

The feelings of the English and the Hessian Troops were manifestly different from each other on this occasion. The former observed no regularity in their movements; the intervals between the plattoons were by no means uniform; their steps did not appear to be measured by the music; the officers held down their heads, their countenances were sullen, and they marched with their arms akimbo:[106] Whereas the latter discovered no mortification in their features, and they exhibited the same cleanliness and order as on a day of Review or Inspections. The contrast, indeed, was striking, and the cause needs no explanation.

The day after the surrender, I was one of thirteen, commanded by Lieuᵗ Price of the Artillery,[107] who entered the town. We struck the British flag, and hoisted our own —took an account of their ordinance, as also of all the stores belonging to that department. I well remember to have numbered 169 Iron, and 75 brass pieces of all descriptions. On opening a box in the Laboratory, a blue suit of clothes was found. It was the uniform of a hessian Sergeant. The coat was covered with lace of an inferior kind. Lᵗ Price observed that I was destitute of clothing, and at the same time afflicted with the fever and ague,[108] and therefore gave me the articles I had found. I soon ripped the lace from the coat —and before I left the laboratory was covered with a warm winter suit. The nights were frosty during the siege —and the cold rains fell in abundance —yet I had not so much as a vest to put on —and when not actively engaged at the piece, I was obliged to put my blanket round me. This was the case with nearly all of us.

Late in the season we started for the northward —and the detachment to which I belonged wintered at Burlington in New Jersey. I was one of the Guard dispatched to Lancaster after Captain Asgill,[109] on whom it was intended to retaliate the outrage committed on one of our own Captains,[110] whose life was taken in an unjustifiable manner. At Burlington I assisted in making the fire works, which were displayed in Philadelphia in honor of the birth of the Dauphin of France.[111] In the early part of the summer of 1782, I joined my Company at West point, where the birth of the Dauphin was celebrated.[112] The whole army was paraded on this occasion, and mostly in the mountains. A large colonnade was erected on west point, and its emblematical figures were invented by some French officers of the Engineers.[113] The Commander in Chief, with most of the Generals, and all of the Ladies of distinction,[114] assembled in the evening in the Colonnade, which was superbly lighted, and furnished with excellent music. I was attached to some heavy Cannons[115] placed about two hundred yards from it —and to increase the report we were directed to point them towards the Colonnade. Some of our wads happened to be to be wound on three pound shot —and at the first fire the shot past just over the heads of the company, and cut away some of the festoon.[116] A terrible outcry ensued —but as no one was injured, tranquility was soon restored. The fire works were brilliant —and the <u>feu de joy</u> fired in the mountains by the troops, had a pleasing effect.

About this time, I was appointed a non Commissioned officer of the lowest grade, tho' I had performed the duty for some time. As none of the Sergeants wrote a good hand, or with any facility, I was deputed by my Captain to take the orders, which I continued to do till the army was disbanded. We spent the ensuing winter at Fort Putnam.[117] The wood we used was carried over the rocky hills upwards of a mile on our backs —but we took care to procure a stock in Septr and October, and during the winter remained quiet.

At length, in the early part of 1783, the signing of the preliminary articles was announced to the army in General orders. What were our sensations, when we began to copy them in the Adjutant Office! I arrived at my Company just before the Retreat beat —the orderly Serg^t as usual was directed to read the orders —but, from the agitation of my mind, I had written them so illegibly, that he could not perform this part of his duty. The Captain directed me to read them —and no sooner was the parade dismissed than the Soldiery gave three cheers. This was repeated in all the cantonments about the Point —and eventually many Disorders, not to say mutinies, were committed. The Troops were soon Discharged, and authorized by their beloved General "to return to the tranquil walks of civil life."

The dissolution of the army excited the mingled sensations of pleasure and pain —pleasure at the prospects of national peace and independence —pain at separating from each other. None but those who have shared the fatigues and privations of our arduous conflict, and mingled their friendships, and sorrows together, can well conceive the feelings, which a sudden, and probably an eternal separation inspired. We were all at once ushered into a new state of existence; —our pursuits and views, our occupations, and even modes of thinking, were utterly changed —and this change was the most sensibly felt by those who entered young into the army; these had nearly forgotten the duties of citizens, and were in a manner ignorant of the means of subsistence. With emotions of regret we parted from each other —and the tears we shed afforded abundant proofs of our mutual esteem. We bid adieu to the character of soldiers, and assumed that of citizens.~

Perhaps no disruption of the army was rendered more painful than that of the officers. Many of them were elevated by their commissions to the first grades in society —to which they otherwise had no pretensions. To descend to their former occupation, and to mingle with their former companions, was extremely disagreeable —especially as their claims on the public, if once satisfied, were sufficient to place them above want, and to enable them to occupy a respectable grade in society. Others again, and these composed the less numerous class, were connected with the first families —and did not conceive themselves elevated by their standing in the army —nor degraded by returning to the great mass of society. Such was the situation of the officers, when the anonymous letters were published[118] —calculated to keep the sword unsheathed till the public debt was paid —and the demands of the army completely extinguished. Genl Armstrong,[119] then a Major, is the reputed Author of these letters —and indeed he is said to have acknowledged the fact. Perhaps several had a hand in them. Genl Gates,[120] Major Armstrong, and Doctors Eustis[121] and Townsend,[122] were at the time very intimate, and if one was the writer, no doubt the others were advisors. Captain Patrick Phelon,[123] who was killed in St Clair's defeat,[124] once declared to me, that Dr Eustis was the Author, and that it was within his knowledge. The design, however, of these letters was frustrated; and whatever were the sufferings of the officers, no one could be found sufficiently corrupt in principle to kindle the fire of discord between the civil and military power. The Gentlemen I have named were never the admirers of Washington, and owning to the suspicions entertained of them, they remained in obscurity till a revolution in our political system ushered them into public view. Indeed, so bitter was Dr Eustis[125] against the father of his Country, that he strenuously opposed, in the Legislature of Massachusetts, an address to him on his retiring from the Presidency to private life.~

During the time I belonged to the army, the Legislature of Massachusetts advanced to the troops of the State three months pay in specie[126] —and this was all I received. Our wants created discontents, —and I confess with shame, that I once contemplated Desertion as a remedy —but reflection cured me of this passion. Our army was composed of the best blood of the Country —and to this may be ascribed the order and patience observed in it. The Troops from some of the Middle and Southern States had many foreigners among them —and no doubt this circumstance contributed to the mutiny of some, and the frequent disorder of others. I wish not to censure —but it is a fact, that the New England troops were unquestionably the best in service.

I have before said, that I was extremely small when I joined the Army. The sudden change of diet and accommodation produced a short sickness, and I afterwards experienced no other indisposition than an attack of the fever and ague during the siege at Yorktown. Ardent spirits[127] were always disagreeable to me, and therefore I mostly refrained from the use of them during the time I was a soldier. Notwithstanding the vicissitudes[128] of several campaigns, the vigor of my constitution was much increased. At the close of the war I was six feet in height, and sufficiently active —and a march of 40 miles in a day created little or no fatigue. Indeed, the day I arrived at my father's house, after dissolution of the army, I travelled on foot 55 computed miles.~

Thrown at once on the wide world at less than 21 years of age, the future occupied my mind. I disliked the occupation of my father[129] —and resolved to obtain a livelihood by means of the head rather than of the hands —but I was unable to designate the profession, which was best suited to my capacity, and I had no friend capable of giving me advice. I had made some progress in what was called learning before I became a soldier —but it was in a great measure interrupted in the army, where my duties occupied much of my time, and where it was difficult to obtain a supply of books. Those I did obtain, I literally devoured —and among them was the translation of Cicero.[130] The first winter of my freedom, I undertook to superintend a Grammar school, and I believe to the satisfaction of my employers. [131] I was now in a situation to procure some useful books —and I studied them in the best manner I was able. History and the Belles Lettres[132] now attracted my notice, and Blair's lectures[133] afforded me many sleepless nights. My mind was ardent in the pursuit of knowledge —and had I been blessed with a director of my studies, my progress would no doubt have been greater, and more useful.

My father lived in the western part of Massachusetts, and in the spring of 1784, I set out for Boston in pursuit of the army pay due me. This I received in certificates, and these, from the depreciation, were not worth more than 2/6 on the pound. A circumstance, which took place the preceding year, was fresh on my mind, and I resolved to profit by it. In traveling home from the army I accidentally fell in Company with two Gentlemen who were returning from the neighborhood of New York in a Phaeton.[134] I first met with them at a tavern, where we took breakfast —and before our departure, I found that my reckoning was paid. Whether I manifested any thing to attract their attention, I cannot say —but as we travelled two days together, they were very inquisitive —they asked me many questions about my family and former pursuits —and at last wished to know what occupation I intended to follow now I was out of the army? —My answer was, that I intended to <u>Drive the quill</u>, provided I could find any one to employ me. One of them said, "If ever you go to Boston, make yourself known to me —my name is Oliver Wendall."[135] The other was Mr Appleton,[136] late Loan officer of Massachusetts. While therefore I was contriving means to make myself known, my fellow traveler asked me to walk into the Clerk's office of the Supreme Judicial Court,[137] where he has some business. While in that office I found, from the conversation of the two strangers, that a writer was wanted. The Clerk of that Court was the very respectable Charles Cushing, Esq[138] —brother to the Chief Justice —and before my departure I told him that I had something to communicate —and he walked out of the office with me. I then unfolded to him my history and wishes —apologized to him for not producing recommendations —as I did not expect, when I left home, that I should have occasion to trouble him —but named to him some Gentlemen, from whom I expected a character, and these he happened to know. I told him that, for the first year or two, the emolument[139] was no great object —that I wished to lay the foundation of future pursuits, and at the same time to pursue my studies. Mr Cushing treated me with attention and civility —he said that in about two months he should want a Clerk, whom he should wish to board in his own family, as he could not afford to hire a large salary —and concluded by expressing a wish, that I would forward him some recommendations, and then he would decide. I therefore hastened home, a distance of 150 miles, and soon transmitted him the papers required. He then accepted of my offer — and I returned back to Boston, and became an inmate in his family. I have been thus particular in relating these apparently trifling incidents, —as I consider the connection formed with this worthy man as the foundation of whatever subsequent distinction I acquired in society. He was to me a father and a friend —and his indulgence and advice contributed in no small degree to put me forward in life. I came into his hands a mere rustic, and whatever little polish I afterwards acquired, (and I was always too different to profit much) I owe to him and his amiable family. I never ceased to respect Messrs Wendall and Appleton; and altho' I afterwards became personally known to them, at least in the way of official business, I never had courage to put them in mind of our old acquaintance, or to express the gratitude I owed to their kindness.~

As the office did not occupy much of my time during the first year, I was at liberty to indulge in my favorite pursuit —study. I soon found access to a large book store, and in the course of that year, I perused upwards of 150 volumes. I never had much taste for Novels —perhaps because there are so few good ones in the world —and I considered the time spent in reading them as thrown away. My mind was particularly drawn to treaties on eloquence, and to eloquent productions. The Boston orations, delivered in commemoration of the massacre of the 5th of March 1770,[140] were almost the first specimens of the kind, which came in my way —and the rapture they inspired is almost inconceivable. Indeed, it must be acknowledged, that these productions are highly colored, and admirably calculated to awaken the populace to fury —and in this respect they are undoubtedly superior to all other specimens of American <u>eloquence</u>. The flight of these orators are equal to those of the best masters of Greece and Rome —and the tone and sentiments uttered on this gloomy anniversary served to initiate —impel, and animate the auditory to deeds of blood. Those who read those orations at this time must make great allowances; the cause then at stake —and the means of our political salvation must be taken into view; many of the doctrines taken in the abstract, are highly objectionable; like those contained in <u>Common Sense,</u>[141] they were calculated to undermine and pull down government —not to build it up, or to support it. Hence it is, that the celebrated productions of our revolutionary patriots and Statesmen suffered to pass into oblivion. The maxims contained in them are opposed to our free institutions —and they are remembered and quoted by those only, who meditate their destruction —and for this purpose they are fit instruments —the more so, as the original object of them is not distinguished from their practical effects at this day.

I think it was in the latter part of 1785, when I first endeavored to obtain a correct knowledge of composition. I perused and reperused the lectures of Blair —and carefully watched the structure of the sentences and paragraphs of the best writers. Long before this, however, I had habituated myself to writing with some facility, <u>according to the dictates of nature</u> —but I paid little attention to language or punctuation. I was not wholly destitute of ideas —but I found it difficult to arrange them properly, or to express them in suitable language. I very erroneously took Rollin's ancient history[142] as a model for style —the consequence was, that all my compositions, even my letters, were stuffed with swilling language, and by no means adapted to the subject. My first compositions cost me much labor —but I soon acquired a habit of writing with facility, and with a considerable degree of correctness. Such indeed —is the force of habit, that a man without it, whatever may be his learning, cannot expect to write with ease, or in a correct style —while another with less than half his knowledge, if accustomed to the pen, may extort the need of praise. Soon after I began to write, I began also to publish my lucubrations in the newspapers —I became acquainted with the Editors, and they were disposed to indulge my whims. I usually selected some occurrences of the times, and as I then conceived, that the merit of every piece consisted in the length. I not unfrequently occupied two or three columns. I was likewise prone to seize on occasions to raise the laugh against individuals, who happened to expose themselves to the lash, and more than once narrowly escaped from difficulty. I now look back on these things as the ebullition of youth, and should be sorry at this day to acknowledge the best of them. I frequently amused myself in publishing the speeches of some of the members of the legislature, delivered on interesting occasions; —and I recollect to have published a very long one delivered by Mr Sedgwick,[143] urging the necessity of maintaining a force in the western County of the State, during the summer subsequent to the suppression of the rebellion. I took down these speeches several hours after their delivery; —and such was the strength of my memory, that I never failed to exhibit the orator in his own dress.

In the year 1786, symptoms of rebellion and insurrection were manifested in various parts of the State. The war of our revolution was at an end —but the demands on the State were heavy —public credit no longer existed —the paper medium had vanished —and the specie, from the want of confidence, was deposited in the coffers of the rich. The people were in a manner wealthy —but they had no market for their surplus produce — at least they were unable to convert it into cash —and the consequence was, that they could not pay their debts, either to the individuals or to the public. If the tax gatherers seized a horse worth 40 Dollars, and exposed him to vendue,[144] he was struck off at 5 or 6 Dollars —and every other article was sacrificed the same way. The monied men followed the sheriffs and tax gatherers about the Country; they took advantage of the necessities of the people to augment their own wealth —and this served to irritate the public mind. Demagogues were not wanting to suggest bad remedies for unavoidable evils —and in this they had in view their own interest, not that of their neighbors. The people finally assembled in some of the Counties, and arrested the proceedings of the Courts of Justice and dispersed the Judges; aware, that, by this step, the judgments on the various demands would be suspended, and of course, that no executions could be issued on them. Resistance to the tax gatherers also became general; and these rebellious proceedings at last assumed such a character, that it became a question, whether to tolerate them, or to resist them by military force of the State. The latter was resolved on.

During this awful period, the Congress of the union was not inattentive to the progress of dissatisfaction in Massachusetts —and to check it in season, that body resolved to raise two Regiments for the ostensible purpose of guarding our western frontier from the incursions of the Indians, but in reality to be employed against the insurgents. These were commanded by Colonels Jackson[145] and Humphrey[146] —and in this corps I was appointed an Ensign.[147] I received orders to reveal in Berkshire —and on my waiting on Governor Bowdoin to know if he had any commands, I found General Lincoln[148] and the adjutant General of the State closeted with him.

The Governor requested to wait for a few days —and finally entrusted me with dispatches to Gen[l] Warner of Worcester County,[149] Gen[l] Sheppard of Hampshire County,[150] and General Patterson of Berkshire[151] —and I set out on my journey about the first of January 1787. As I appeared in a military undress,[152] the people were very suspicious of me. In Hardwick, a number of them arrested my progress —and I was obliged to exhibit my commission and recruiting instructions. They examined my pocket book —but as the dispatches were concealed in my boots, they were not discovered. The same night I slept at a tavern in Greenwich,[153] kept by one Hazeltine,[154] who was a subaltern[155] in our revolutionary army. His wife informed me, that it was rumored, that General Lincoln, was about marching an army into the Country to subdue the insurgents —that Gen[l] Shays, who was a great leader of theirs, had that day called a council of which her husband was one of the members, to concert the necessary measures of opposition. I signified that I was an entire stranger to the designs of both parties. Sometime in the night her husband came home, and appeared extremely uneasy at the military appearance of my saddle, which attracted his notice. The next morning I procured my breakfast at a tavern about five miles from the house of General Shays.[156] Several men about the house had their hats adorned with some evergreen, which was the badge of that party. They appeared very impertinent and disposed to pick a quarrel with me. Just as my breakfast was placed on the table, a M[r] Hathaway of Spencer[157] arrived —asked how far it was to Gen[l] Shays' —observed, that he was one of the council, and ought to have been with him the day before —but the snow was so deep as to retard his progress, —called for breakfast, appeared to be in great haste, and seized on my breakfast before I had time to seat myself by the table. I know this man to be a member of the Legislature of Massachusetts —and it came into my mind to disguise my sentiments, and to try the effect of duplicity.

I therefore took no notice of his impertinence, —but dropped some expressions, which indicated a friendly disposition to the cause he was engaged in. He immediately asked me my name, and the place of my residence. After disclosing the first I told him that I had served in the revolutionary war —that I still belonged to the army —that my Station was at West Point —that I was there bound on a visit to my friends in Berkshire —that I was sorry to see the Country in such a flame —but as the people had once bled to obtain liberty, I hoped they would bleed again, if necessary, to preserve it. This had the desired effect: —he shook me by the hand, and the gaping spectators, adorned with evergreen, seemed to smile with complacency. The Legislator and myself ate our breakfast together, and he declared, that, as I was so good a patriot, I should accompany him on a visit to Gen[l] Shays,[158] who lived only a very short distance from my route. I did not much relish this visit, as I was fearful of detection —but I was induced to gratify my companion.

We arrived at the home of this noisy and infatuated man about twelve o'clock the same day. Shays startled at my appearance —Hathaway made him easy, by saying, "all friends —all friends General." On answering his questions, I repeated the story I had previously told his councillor. "Ah, said he, are you the Captain Stoddard, which served, "in the — Regiment of Infantry"? alluding to Captain Orange Stoddard, a distant cousin of mine.[159] "The very one," said I. He then enquired after many old officers, and as I happened to know them, I was able to give him proper answers. He then asked me, if "General Lincoln was about marching troops into that Country"? I told him, "that I had never heard a whispering of the kind till two days before, and therefore doubted the truth of the report". He observed, "that General Lincoln was an able soldier, and that he should be very sorry to fight him —but supposed he should be obliged to do it". He then explained the proceedings of his Council the day before —one was to set fire to the town of Boston, and destroy it —as this place, like pandora's box, vomited its plagues to every part of the State. —Another was to assemble two armies; —one was to be placed at Springfield; —the other at Pelham, the Head Quarters and abode of Shays, which would serve to take an opposing army in flank. A third was to make General Lincoln and his army prisoners of war —send them to Berkshire, where they were to be kept till the contest subsided.

Previously to my interview with Shays, the Legislature had offered a reward of One Thousand Dollars for his apprehension. To defend himself he constantly kept four or five loaded muskets in his room, exclusive of some missile weapons adapted to defense, and from 15 to 20 men slept every night in his house. The vanity of this man was greatly excited by the title of General given him by his deluded followers. He had nothing to recommend him but an athletic frame, and the Commission of a Subaltern, which he bore in the revolutionary army. He was probably capacitated to lead a plattoon —but not to conduct the operations of a campaign. During the revolution he disgraced himself in the eyes of his brother Officers. He at one time was attached to Infantry commanded by the Marquis De lafayette. That General presented each officer in his brigade or corps with an elegant uniform sword imported from France. Shays was mean enough to dispose of his to a tavern– keeper —and for this breach of decorum he was obliged to quit this partizan corps, and join his regiment.

After taking dinner with Shays, I proceeded on my way, and arrived at Northampton the same evening. I immediately wrote to General Lincoln, and stated the particulars of my interview with Shays —and observed, that if I had been furnished with the assistance of two or three men, I might easily have conducted him to Boston. His Secretary[160] was imprudent enough to publish my letter,[161] which induced Shays and his party to denounce me as a spy —and was of great disservice to me in our subsequent operations.

[Images of two newspaper articles published at that time, referencing excerpts of this letter, are presented on the following page.]

AMERICA.

BOSTON, Jan. 23.

Extract of a letter from an officer on the recruiting service, dated at Northampton the 20th inst.

"I found on my journey from Boston, in passing through Holden, Hardwick, Greenwich and Pelham, great part of their inhabitants much exasperated against government; and so jealous are they of every person passing through them, that I was taken up as a spy, and had to produce my enlisting orders, &c. before I could undeceive them.

"Yesterday morning I fell in company with two men, who were on their way to visit their great leader Shays;—after prying into my principles, they thought, to their great joy, I was friendly to their cause, and as I came from Boston, and could give some intelligence about the court party, they gave me an invitation to ride through Pelham and visit their general.—As it was but a little out of my way, I accepted it, and about 10 o'clock arrived at his cottage, situated between two very high mountains, and half a mile either way from any house; he received us kindly, but was suspicious of me, and had not the two men strongly pleaded in my behalf, I am conscious I should have undergone a rude examination.—In the conversation Shays informed me he expected the court party from below, to support the court at Worcester, the week after next; and that he had dispatched expresses into the different parts of the country to rally the people. But he thought the court party would not dare to appear, if they knew of the strength of his party, which, he assured me, consisted of three western counties, except about 50 men in Northampton and Hadley, but I find on enquiry, that all the inhabitants of those two towns, 12 excepted, are in favour of government. He also said, that he expected general Lincoln, whom he dreaded, but was ready for him, that he wished to have him take the ground first, in order that he (Shays) might cut off his retreat below, surround him, and make his whole party prisoners. That he was not afraid, as he was conscious he had done nothing to merit the frowns of government, or the resentment of indivi-

duals; but that he thought proper to keep guarded by a number of men every night. He also expressed his highest disapprobation of the measures government had taken to secure Shattuck, &c. and if they were condemned, there were plans laid to lay the town of Boston in ashes, which he thought could easily be executed, and that it was entirely owing to his unremitted exertions, that the men were prevented from doing it. And concluded by saying, that times would soon be better, in a-massing large fortunes by extortion, rather than the good of their subjects, &c. Such was the drift of his conversation as near as I can recollect; what the end will be I know not. However, the friends of government are preparing to oppose their insur-gents.

"I took particular observation of Shay's house and its situation, and am of opinion, that had I a warrant, with three men, I could make a prisoner of him, and convey him safe to Boston."

Last Friday afternoon, the company of artillery and the two companies of militia, furnished by this town as its quota of the army ordered to Worcester, for the protection of the courts of law, began their march for that place. 'Tis said, on the junction of the troops, the army will consist of 5000 chosen men, and are to be commanded by the honorable major-general Benjamin Lincoln, Esq.

Massachusetts Insurgents!

MASSACHUSETTS,

BOSTON, Jan. 20.

Extract of a letter from an officer on the recruiting service, dated at Northampton, the 20th inst.

"I found, on my journey from Boston, in passing through Holden, Hardwick, Greenwich, and Pelham, great part of their inhabitants much exasperated against government—and so jealous are they of every person passing through them, that I was twice taken up as a spy, and had to produce my enlisting orders, &c. before I could undeceive them.

"Yesterday morning I fell in company with two men, who were on their way to visit their great leader, Shays;—after prying into my principles, they thought, to their great joy, I was friendly to their cause—and as I came from Boston, and could give some intelligence about the Court Party, they gave me an invitation to ride through Pelham, and visit their General—as it was but a little out of my way, I accepted it, and about to o'clock arrived at his cottage, situated between two very high mountains, and half a mile either way from any house—he received us kindly, but was suspicious of me, and had not the two men strongly plead in my behalf, I am conscious I should have undergone a rude examination. In conversation, Shays informed me he expected the Court party from below, the week after next: and that he had dispatched expresses into the different parts of the country to rally the people.—But he thought the Court party would not dare to appear, if they knew of the strength of his party, which he assured me, consisted of the three western counties, except about 50 men in Northampton and Hadley—but I find on enquiry that all the inhabitants of those two towns, 12 excepted, are in favour of government.—

He also said, he expected Gen. Lincoln, whom he dreaded, but was ready for him—that he wished to have him take the ground first, in order that he (Shays) might cut off his retreat below, surround him, and make his whole party prisoners. That he was not afraid, as he was conscious he had done nothing to merit the frowns of government, or the resentment of individuals—but that he thought proper to keep guarded by a number of men every night—He also expressed his highest disapprobation of the measures government had taken to secure Shattuck, &c. and that if they were condemned, there were plans laid to lay the town of Boston in ashes, which he thought could be easily executed; and that it was but a little owing to his unremitted exertions, that his men were prevented from doing it. And concluded by saying that times would soon be better, as he was endeavouring to put matters on a footing, whereby every man should enjoy his liberty, free from mercenary rulers, who study their own interest, in amassing large fortunes by extortion, rather than the good of their subjects, &c. Such was the drift of their conversation, as near as I can recol-lect—what they said will be known.—However, the friends to government are preparing to oppose these in-surgents.

"I took particular observation of Shays' house and its situation, and am of opinion, that had I a warrant, with three men, I could make a prisoner of him, and convey him safe to Boston."

[The above letter is from a gentleman of very good intelligence—the informa-tion it contains may be relied on as au-thentick.]

The New Hampshire Spy and Pennsylvania Packet
Newspaper Articles
January 23 & February 1, 1787
Courtesy of the Serial and Government Publications,
Division of the Library of Congress, Washington, DC

I soon after reached Lenox,[162] where I delivered the last of my dispatches to General Patterson. These dispatches gave the first notice of a design to oppose the insurgents by force of arms. The Major Generals were informed of the time when Gen[l] Lincoln would begin his march. They were directed to aid him with all the well affected militia they could rally around the standard of Government, and to make every possible exertion to disperse the Insurgents, thro' strongly cautioned not to shed blood, if it could possibly be avoided.

I was now with my Mother, who was a widow. My father took the small pox in 1785 and died of that distemper.[163] His farm was small, but of a good soil, and under good cultivation. I enjoyed the right of primogeniture[164] —but when the property was divided among nine children, my share tho' double to any of the rest was extremely moderate. My father left six sons[165] and three daughters.[166] One brother[167] and two sisters[168] are now dead (1812).

Agreeably to my instructions, I endeavored to procure recruits for the army. But my lot was cast in a hot bed of Insurgents —even nine tenths of my old school mates were of this description; and so strongly were they impressed with the idea of my enlisting men to oppose their views —particularly after the publication of my letter to General Lincoln —that I could not hope for success, and indeed my personal safety was threatened from every quarter. I therefore found it necessary to join the militia assembled under General Patterson, who had for his aids Major Egleston,[169] his son–in–law, and M[r] Sedgwick.[170] Two brass six pounders were attached to the militia under the charge of Major Fellows;[171] he politely offered to act as my Subaltern —and with the approbation of the General I assumed the command of them.

Previously, to the arrival of General Lincoln, Shays made an attempt on the public arsenal and stores at Springfield. These were defended by a small band under Gen[l] Sheppard. —A single Cannon shot, leveled at the ranks of the Insurgents, caused them to retire with precipitation and in disorder. Shays assembled his adherents at Petersham.[172] General Lincoln, by forced march in one of the coldest nights in winter, came on them by surprise, took many prisoners; —the rest fled and most took refuge in Vermont.

During these operations, General Patterson had to rely on the militia of Berkshire —and, owing to the disaffection to Government, these seldom amounted to more than 250. The Insurgents were five times more numerous —but as they had no concert among them, we were able to succeed in all our measures. We kept in a body, and were well provided with horses. No sooner had the Insurgents formed a rendezvous, and began to assemble, than by a rapid movement we dispersed them before they became sufficiently numerous to oppose us. And indeed we kept playing this game during the first part of winter —sometimes we were at one extremity of the County —sometimes at the other —and we never quartered longer at any one place than the arrival of intelligence of some assemblage of Insurgents. To disperse such assemblages before they became powerful, was our only safety —tho' in one or two instances they nearly eluded our vigilance; their number was considerably superior to our own, and nothing but a sudden attack enabled us to triumph over them.

The insurgents attempted to assemble at Williamstown, Lee, Sheffield, and West Stockbridge. We successively broke them up at these places. While the Gov^t militia were billeted in Stockbridge, the Insurgents began to rendezvous at West Stockbridge, about seven miles from them; and such was the secrecy of their movements, that about two hundred had united before we had notice of it. They were about to turn the tables on us —and attack us in the night; and as we were scattered about in the village on account of the extreme cold, we stood a chance of falling in detail. To avoid this we concluded to attack them without delay. We divided our forces into three parties. —One started by way of Richmond —another by way of Great Barrington —and a third, consisting of the artillery and about 30 on horseback, took the road leading to the crossroads at West Stockbridge, where the Insurgents had collected; and as the distances were very unequal, the parties started at different periods, so as to arrive at the same time. But this was not the case: The artillery arrived first. On approaching the village, one of the Sentinels of the outguard of the Insurgents fired on us, and then the guard precipitously retired. The pieces and wheels were taken [from] the Carriages, and then all were lashed on, and conveyed in Sleighs. On the firing of the guard, I ordered the pieces mounted —and they began to move forward before the 30 men with us were able to dismount and form. We followed close on the heels of the guard —and on turning a corner, we beheld the Insurgents crowed up together in the road about 30 or 40 yards in front of us. I brought the pieces to bear on them —expecting the General, who was with us, to order us to fire. The artillery intimidated them —and they moved from their line of direction. The pieces moved also, and I kept them pointed to the thickest of them. At this instance, their commander, Capt Hubbard,[173] whom I knew as a member of the Legislature, gave the words, make–ready! They did so. Take–aim! Their muskets were instantly levelled at the Artillery —fire! not one dare obey —fire! Dam you —fire! was repeated. At this critical moment I waited for orders —but received none. The discharge of a single musket would no doubt have produced that of all the rest —but the pieces created a panic, tho' the discharge of about 200 men must have killed or disabled every man attached to them. Perhaps another circumstance served to disconcert them. When we first presented ourselves to their view, the General[174] accompanied by his aide and some of the magistrates of the County, particularly Judges Edwards and Woodbridge,[175] rode up to the Insurgents, and expostulated with them. Mr Sedgwick, with a thundering tone of voice, and his accustomed eloquence, worked on their fears and hopes —he finally directed them to ground their arms and not to run —The last injunction was mistaken —they understood him to say run —the consequence was, they leaped over a board fence, and waded a small river just below some forges and mills, up to their middles in water —and then scattered over a large field, directing their course to the road in the edge of the woods on the back of it. The men attached to the pieces immediately secured a musket each, and they proved to be loaded with a ball and eleven buck shot. Genl Fellows[176] placed his Son of about 12 or 13 years under my charge. He came to me with a fine musket in his hands, and said, "Captain shall I fire?" I answered yes —because I discovered no Insurgents within his reach. He directly after rested over the board fence, and fired at a lad of about 18, who was who was rising the bank on the opposite side of the river. The ball entered near his back bone —and came near his naval. I hastened to the relief of the poor boy —and procured good quarters for him, as also the assistance of a surgeon. He regained his health after about 18 months confinement —and I understood, that Genl Fellows paid the expenses occurred on this occasion. At the time the insurgents had retired just out of reach of our shot, one of our parties, in advancing to our assistance, met them in the road, and made prisoners of a large number. We secured in the whole 104, together with their arms, horses and sleighs.

Soon after this adventure, Genl Lincoln, with a considerable body of militias, arrived at Pittsfield, when those under Genl Patterson, were deemed unnecessary, and permitted to return to their homes. As my connection with them was now dissolved, I conceived it best to open a rendezvous in Stockbridge, and to endeavor to obtain some recruits. During my stay there, a sudden inception of Insurgents, who had fled for protection to the state of New York, took place, and I was nearly falling into their hands. Their object was to seize some of the most influential characters in Stockbridge, particularly Mr Sedgwick, and to liberate their friends confined in the goal[177] at Great Barrington. A few moments warning enabled me to secure and mount my horse —the people fled in all directions —and as soon as I perceived, that they mediated a visit to Great Barrington, I hastened to that place before them. Not finding a sufficient number of men to oppose them, I rode to Sheffield and apprised Genl Ashley[178] of what was going on. He immediately rallied about 30 men — and as considerable time had been lost, we concluded it best, by a circuitous route to intercept them in the road heading from Great Barrington to the New York line, well aware that they would retire with all possible speed to their hiding place beyond the limits of our jurisdiction.~

Soon after we entered the road, we perceived thirty or forty Sleighs approaching us, with about four men in each sleigh. We immediately dismounted and waited for them in an advantageous position. A man of our party, rather of a delirious disposition, fired on them as they approached, and wounded Hamblin,[179] their leader, in the ankle. Several other shot were then fired by us, while they were endeavoring to disengage themselves from their Sleighs, and to form in front of them. Three or four others were slightly wounded —and Hamblin received another shot, which passed through his body. They then placed about 20 prisoners in their front, most of whom they had taken from Stockbridge, expecting by this means to check our fire. The prisoners, finding themselves between two fires, suddenly started for us, when one of them by the name of Gleason,[180] with whom I boarded in Stockbridge, was shot dead by one of the Insurgents. The rest joined us, when the insurgents gave way —they had not time to rescue their horses and Sleighs —but precipitated themselves into the snow up to their middles, and finally disappeared in the woods. Those prisoners, whom they had liberated from Goal, escaped with them. We immediately secured their horses and Sleighs, and returned to Great Barrington.

Gleason was the only one killed —but several were wounded on both sides —and among them was a young man by the name of Burghat.[181] He was a student at Yale College —and was on his way to that place, when, falling in with our party, he joined us; a number of buck shot entered his breast and arms —but he finally recovered of his wounds, and gained great credit for his gallantry.

The Insurgents, as they passed through Great Barrington, liberated a number of their friends from Goal. They directed the wife of the keeper to open the Goal doors —and as she passed from her own apartment to that of the prisoners, she sung in a humorous strain the following stanza —

"Hark! From the tombs of a doleful sound,

"Mine ears attend thee cry,

"Ye living men come view the ground,

"Where you must shortly lie" —

This was literally fulfilled —for not many weeks elapsed before many of the leaders were confined within the same Goal, several of whom were tried, convicted, and hung.

As some movements in the north part of the county indicated an attack on the militia at Pittsfield, General Lincoln sent for me, and gave me the command of two brass six pounders. I formed a Company from those who voluntarily offered their services from the line —and I took no small pains in drilling them. One night, while visiting an out guard, I gained intelligence of the approach of a large body of Insurgents —I hastened back to Head Quarters, and informed the General[182] of the discovery I had made. He leaped [from] his bed, and began writing an order, when he suddenly fell a sleep, and snored very loud. It is impossible to conceive my anxiety on the occasion —he soon awoke, and finished the order. The Insurgents, finding they had given the alarm, did not think proper to attack us —and from this period peace seems to have been restored. They found it in vain to contend, and voluntarily came in and took the oath of allegiance. Gen¹ Lincoln had predicted, that he should be able to conquer the Insurgents without spilling their blood. Not a drop was spilt where he had command —and very little in other quarters. The Country owed much to his policy and humanity. He inherited a lethargic habit from his childhood —it would frequently overcome him in the midst of anger —but the fits or instances of it were so extremely short in their duration, as not to prove injurious. At other times, he was remarkably quick in his perceptions, and possessed a sound judgment. His principles were of the most pure and elevated kind —and perhaps it was the least of the praise due him, that he was the confidant and companion of Washington during the war of our revolution.

In the spring of 1787, a special Session of the Supreme Judicial Court was [held] at Great Barrington for the trial of the Insurgents, when Chief Justice Cushing[183] delivered one of the best charges to the Grand Jury ever witnessed. Out of about 200, the Grand Jury found bills of Indictment against 10 or 12 for treason; two or three of whom were also indicted and tried for Burglary. Those designated for trial were separated from the rest; and before it was known who were of this description, the Chief Justice, to aid the recruiting service, authorized me to proclaim a liberation from prison to such as would enlist. Between 50 and 60 offered their services. They were conducted to Boston by John Blake, Esquire,[184] who had signalized himself against the Insurgents. I proceeded to Boston in the stage with Gen¹ Lincoln —and perfectly recollect a long conversation between him and General Ward[185] on the nature of the soul, and of its existence after death, which made a strong impression on my mind. Gen¹ Lincoln said, that the belief of such an existence supported him in life, and that without such a belief, or had he any reason to doubt on the subject, life would be a burden, and his mind tormented with the dreadful apprehension of non–existence. Gen¹ Ward was not much respected in the revolution as a soldier —but he was a man of sound sense, and of a fair character.

Several of the Insurgents were convicted of Treason at Great Barrington and Northampton —but Govʳ Hancock, who was now the Chief Magistrate of the State, pardoned them. Some of them were likewise convicted of Burglary, and were executed. John Hancock was chosen Govʳ in 1780, and was continued in his office till 1785; when, foreseeing the rebellion, he voluntarily retired to private life —and left Govʳ Bowdoin, who succeeded him for two years, to buffet the storm. Hancock was a weak man —but the madness of the times made him popular, and popularity was the object of his soul. Bowdoin, on the contrary, was esteemed a philosopher, and in science stood among the first of its votaries. He had many difficulties to combat, and he combated them like a wise man. After the storm had abated, Hancock peeped again from his hiding place, and again became Governor of the State, which office he held till 1793. His money and patriotism, real or pretended, produced wonders; while deep penetration, and the regular management of public affairs, were unnoticed by the multitude.

Notwithstanding the phalanx of rebellion was completely broken —yet the legislature conceived it prudent to station a regiment in the western Counties. This regiment was raised for six months, commanded by Colonel William Lyman[186] —and I was placed at the head of a Company of Artillery, which was attached to it. Great Barrington was our station —and here we spent the summer of 1787 in an agreeable manner. One incident only served to interrupt our repose, and as I was the principle actor, it shall be distinctly related. We had three state criminals in Goal —and the Goal was guarded by the troops, and during the night by an additional number of Sentinels, who were placed on these posts just before dark by the officer of the day. These prisoners had been some time preparing for an escape. They excavated the Earth from under the bottom of the Goal, and the evening when I was officer of the day, and just before I placed the Sentinels, they made their escape from the back part of the Goal, and soon disappeared in an orchard. Pursuit was in vain, as they had entered a wood at no great distance, and the trail was not discernable. An old Negro, confined with them, informed us the next morning of their plans. After leaving Goal, they agreed to separate, and the next night to meet at the house of one Turner on Green river in the State of New York, or at the house of one Andrews about two miles beyond. I applied to Col. Lyman for leave to pursue them with a detachment of troops. The plan was arranged. In the afternoon of the next day, Capt Ingersol[187] of the militia, who had volunteered his services, set out for Green river, a distance of about 20 miles. His object was to procure a sheriff or some civil officer, to meet us in the night on the divisional line of the two states, and to conduct us to the house of Turner, or to any other place, where it was likely the refugees might be found. This precaution was necessary, as we had no right to march an armed party beyond our jurisdiction; yet we resolved to extenuate the offense under the plea, that we were headed by a civil officer of the State of New York. Our intentions were kept a profound secret. At a late retreat beat, after the rolls were called, about 50 men were taken from one of the flanks, and to them were added about 30 on horseback. We left the parade in the dusk of the evening, and proceeded on the road to Green River. The night was extremely dark, and not one among us was acquainted with the route. The plan was, that we should proceed till we met with Capt Ingersol, who had promised to wait for us in the road after he had procured a civil officer. Our march was rapid, and as we came to a populous settlement, I was apprehensive, that we had passed Capt Ingersol, and therefore halted in a secure place. I ordered two men to advance, and two to return back in search of our guide. Soon after their departure, I discovered two armed men in the road —and supposing them to be one of the parties I had just sent out, I advanced to them, when they cocked their pieces, pointed them to my breast, and demanded my name and business. These were citizens of the State of New York, who had by some unknown means discovered our designs, and were determined to frustrate them. During all this time they saw no one with me —but from a rusting noise under the fence nearby, they rightly suspected, I had a party at no great distance. This suspicion added to the conciliatory language I used, induced them to alter the position of their muskets, and to assume a tranquil air. They then informed me that they knew I was in pursuit of the refugees —that I was bound to Green River settlement about two miles ahead, where I must not expect to find them —and that if we attempted to enter the settlement, not one of us would escape with life.

While I was in communication with these men, who appeared respectable, and endeavoring to penetrate their views, and to modify their passions, the two men sent in advance made their appearance, and informed me that the settlement was a considerable distance ahead, and that Cap[t] Ingersoll was waiting for me, with a Sheriff, on the road, which extended through a thick wood. The Sheriff pointed out the house of Turner to me, which we instantly surrounded, and searched with permission of the owner. As the refugees were not found here, I directed the horsemen to dismount, and a Sergeant and six men to be left as a guard over the houses. We then hastened to the house of Andrews, but as the refugees were not here, we set out on our return, and found on our arrival, that our guard had been seized, and taken away —and the holsters and furniture of the horses adorned with evergreen, the badge of the Insurgents. The alarm had been given —more than a hundred lights were discovered —huzza for Shays! resounded from every quarter —and as I knew, that several hundred of the Insurgents had taken refuge in this quarter, I was apprehensive of an attack —and therefore put the troops in motion on their return. The road led through a wood of nearly two miles in extent, and it was so dark as to render it difficult to pursue our way. About ten minutes after we entered the wood, a musket was fired at us —and the ball glazed my hat. I peremptorily[188] directed my men not to return the fire in any case, till ordered, on their peril, as I was determined not to commit any aggression while in the State of New York. We had about 20 shot fired at us before we escaped from the wood, and some of them less than as many feet from us, tho' without any damage. We soon arrived opposite to a large house, which appeared to be a Tavern, when a man a man rose at the corner of a stone wall, and hailed us three times in rapid succession, and then fired, the ball making a slight contusion across the breast of the soldier behind and nearest to me. As the man stood his ground after firing, Captains Ingersoll and Lovell[189] cried out, "cut the rascal to pieces," when the Soldiery prepared to fire, and I found it extremely difficult to restrain them. The stone wall above mentioned extended nearly half a mile along the road, and about every minute as we passed it a shot was fired at us. After a very severe fatigue of about 13 hours we returned to Great Barrington.

It was soon discovered, that about 200 of the Insurgents collected, and tried every means to provoke us to fire at them —they were unwilling to spill the first blood —they wished us to do it, and then they resolved to destroy our whole party. For this purpose, they planted parties in the woods, and along the house wall —and as we were not disposed to commence hostilities, they did not like to take the responsibility of that act on themselves. My conduct was highly approved by my superiors —but some of my hot headed subalterns wished for a little sport.

Not hours after my return to my quarters, I received a note from a magistrate in the State of New York, by the name of Ford, demanding to know by what authority I had violated the laws of the state, requesting me to appear before him, and promising me protection. As I knew this magistrate to be displeased with the Insurgents and friendly to good Government, I did not hesitate, particularly as I had the release of my Guard much at heart. On my arrival at the house of the magistrate, I found it surrounded hundreds of these scoundrels, who demanded my commitment. In the presence of them, the magistrate was obliged to act with some duplicity; he spoke to me in a severe tone of voice; I understood him, and avoided enticing minutely into any justification; he told me, that I must dine with him, and after Dinner he would enter on business. The multitude then dispersed. —I told the magistrate, that we had a civil officer with us. This he suspected, and wanted an affidavit of that fact, which would serve to liberate the Guard at the evening session. I refused to disclose the name of the civil officer, and in fact I did not know his name. He said, that my conduct had made the more noise, as their legislature, at the instance of our own, had sometime before passed an act to favor the cause of Government, in which it was declared, that if three or more men found together in arms, they should be deemed guilty of a riot. This was intended to operate on the Insurgents, who had taken refuge in the State of New York —and therefore it was the less excusable in as to become the first violators.

In about a week after this interview, the Court commenced its Session. Colonel Lyman and Mr Sedgwick attended; the Sergeant and six men were acquitted —and soon after rejoined their corps.

On the dissolution of the Regiment I returned to Boston. I again resumed my employment in the office of the Supreme Judicial Court.[190] This Court had a general superintendence over the records of the Common pleas in the various counties, and in case the Clerks of the Common pleas neglected to bring up the records, the Supreme Judicial Court had a right to replace them by new appointments. The Clerk of the Common pleas of Middlesex County was a very old man, upwards of 70 —and as he had neglected to record the Judgments of the Court for several of the preceding years, he was threatened with a mandamus to oust him of his office. He therefore applied to Mr Cushing for my services —and I spent six or eight months in Cambridge much to my satisfaction. During this period the old clerk, to whom I have alluded, signified his intention to resign, and I had a desire to fill the vacancy, conscious that I was able to discharge the duties of it with accuracy and dispatch. The Judges of the Supreme Judicial Court addressed a joint note to the Judges of the Common pleas in Middlesex, recommending me as a person suitably qualified for the office. This note was put into the hands of the Chief Justice of the latter Court to be communicated to his brethren —but he never did communicate it, because he wished to obtain the office for a friend, and I felt the less regret, as this friend was in every respect worthy of the partiality shown him.

The Supreme Judicial Court had two clerks; —one was denominated the recording, the other the riding clerk. In 1789 the riding clerk was out of health, and I was appointed to perform his duty on the eastern circuit, on which we had a variety of important trials —and among them one of a capital nature. The next year I performed the same duty on the western circuit; and I feel a pleasure in the recollection, that the Judges approved of my conduct.

And here I beg leave to relate one short antidote. It was customary for the Judges on the first day of the Session in every County to invite the Clergyman of the Parish to address the throne of grace, and to dine with them. This practice was repeated at Taunton, a beautiful village between Newport and Boston, where I acted as a clerk. The Clergyman of that place was a contemporary with my father and mother, and had been educated in the same parish.[191] While at Dinner, he was informed of my name —and interrupted the conversations of the Judges, Lawyers, and Magistrates of the County, by asking from whom I descended. He then told a long story of the pious habits of my Great Grand father,[192] under whose ministry he had been educated —that he was the only magistrate in the town where he lived —and that he possessed an extraordinary influence over the affections, the hopes and the fears of the people about him —"but alas!" said he, "his posterity has become amazingly degenerated". The gentlemen about the table almost burst with laughter at the compliment. —I probably blushed —certain it is that I felt the truth of this rude declaration too much to be offended with the pious Calvinist. We afterwards, however, become better acquainted —and I endeavored to convince him by my conduct, that I was not unworthy of the name I bore.

While attending the Court at Taunton I became acquainted with the honorable Seth Padelford,[193] a Gentleman of considerable note at the Bar —he was at the head of his profession in his own County, and his practice extensive. He advised me as a friend to enter on the study of law —my reply was, that I had not funds to discharge my board, tuition, and other expenses, for so long a term as 3 or 4 years. We entered into calculations —and he offered to bestow on me some prerequisites. I left him, however, without coming to a conclusion on the subject.

From this period, I began to think, that I was wasting my life to no purpose —that I ought to resolve on a course of business adapted to my means and capacity, and endeavor to become, what is called, settled in life. General Lincoln offered me a place in the Customs house,[194] which was established about this period under the new order of things —but as long as Quill driving was my business, I had no disposition to quit the Judicial department, under which I had in a manner served an apprenticeship. I owed too much to Mr Cushing to leave him as long as he stood in need of my services. I, however, ventured to open my mind to him on the subject, and to ask his advice. It was his opinion, that I ought to read law, and gave as one reason among many others, that the knowledge of forms obtained in his office eminently qualified me for it. The fact is, that, as a recorder, I had treasured up in my memory the technical forms of all kinds of declarations, Indictments, and particularly Special pleadings, grounded both on the statute and common law. —These were complicated; and as much nicety was required in our Massachusetts Courts as in those of Great Britain; —the forms, indeed, were the same. I wanted only the principles of law to qualify me for practice, and I at last concluded to study them. The common rules and practice of our Courts were perfectly familiar to me.

The late Govr Sullivan[195] offered me a place in his office —but I had no disposition to study in Boston, because students were there kept too much at writing, to the neglect of their books. I therefore repaired to my friend Padelford—and he agreed to liberate me from all writing, except in his absence. In his office I spent four of the most happy years of my life. I had one, and sometimes two fellow students, and Leonard Baines, Esq.[196] had two more. Friendship and harmony prevailed between us. Mr Padelford took pleasure in directing our studies by points, and in explaining difficult parts of the common law, as also some of the most important decisions under our penal and other statutes. The village of Taunton afforded a charming society —and the evenings glided away in a manner unperceived. The young ladies of this place were remarkably gay and attractive —and we were sure to be in their society when not engaged in our studies. Happy days! But they are fled on the pinions of time —and the recollection only is left us.~

While engaged in my studies, I was induced me to take a trip to England in pursuit of a family estate. This estate is situated in the Hamlet of Mottingham in kent, near Eltham, and about seven miles from London Bridge. It was the residence of one of my ancestors in 1490 —and was successively occupied by his descendants till 1765, when that branch of the family became extinct in the death of Nicholas Stoddard. This gentleman died a bachelor and intestate. —He left his estate in possession of a disscipated[197] [and illegitimate] Son, directing him to enjoy it till his heirs, (belonging, as he alleged, to a collateral branch of his family settled in Boston, in America) should make good their claims to it. This natural son[198] did not long survive his reputed father; the tenants were in quiet possession, and knew not to whom their rents were due. By some means or other, my eldest Uncle,[199] who was in the eldest line of male decent from the Boston family, found out in what manner the estate was left, and resolved to prosecute his claims to it. He therefore went to England just before the commencement of the American war. He had letters to an eminent legal character —but before his arrival this character was removed to the House of Lords, and therefore did not present them. My Uncle now in London, like a man in the wilderness, knew not what course to pursue —he was known to no one —nor was he calculated in all respects to proceed without a judicious friend. He first sent about for a Lawyer, and chance threw him into the hands of Mr Life,[200] who was disposed to do more for himself then his client. He visited the Estate he claimed, and resided on it some months; He satisfied the tenants, that he was the legal heir; the account he gave of himself and family comported with the declarations of Nicholas Stoddard —and they offered to attorn,[201] and pay to pay him the rents. But he did not think it prudent to take a simple step without consulting Mr Life, who, jesuit like, told him, that if he got in possession, pretended heirs might start up, and he would be obliged successively to defend himself against their suits, the expenses of which would operate to his ruin —even if he succeeded at last; that his best way was to return home, suffer the Estate to fall into the hands of some claimant, and then he would have one only to contend with. My uncle did not understand the advantages derived from actual and peaceable possession, which is said to be eleven points in the law,[202] and therefore too easily fell into the snare laid for him. Another circumstance had its weight. The trouble in America began to assume a serious aspect —and he was not disposed to be absent from his Country and friends in the time of hostilities. He therefore unfortunately concluded to follow the advice of Mr Life. The evening before he sailed Mr Life invited him to supper, and he was introduced to a Mr Bowman,[203] who was at that time an articles Clerk in his office. He pretended, that Colonel Bowman of the Isle of Wight, one of his ancestors, married Mary, the daughter of William Stoddard of Mottingham, about the year 1662; That the estate in question was gavelkind[204] —of course descended to the female branch in preference to a younger male branch; and indeed the title of Bowman, if correctly deduced in the manner stated by him, was certainly preferred by the laws of England to that of my Uncle. The day my Uncle went on board of ship, he was taken extremely ill, and never fully recovered, tho' he lived upwards of 20 years afterwards. The physicians were of opinion, that his disorder was the effect of poison; perhaps they were mistaken.

Things remained in this situation till the early part of 1791, when one of the tenants addressed a letter to the family of Stoddards of Boston, which fell into my hands. He gave information that Mr Dyneley and Mr Graham,[205] two eminent lawyers in London, had obtained possession of the estate in question —that they had turned away most of the old tenants, and begged the heirs to prosecute their claims. I immediately hastened to my Uncle, who lived in Connecticut,[206] who was some what debilitated by age, but still more by disease; He was unable to prosecute his claim from want of means, and therefore requested me to do it for him, promising me one half of what I should obtain to remunerate me for my trouble and expenses. I contacted the late Judge Wm Cushing[207] on the subject, who drafted a power of attorney for my Uncle to sign, authorizing me to prosecute in his name, and to sell and dispose of the Estate in case I obtained it. After my papers were duly authenticated (and among others was the pedigree of my family from their first arrival at Boston) I sailed for London, and went on shore at Deal, on the 16th Decr 1791.[208] I did not fail to recollect that I landed in the same place where Julius Caesar debarked his legions, when he invaded Britain, more than eighteen hundred years before[209] —and the circumstance gave rise to many reflections. —We dined at Deal, and in the afternoon we proceeded to the City of Canterbury. The next morning we visited the Cathedral, where we paid sixpence for an examination of its curiosities. Edward, the black Prince, his coat of mail, and ponderous shield and sword, attracted more of my attention than the stains at the foot of the alter, occasioned by the blood of Thomas A. Becket. We reached London the same day, and took lodging for the night at the New England Coffee house.

Our passage was a boisterous one —we experienced a gale of seven days, before which we scudded,[210] and most of the time under bare poles.[211] The sight of land, and the first we made was the Isle of Wight,[212] made a delightful impression on the mind. The verdant fields formed a striking contrast to the wide and dreary expanse of waters. The plough was still in use —and the pursuits of the husbandman[213] seemed to announce the approach of summer rather than of winter. The Isle of Wight presented some cliffs of considerable altitude; —and those at Dover (so nobly described by Shakespeare) as we sailed along under them, inspired both delight and Terror —but these were soon exchanged for the low and sandy level on which the town of Deal is situated. Kent is reckoned one of the best Counties in England. The soil is excellent, supported by a solid chalk rock of different depths below the surface —the undulations of the land afford many charming views, and delightful inclinations for County seats. The contrast between the English and American cultivation is remarkable. The fields in England have the appearance of so many gardens; this is considered necessary from the crowded population: In America the population is comparatively small; —and were our agriculturists possessed of a less quantity of land, it would be more highly cultivated, and at the same time more profitable.

No stranger is likely to be known, or noticed in London, without letters of introduction. The late Thomas Russell[214] of Boston gave me letters to the house of Lane, Son, and Frazer.[215] Mr Lane, indeed, one of the firm, was a passenger in the ship with me; and the civilities and assistance afforded me by those Gentlemen will always occupy a place in my memory and affections. The first step, after I had taken my lodgings, was to engage a solicitor. From the Herald's office, Doctors Commons, Parish Registers, I collected all the papers necessary to connect the Boston family with its English ancestry, and particularly with the one settled at Mottingham. My uncle indeed had done much before me. —My counsel were Mr Stainsbury,[216] and Sir John Mitford.[217] In the first place, I took their written opinions separately. —They afterwards had a consultation and gave an opinion conjointly. They both agreed, that the claim of my uncle would prevail, unless it appeared in evidence that he had been in England —in which case he would be barred by the Statute of Limitations. Apprehensive, that the evidence would appear, I became some what discouraged, and to undertake a compromise.

["*Pages 53 & 54 never came to my hands —they were lost*" "*H.S.*"] [218]

[The remaining pages 55-60 were recovered damaged and some text is missing - Editor]

[Missing Text] and a new leaf inserted on to which all [new] marriages were transferred, together with the addition [of the] one in question. We took out the new leaf, which [was made of] parchment, and found that it was cut from the end [of the] volume, as all the indentations or curvatures equally corresponded. This [manufacture] of wickedness was no doubt laid in this obscure corner from the persuasion, that the heir would not take the trouble to examine the records. The copy was left in the Herald's office to prevent further enquiry, and to deceive the heirs into a belief, that he had no legal claim. Mr Duncan[219] was so well convinced of the forgery, that he offered to appear with the book before any tribunal. I put certain queries to him in writing, calculated to unfold the whole business, and requested him to address his answer to me in London. On my arrival there, I found it, and it was such as I desired. I reflected some days on the measures most proper to take. The forgery was not likely to be fixed on Mr Dyneley —I well knew, that the success of my claim would not depend on the weakness of his title, but on the soundness of the title of my Uncle. I consulted my Solicitor —and concluded to address a letter to Mr Dyneley —my object was to intimidate him —or at least to induce him to express a wish to compromise our affairs. I therefore told him in my letter, that he was [probably] apprised of my claim —that I had understand he held the [?] under Bowman and that if Bowman [succeeded] in the maternal line, as was [the apparent] weakness of my claim, and was ready [to disclose it in order to] avoid [a legal suit by] providing [evidence] sensible of the correctness of his title, and therefore [I proposed] a conference, and an examination of his title papers. To this note he returned a polite answer, and proposed my calling at his house in Bloomsbury square[220] the next morning at ten o'clock. I waited on him accordingly, and was treated with great civility. He first produced the Deed of Bowman, duly executed —next his pedigree from Col. Bowman of the Isle of Wight —and last of all the record of the marriage between him and Mary Stoddard, certified [in the] manner already stated. I then addressed him thus —"[The] papers all appear fair —but there is one circumstance [which] it becomes me to mention; because I believe you to [be] totally ignorant of it — This record of a marriage [is a] palpable forgery —and to convince you of the fact, be so good as to read this letter," at the same time putting into his hand the letter of Mr Duncan. He read it with a trembling hand, and a chargeable or disconcerted countenance —and in finishing it he exclaimed —"Is It Possible?! Is It Possible?!" and sunk into his chair. I replied that it was extremely probable, and immediately took my leave of him. A correspondence ensued —but it was rather calculated to irritate the passions than to compose difficulties.

On my next visit to the tenant, I was much surprised to find, that Mr Dyneley had resumed his work on the house. This convinced me, that he had discovered what I was disposed to conceal. He had hitherto supposed me the real heir —but now he was informed that I represented my Uncle, who was the heir, and who was in England about the year 1774. He now [changed his attitude] and bid defiance.

Of the motives of [Missing Text]. He had [?] obtained the Estate in a clandestine [Missing Text] by him or Bowman —perhaps during [the war with] England. But surely the levy at this [Missing Text] of the heirs at law, [?] who is entitled to his [Missing and Illegible Text] within sixty years as from the death of the Intestate. [A portion of crossed–out but legible text reads: "It has been said, that the right of my uncle ceased to exist at the end of 10 years subsequent to his arrival in England, tho' the principle of the English Law appears to be different.] At any rate, Mr Dyneley considered that the claim of my Uncle was barred by the Statute of Limitations; and as I began to grow low in cash, I was obliged to suspend my pursuit and to return home. I was not disposed to take advantage of the kindness of my friends, and to borrow money under the explanation of recovering the estate.

During the eight months I was in England, I made it a point to attend the Courts of Nisi prius,[221] where I attended to the decisions of Lord Kenyon.[222] I also attended the Courts in Westminster Hall —part of the trail of Warren Hastings[223] before the house of Lords —and the debates in the house of Commons —particularly the interesting one on the Quebec bill,[224] when Burke[225] and Fox[226] indulged their political prejudices to great excess. If on that occasion I admired the firm and indignant manner of Burke, I was led to pity the feelings of Fox, who found himself discarded forever from the confidence and friendship of his political father. Their speeches are yet fresh in my mind. The harmonious and diversified elocution of the first, and the rapid argumentative strains of the second, still vibrate on my ears. Notwithstanding the English house of Commons always contains some splendid orators —yet much the greatest number of the members are not able to deliver their sentiments. There was a time, now past, when the Congress of the United States boasted of more good speakers than the British Parliament —; and if the eloquence of a King[227] and an Ames[228] was ever exceeded by contemporary Statesman, it was alone by that of a Burke and a Fox. The bar in England was deficient in eloquent men —perhaps Erskine[229] was the first —but they were profound, and discovered great erudition. Their [?] wholly grounded on authorities —and hence their [?] appeared to contain the essence of metaphysics. [Those] of our legal characters, merely from their loose mode of reasoning, would [?] in Westminster hall. Perhaps a Parsons, a Marshall, a Chace, a Hamilton, and a Dexter would command the attention of the English Courts; their argumentative process differs in no respect from that of English Lawyers —and the eloquence of some of them is much superior.

I was there at a period of life where curiosity is wide awake, and seldom gratified. I visited all, or nearly all, the places of public resort. I divided my evenings between the Theatres, Vauxhall, and [Ranelagh].[230] I visited the curiosities at Richmond, Hampton Court and Kensington —Shakespeare Gallery, the Tower, and a vast number of minor objects. My excursions did not exceed 50 miles from London —but within that distance curiously examined whatever usually attracts the attention of strangers.

Political disputations ran high. Paine had just before published his "Rights of Man" in answer to the "Reflections" of Mr Burke. I must confess that I was a real admirer of the French Revolution. —I was even foolish enough to identify their cause with the one, in which I had been an humble actor —and I continued in the same sentiments till the unfortunate Louis expired under the goulatine.[231] In the course of my political reading, a pamphlet in answer to Paine, written by Dr Tatham of Oxford,[232] attracted my attention. The blunders and misstatements of that political divine awakened my resentment, and induced me to write an answer of about 120 pages. This I completed in 4 or 5 days; it found its way to the press and was published. I forbear to name the title page, as I am heartily ashamed of that effort at political disquisition[233] —much more, indeed, of the sentiments it contained than of the style and language of the work.

I am induced to mention [for the] singularity of it —especially as it will serve to explain a custom not generally known in the United States —I mean the practice of advertising for wives or husbands. In procuring the papers one morning in company with several Gentlemen at breakfast, I found an advertisement of this nature. —The writer observed that he had spent many years in the East Indies where he had acquired a fortune —that he was almost a stranger in England, and for this reason made known, that he was desirous of marrying a young Lady of good character and convictions —that property was no object with him —and if any one was desirous of the connection, they were directed to address a line to A. B. to be left at a certain place [stated] out —and it was suggested that an interview would probably be the consequence. The writer has lodgings in the [same] house with me —but of this I was ignorant —and he soon after married the daughter of a country clergyman and a distant relation of the Duke of Bedford. On reading the advertisement, I was disposed to be merry, and ridiculed the practice, observing the light in which such a step would be viewed in my own Country. I carried the joke to such lengths, that I immediately wrote an advertisement for myself —in which I stated, that a Gentleman of <u>NO</u> fortune wished to marry a Lady whose income was not less than 200 pounds annually —I then described my person and education, my disposition and [convictions] in the most flattering terms. I intended this advertisement to ridicule the custom, and then reading it produced considerable sport. A Lady present requested to see my manuscript —and after she had got it, she declared, that she would publish it. This however I did not believe. A few days afterwards a letter was left at my lodging addressed to S. A. —The lady, smiling, said, "I put your advertisement in the paper, and this must be an answer to it." The answer was in a female hand —and I was requested to address Z to be left at a place near Charring cross.[234] I hastened to the place, and found it was the shop of Lady–hair–dresser. I next procured the paper in which the advertisement was inserted. At first I was not without suspicion that a trick was intended to be played on me —but I was eventually convinced to the contrary. The letter in question stated, that the writer was left with an ample fortune under the guardianship of an uncle who appeared disposed to prevent her marriage, because [as he] wished to inherit her property. She informed me, that [the next day at 11 o'clock she] would arrive in her carriage at the upper end of the [walk] —that she would be dressed in white muzlin, trimmed with black —that to enable her to recognize me in the [expansive] walk, where there is always a crowd taking the air in summer season, she requested me to be dressed in black, with a cane in my right hand, and a black handkerchief wound carefully round that hand, by which she would be able to recognize me. I took care to be on the walk before the time specified, tho' I did not appear in the manner she wished —as the advertisement was not serious, I had no Disposition to treat the subsequent affair in any other light. Precisely at the time mentioned a Carriage halted at the [end] of the walk, and out jumped a beautiful female. I began to [think that] I did not assume the character she desired. We passed each other frequently —and I perceived, that she carelessly fixed [her] eye on those whom she met. She walked here near an hour, and as if despairing of the expected discovery, she re–entered her carriage, and drove away. I immediately retired to my lodgings and wrote her as handsome a letter as I was able —apologized for the trouble I had given by hinting at the real truth —informed her, that I had the pleasure of seeing her, and passed such compliments on her appearance as I conceived would not be disagreeable. I signed it Z and left it as I was directed.

Perdition[235] seize me, if ever I wished to sport with the feelings of a female, or in any degree to deceive or ridicule the sex; and I leave it with the reader to judge whether I was in the least to blame, except in not suffering her to recognize me, and in not endeavoring to make her my own. The fact is I never reflected much on the marriage state —my situation in life did not then admit of it —and my roving disposition pleaded strongly against it. I was not unsusceptible of love; on the contrary, I was often the victim of that passion —perhaps too much so for my own good. Though constitutionally of a different turn of mind in the presence of females — particularly among strangers —yet I [often] courted their society, and was never so [?] [?] when in the company of those whom I [?] [?] amiable qualities endeared them to my [?]. I have hitherto lived a bachelor —and should I die one, I hope my memory will escape the stain of undervaluing the best part of creation. ~

Leaving my residence in London, I selected a library of nearly 500 Volumes, consisting of Law, history, and the belle lettres, together with a few political tracts. I disposed of about 100 Volumes soon after my arrival —the remainder I kept for my own use. I returned to my studies with vigor,

The End

Autobiography Manuscript Notes

[1] It is unknown at whose urging Major Stoddard was writing his autobiography.

[2] Meaning; persistent, to the point of annoyance.

[3] Exactly what ancestral or heraldry evidence Major Stoddard may have received from his uncle, or discovered during his research in 1791 connecting the family ancestry back to the year 1490, is unknown today. The Anthony Stoddard of Boston ancestry has been traced back to Rushton Spencer, Staffordshire, England in the early 16th century.

[4] In 1560, a George Stoddard, merchant of London, owned lands, and rebuilt the mansion, called Mottingham Place, in the village of Mottingham, Parish of Eltham, County of Kent, England. His son, Sir Nicholas Stoddard, inherited the estate but died in 1636. The ancestral record from here is not entirely clear, but jumping ahead, we know a descendant, another Nicholas Stoddard, lived on the estate and in 1765 died a bachelor and intestate (without leaving a valid will).

[5] Anthony Stoddard (1606–1687), known as "Anthony Stoddard of Boston," was baptized at St. Michael le Querne, London, England in the year 1606. He was the son of Anthony (or Anthonie) Stoddard, born in 1572 in Rushton Spencer, Staffordshire, England. No ancestral relationship between Anthony Stoddard of Boston and George Stoddard, Sir Nicholas Stoddard, or Nicholas Stoddard of Mottingham, Kent, England has been found. See the introduction for more information on Anthony Stoddard of Boston.

[6] Anthony Stoddard departed London aboard the ship Endemion, or Endymion, sometime after February 1639 and arrived at the Massachusetts Bay Colony in April 1639.

[7] Anthony Stoddard's death was recorded in the diary of Samuel Sewall as March 16, 1686/7 at 1 o'clock. Conversion of the Old Style calendar used at that time to the New Style makes the date March 26, 1687.

[8] Anthony Stoddard fathered seventeen children in his life. In his will, dated December 29, 1684, he left his property to his eight surviving children: Solomon: Samson; Anthony; Christian; Lydia; Dorothy; May; and Jane. He appointed them joint executors. He did not include his son Simeon in his will due to a demand for repayment of a debt. However, his brothers and sisters provided a remedy to allow Simeon to share in the inheritance of their father's estate with them. Therefore, there were nine of his children alive at the time of his death in 1687.

[9] Anthony's shop was located near the present–day intersection of State Street and Congress Street in Boston. His home was nearby. Being a short distance from Long Wharf and the commerce of the harbor, his place of business was a perfect location for the merchant to get his start. The Union Building, home of the State Street Trust Company, was located at that site around 1810. This site is near the location of the famous, "Boston Massacre" of March 5, 1770 at State Street and Washington Street in Boston.

[10] Anthony Stoddard was certainly a leading member of the church congregation and of its governance council. In those early colonial days, there was virtually no separation between church and state. Anthony was an important Boston merchant and businessman. He was a member of the Worshipful Company of Skinners in London, and continued to be a member while living in the Massachusetts Bay Company. His brother William, living in London, was also a member of the Skinners Company. Anthony of Boston was known as a "linen–draper," or a dry goods merchant. However, Anthony's son, Rev. Solomon Stoddard, was the family's first congregationalist minister.

[11] Reverend Solomon Stoddard (1643–1729).

[12] Rev. Solomon Stoddard died on February 11, 1729, and was 85 years old at the time of his death.

[13] The grandson of Rev. Solomon Stoddard, Jonathan Edwards, became his ministry assistant in November 1726, and was ordained a minister at the First Church in Northampton on February 22, 1727.

Jonathan Edwards (1703–1758) succeeded his grandfather as minister of the First Church in Northampton after his death on February 11, 1729. Rev. Jonathan Edwards later became a very controversial minister, changing much of his grandfather's long–held Church doctrine, which created consternation among the people. As a result, he was dismissed as minister of the First Church in Northampton in 1750.

[14] This refers to Reverend Solomon Stoddard's second daughter, Esther Stoddard (1673–1770), who married Reverend Timothy Edwards (1669–1758). Esther Stoddard was the mother of Jonathan Edwards.

[15] Jonathan Edwards became the third president of Princeton College on September 29, 1757. He died a few short months later of a fever from an inoculation for smallpox, on March 22, 1758.

[16] Reverend Doctor Benjamin Colman (1673–1747). Actually, Reverend William Williams of Hatfield, Massachusetts, the son–in–law of Rev. Solomon Stoddard, provided the principal funeral sermon at the First Church in Northampton, followed by a sermon from his grandson, Rev. Jonathan Edwards. Rev. Dr. Benjamin Colman provided a sermon during a lecture at Harvard College in Boston later that year, honoring the late Rev. Solomon Stoddard of Northampton. This sermon was published in Boston in 1729.

[17] Solomon Stoddard (1643–1729) was born September 27, 1643 in Boston, Suffolk County, Massachusetts, at that time the Massachusetts Bay Colony.

[18] Solomon Stoddard fathered 13 children in his life. Four died shortly after birth. One son, Israel, was taken prisoner by the French while on an English ship in 1703, and was removed to Brest, France, where he died. Eight children survived their father Solomon—six daughters, and two sons: Anthony Stoddard known as Rev. Anthony Stoddard of Woodbury, and John Stoddard, known as Colonel John Stoddard.

[19] This was Col. John Stoddard (1682–1748) born Feb. 17, 1682 in Northampton, Massachusetts. He graduated from Harvard College in 1701. As hostilities in the colonies with belligerents occurred, whether it was French or Indian, his ability as a soldier and officer were quickly recognized. He was a common soldier in 1704, a captain in 1706, a major in 1712, and a colonel in 1721. He was first elected selectman of Northampton at the age of 24, and sixteen times reelected. In 1716, he was first chosen representative to the Massachusetts General Court, the provincial legislature. He was seventeen times reelected to that position. He was a member of "His Majesty's Council for the Province of Massachusetts" in 1724, 1727, and 1728. Colonel Stoddard was entrusted with the defense of the frontier during the French and Indian Wars, and in the difficult and arduous task of negotiating with Indian tribes and contiguous colonies. He was a supporter of and loyal to the King, which caused him problems when the spirit of liberty began taking hold in New England. Both of Col. John Stoddard's sons, Solomon and Israel, inherited their father's loyalist sentiments, which caused both of them difficulties during the American Revolution.

[20] Sir William Pepperrell (1696–1759) was a wealthy merchant of Kittery Point, Massachusetts Bay Colony, now a part of the State of Maine. He served in the Massachusetts General Court and in the "His Majesty's Council for the Province of Massachusetts" during the same period as Col. John Stoddard. During "The Kings War," or the "The War of Austrian Succession,"1740–1748, known as the "French and Indian Wars" in North America, Pepperrell was commander–in–chief of an expedition that sailed in April 1745 to the French Fortress of Louisbourg —present–day Cape Breton Island, Nova Scotia, Canada —and after a six–week siege of the fort, succeeded in capturing it. In 1746, Pepperrell was made Baronet, a hereditary title awarded by the Crown for his service.

[21] Therefore, it depreciated.

[22] Col. John Stoddard (1682–1748) inherited his father's house and property in Northampton and expanded the house during his life. His eldest son, Solomon Stoddard (1736–1827), inherited the house and property upon his death on June 19, 1748 and continued to reside at this house until it was sold in 1812. Major Stoddard refers to this Solomon Stoddard, the grandson of Rev. Solomon Stoddard. Solomon Stoddard died in Northampton at age 94 in 1827.

[23] The home, known as, "The Manse," still stands at 54 Prospect Street in Northampton, MA in 2016. It is one of the oldest homes in New England and in America.

[24] Reverend Anthony Stoddard (1678–1760) was born August 9, 1678 in Northampton, Massachusetts. He was the eighth child born and the oldest surviving son of Rev. Solomon Stoddard and his wife Esther Warham Mather Stoddard. Four brothers born prior to him died at birth or shortly after birth. Rev. Anthony Stoddard served as the respected and harmonious minister of the First Congregational Church in Woodbury for 60 years, until his death on September 6, 1760, at the age of 83. See the introduction for more information on Reverend Anthony Stoddard.

[25] Amos is referring to the fact that his great–grandfather, Rev. Anthony Stoddard, was appointed to preach the "Election Sermon" at the May session of the General Assembly of the Colony of Connecticut in 1716. The next day, May 11, 1716, the Assembly passed a resolution that "a Copy of it for the press" should be made available and published. His father, Rev. Solomon Stoddard, also preached the Election Sermon in Massachusetts in 1703.

[26] Reverend Noah Benedict (1737–1813) was selected by the town of Woodbury to succeed Reverend Anthony Stoddard, and the date for the transition was set for October 22, 1760, but Rev. Anthony passed away on September 6, 1760. However, the town waited until the pre–arranged date and Noah Benedict was then ordained its minister.

[27] Reverend Anthony Stoddard (1678–1760) never preached in Woodbury before 1700, to this editor's knowledge, so it was impossible for the "these two divines to preach in the same parish during part of three centuries."

[28] Reverend Noah Benedict died April 20, 1813 at the age of 76 and in the 53rd year of his ministry.

[29] Amos here has confused his grandfather with his uncle Israel Stoddard (1732–1794). Amos' grandfather was Eliakim Stoddard (1705–1749), born April 3, 1705 and died Sept. 30, 1749 in Woodbury, Connecticut at the age of 44, leaving a wife, Joanna Curtiss Stoddard, and 10 children, including Amos' father, Anthony Stoddard, who was not yet 16 years old. Eliakim, at the time of his death, lived in a house built on land gifted to him in 1736 by his father, Reverend Anthony Stoddard (1678–1760). This home, still standing today in Woodbury, is known by the name "Curtis House" and is operated as an inn.

[30] Amos' father, Anthony Stoddard, (1734–1785) was born on October 21, 1734 in Woodbury, Litchfield County, Connecticut

[31] Phebe Reed (1740–). Her birth certificate, dated Nov 25, 1740, lists her name as "Pheby Reed" and her father's name as "Jonathan Reed." From here we shall use the spelling of "Reed" to reference these family members. Phebe first married Anthony Stoddard in 1760, and after his death in 1785, married Samuel Benham of Middlebury, Connecticut sometime after Samuel's wife's death in 1787.

[32] Her father, Jonathan Reed (1707–), his last name sometimes spelled Reid, Read or Reade, was born March 30, 1707. He married Elizabeth Mack, who died on Jan 18, 1723 in her 21st year. Jonathan then married Elizabeth Smith, widow of her cousin Daniel Smith, on March 14, 1734. They had two daughters, Elizabeth and Phebe, among four other children. These sisters had a half–brother, Richard Smith (1728–1807), from their mother's first marriage to Daniel Smith. Richard Smith had two sons born in Woodbury, Connecticut: Nathan Smith (1770–1835), a U.S. Senator for Connecticut, and Judge Nathaniel Smith (1762–1822) who practiced law in Woodbury and served on the Supreme Court of Connecticut from 1806 until 1819. A Jonth Reed is found in Capt. Uriah Stevens Company in Col. Ebenezer Marsh's Regiment for the relief of Fort William Henry in August 1757 during the French and Indian War.

[33] The French and Indian War in North America, and known as the Seven Year War in Europe, 1756–1763.

[34] This is most likely referencing his mother's older sister, Elizabeth Reed Stoddard (1738–) who was married to Israel Stoddard, the brother of Phebe's husband, Anthony Stoddard. Elizabeth Reed Stoddard was born August 30, 1738 and was apparently still living in 1812. She is most likely the "old aunt" to whom Amos refers. No date or location for her death has been determined.

[35] A series of books based on the Old Testament that constitute the theoretical history of the Israelites.

[36] A ferula is a round ruler, or rod.

[37] Anthony Stoddard's (1734–1785) name is included in the list of participants in Capt. Wait Hinman's Company from Woodbury for the relief of Fort William Henry, near Lake George, New York, in August 1757, during the French and Indian War. They were gone for about three weeks.

[38] The Battle of Bennington, New York occurred during the American Revolution, August 14–16, 1777. Anthony may have participated with the Berkshire, Massachusetts militia who arrived on August 15, 1777 to join General Stark's militia forces at the battle. The American victory at Bennington denied British Major General John Burgoyne's army, running low on supplies, the American Continental Army supply depot stored at Bennington that he hoped to capture by winning this battle.

Anthony Stoddard (1734–1785) of Lanesborough, Berkshire County, Massachusetts, was known to have served as a private in Capt. Jesse Bradley's Company, Col. John Brown's Regiment, during June and July 1777. However, it is hard to believe that Anthony left the field in late July with a British Army approaching, returned home, but then returned to New York by September 21st to fight at the Battle of Saratoga (see note 39). Therefore, it is most likely that he continued to serve in a Berkshire County, Massachusetts company of militia between July 22nd and September 20th and participated in the Battle at Bennington, New York.

[39] This refers to British Major General John Burgoyne (1722–1792). Anthony Stoddard is known to have served in 7th Company, 2nd Berkshire County Regiment of the Massachusetts militia, Capt. Oliver Belding's Co., Col. John Brown's Regiment, between Sept. 21 and Oct. 14, 1777. He would have participated in the Battle of Saratoga during this time. British Major General John Burgoyne and his forces were defeated at this battle on October 7, 1777 and surrendered on October 17, 1777.

The Battle of Saratoga and the surrender and capture of Major General Burgoyne was the first victory over the British since the crossing of the Delaware River and defeating the Hessian forces at Trenton, New Jersey on Christmas Eve 1776, and a major turning point in the Revolutionary War. It provided the King of France with the confidence in the American Patriots to formally join their side in the war against England.

[40] Inspector General Friedrich Wilhelm Baron de Steuben (1730–1794) —usually and incorrectly referred to as General Baron *von* Steuben —was a former Prussian military officer in the services of Frederick the Great. After the Seven Years' War in Europe, his military services were no longer required, and he wasn't particularly well suited for civilian endeavors. Therefore, he began looking for opportunities of a military nature around the time of the American Revolution. He met with the American commissioner in Paris, France, Benjamin Franklin, in 1777, and offered to serve as a military officer in the Continental Army. However, Franklin was unable to offer him a commission and he left feeling somewhat dejected. However, since his expenses would be paid by the French, Baron de Steuben decided to come to America anyway and to offer his services as a volunteer to start, anticipating that he would prove his value, and that he would ultimately be hired for pay and earn his own promotion. In this regard, he was quite correct.

He arrived at Valley Forge in February 1778, and offered himself to General Washington as a volunteer —at a time when the condition and organization of the Army was at its lowest ebb. He was appointed Inspector General and immediately set himself towards improving discipline and morale of the Continental Army encamped at Valley Forge through professional training and drill. He is credited with helping to turn around a desperate situation at Valley Forge and preparing the American Continental Army in discipline and formation fighting in time for its first major test of the 1778 spring campaign: The Battle of Monmouth Courthouse, New Jersey in June 1778. He documented his training techniques, taught at Valley Forge, into a training manual while in winter quarters in Philadelphia in 1778/9. The *Regulations for the Order and Discipline of the Troops of the United States*, known as the "Blue Book" because of its blue paper cover, was first published in Philadelphia in March 1779. It remained the principal American military training manual until 1812 and is considered one of de Steuben's greatest contributions to the cause of liberty.

When Amos Stoddard mustered in with General de Steuben in early 1779, General de Steuben had just completed publication of this manual in Philadelphia, and had likely only recently arrived at West Point to begin the process of distributing the "Blue Book" training manual and providing instruction in its use and application. This was his primary duty and responsibility as Inspector General during most of 1779.

[41] General Baron de Steuben is wearing the large, jeweled, Star of Fidelity of Baden, on the left breast of his uniform, an award that was bestowed on him through the favor of Princess Frederica, a niece of Frederick the Great.

[42] Initially, upon enlistment, Amos was assigned into the 3rd Berkshire County Massachusetts militia, Capt. Dibbell's Company, Col. David Rossiter's Regiment. He then integrated into the 12th Massachusetts Infantry Regiment of the Continental Army, under the command of Lt. Col. Ebenezer Sproat, or Sprout, who was in command of the regiment from September 28, 1779 until January 1, 1780.

[43] He is referring to the duty of going to the mountains to gather wood (for fires) and returning with logs carried on the shoulders of 6–8 men over uneven ground.

[44] Captain Henry Burbeck (1754–1848) commanded a company of the 3rd Artillery Regiment. Henry Burbeck was from Boston and served nearly forty years in the military. He was charged with the defense of West Point in the Highlands in 1779. He continued to serve in the 3rd Artillery Regiment until the end of the war. He later served as Lt.–Colonel Commandant of the 1st Artillerists and Engineers in May 1798 and as a Colonel in the Regiment of Artillerists in April 1802. Captain Burbeck was Amos Stoddard's direct commander at West Point in the 3rd Continental Artillery Regiment, and later in the 1st Artillerists and Engineers and in the 1st Regiment of Artillerists before and during part of the War of 1812. Their military careers ran very much in parallel. Since they had known each other since those Revolutionary War days at West Point in 1780, when Amos was still just a 17–year–old, greenhorn private, it is likely that Henry Burbeck became a both a friend and mentor as well as a commander to Amos Stoddard during his life and military career.

[45] Stony Point, New York, on the west side of the Hudson River, south of West Point.

[46] On September 24, 1780, Arnold fled West Point from the east side of the Hudson River on his barge, and escaped on the British ship HMS *Vulture* anchored in Haverstraw Bay.

[47] Major General Alexander McDougall (1732–1786) from New York was charged with overall command of the forces at Fort Clinton (West Point, the "Highlands") after the defection of General Benedict Arnold.

[48] Meaning; waste material.

[49] King's Ferry is the name of a narrow, shallow span of water on the Hudson River that separates Verplank's Point on the east side of the Hudson River from Stony Point on the west side of the river.

[50] The Corps of Light Infantry, under the command of Brigadier General Anthony Wayne (1745–1796), crossed from the east side of the Hudson River, across King's Ferry, to the Stony Point side of the river on the west, in two columns, one to the north and one to the south of the river at the designated crossing, under the cover of darkness on the night of July 15, 1780. Their muskets were not loaded —only their bayonets were attached —to ensure no accidental shots were fired to warn the enemy. The Battle of Stony Point ensued. General Anthony Wayne's Corps of Light Infantry took the place after a brief bayonet assault on the morning of July 16, 1779.

[51] Orangetown, or Tappen, New York.

[52] Old word for "the gallows."

[53] Old word for "linen neckwear."

[54] Lampblack is a black pigment made from soot.

[55] Major John Andre (1750–1780) was sentenced to death by a Board of General Officers on September 29, 1780, and his sentence was carried out on October 2, 1780 at Tappen, New York.

[56] Brigadier General John Stark (1728–1822), from Londonberry, New Hampshire, served as a captain during the French and Indian War and as a colonel during the beginning of the American Revolution. He was passed over for promotion by General Washington, and feeling slighted, resigned from the Continental Army in March 1777. As a result, he was made a brigadier general in command of a New Hampshire militia unit under the condition he wouldn't have to take orders from the Continental Army command. He participated in the Battle of Saratoga in August 1777. Brigadier General Stark was one of 14 generals that served on the Board of General Officers that sentenced Major John Andre on September 29, 1780 at Tappen, New York. He obviously stayed to see that justice was carried out on October 2, 1780.

[57] The First Brigade, a division of light infantry under the overall command of Major General Marquis de Lafayette (1757–1834), was divided into three infantry battalions, and were supported by an artillery detachment, from the 2nd Continental Artillery Regiment and the 4th Continental Artillery Regiment, with 8–10 pieces. General Lafayette referred to these men as, "the flower of General Washington's Army."

[58] Hackensack, New Jersey. The army was encamped at Teaneck, New Jersey, on the east side of the Hackensack River and west of the Hudson River.

[59] Colonel Joseph Vose (1738–1816) of Milton, Massachusetts commanded First Battalion, First Brigade, under the overall command of General Lafayette. This was also referred to as the 1st Massachusetts Regiment.

[60] French volunteer officer, Jean–Joseph Sourbader de Gimat (1747–1792), or Lt.–Col. "James" Gimat, commanded Second Battalion, First Brigade, under the overall command of General Lafayette. His command consisted of five Connecticut regiments, two Massachusetts regiments, and one Rhode Island light infantry company.

[61] Lt.–Col. Francis Barber (1751–1783) of Princeton, New Jersey commanded Third Battalion, First Brigade, under the overall command of General Lafayette. His command consisted of the 1st and 2nd New Jersey Regiments, the 1st and 2nd Hampshire Regiments, and the Congress Regiment, or Canadian Regiment.

[62] Capt. Joseph Savage (1756–1814), from Lancaster, Massachusetts, was in command of a company of the 2nd Continental Artillery Regiment previously under the command of Colonel John Lamb. It appears that Private Amos Stoddard was transferred from the 3rd Artillery Regiment, Capt. Burbeck's Company, into the 2nd Artillery Regiment, Capt. Joseph Savage's Company, which was ordered to support General Lafayette's operations in Maryland and Virginia.

[63] Major General Marquis de Lafayette (1757–1834), of Chevaniac, France, was placed in command of a brigade of light infantry by General Washington, which consisted of three regiments commanded by Col. Joseph Vose of Massachusetts, Lt. Col. Jean–Joseph Gimat, a volunteer French officer, and Lt. Col. Francis Barber of New Jersey. They were supported by a company of the 2nd Continental Artillery Regiment. With only about 1,000 men under his command, Lafayette complained in a letter written on May 24, 1781 to General Washington, that "Was I any ways equal to the Ennemy, I would be extremely Happy in my present Command —But I am not Strong Enough even to get Beaten."

[64] Head of Elk, Maryland is now Elkton, Maryland located at the confluence of the Elk River, at the north end of the Chesapeake Bay.

[65] Possibly Plum's Point, Maryland, south of Annapolis on Chesapeake Bay.

[66] A two–masted sailing ship.

[67] Quote from William Shakespeare's play, "Julius Caesar," Act 3, Scene 1, Line 273: "Cry 'Havoc!', and let slip the dogs of war."

[68] On April 8, 1780, Major General Lafayette received orders from General Washington, written April 6, 1780, to return back south (from Head of Elk, Maryland, to Virginia) and place himself under the command of Major General Nathanael Green. This order was later countermanded when he reached Virginia, and he was allowed to continue to command independently of General Green. The order to Virginia was intended to keep British forces from leaving Virginia and joining General Cornwallis in South Carolina and further threatening General Green's Continental forces there.

[69] The Susquehanna River, the longest river that drains into the Atlantic Ocean and which passes through New York, Pennsylvania, and Maryland where it flows into the Chesapeake Bay.

[70] A drumhead court martial is held in the field to hear charges of an urgent nature.

[71] April 17, 1781.

[72] Patapsco River in central Maryland, which flows into the Chesapeake Bay west of Baltimore.

[73] General Lafayette arrived at Alexandria, Virginia April 21, 1781.

[74] General Lafayette arrived at Richmond, Virginia on the evening of April 29, 1781.

[75] British forces under Major General William Phillips (1731–1781), with Benedict Arnold, reached Manchester, across the James River from Richmond, on May 30, 1781.

[76] The James River.

[77] Lafayette crossed the Rapidan at Ely's Ford near Culpepper on June 4, 1781.

[78] Brigadier General Thomas Nelson, Jr. (1738–1789) in command of the Virginia militia, a force he personally raised and financed. In June 1781, Nelson was elected to succeed Thomas Jefferson as governor. He coordinated his Virginia militia forces with Continental forces in defense of Virginia and at the Siege of Yorktown.

[79] Meaning; chicken–hearted.

[80] Meaning; swiftness of movement.

[81] Near Charlottesville, Virginia, approximately 70 miles northwest of Richmond, in close proximity of the Blue Ridge Mountains.

[82] Brigadier General Anthony Wayne (1745–1796) of Easttown Township, near present–day Paoli, Pennsylvania, commanding regiments of the Pennsylvania Line, joined with General Lafayette's forces near Charlottesville, Virginia on June 10, 1781. Regarding the tardiness of the arrival of Wayne's brigade, Lafayette wrote to Hamilton on May 23rd: "They are to go to Carolina, But should I want them for a few days I am at liberty to keep them; this permission I will improve so as to receive one Blow that, Being Beat, I may at least Be Beat with some decency."

It should be noted that events are out of sequence here. General Wayne did not join General Lafayette until June 10th, while the preceding events in Petersburg, Virginia took place May 7–10th.

[83] General Lafayette crossed to the south side of the James River below Richmond, possibly near Westover, on May 7th to take his position at Baker's Hill, present–day Colonial Heights, Virginia, on the opposite side of the river from Petersburg and the British encampment there. It was from here that he bombarded the British encampment at Petersburg on May 10, 1781.

[84] Command of a piece of artillery.

[85] This was Major James Randolph Reid (1750–1789), of Hamiltonban Township, Pennsylvania and of the 2nd Canadian Regiment. The regiment was also known as the Congress Regiment because it was the direct responsibility of the Continental Congress as opposed to being supplied and funded by any particular state.

[86] The "seat of the late Colonel Bird" refers to the town of Westover, Virginia, and specifically, the site of the mansion, "Westover Plantation," built around 1750 by William Byrd III. Westover Plantation is below Richmond on the north side of the James River. William Byrd III (1728–1777) was in military service during the French and Indian War, and in 1758 he became colonel of the 2nd Virginia Regiment. The following year, he succeeded George Washington as commander of the 1st Virginia Regiment. However, gambling and debts caused him such distress that in the early part of 1777 he took his own life.

[87] May 8–10, 1781.

[88] Petersburg, Virginia.

[89] Colonial Hills, Virginia today, at the intersection of Jefferson Davis Highway and Arlington Avenue, on the north side of the Appomattox River.

[90] British Major General William Phillips (1731–1781). During his attempt to link up his forces with General Cornwallis, he became sick with malaria. He died on May 13, 1781 in Petersburg, VA —just shortly after this encounter. He was secretly buried in an unmarked grave in the cemetery at Blandford Church where he is still interred today.

[91] Benedict Arnold (1741–1801), former Continental Army general and traitor.

[92] Most likely the home of Thomas Shore on Baker's Hill, known today as Violet Bank House at Colonial Heights, Virginia, across the Appomattox River from Petersburg, Virginia.

[93] Jamestown, Virginia.

[94] Feu de joie: A ceremonial rifle salute consisting of each soldier firing in succession along the ranks to make a continuous sound.

[95] Known as the Battle of Green Springs which took place on July 6, 1781.

[96] Oblique Firing: Firing into a column instead of a line.

[97] Williamsburg, Virginia, on or about September 1, 1781.

[98] About September 14, 1781.

[99] General Thomas Nelson, Jr. (1738–1789) was mentioned earlier in note 73. However, it is worth mentioning here that General Thomas Nelson, Jr. was a signer of the Declaration of Independence and served in the Continental Congress during 1781. He lived in Yorktown, Virginia.

Legend has it that General Nelson requested General Washington, or General Lafayette, to fire upon his own home at Yorktown where General Cornwallis had his headquarters, offering five guineas to the first man to hit his house. This is entirely myth. However, it is interesting to note that General Nelson here orders Private Amos Stoddard, manning an artillery battery, to fire on the "subterranean quarters" of General Cornwallis.

The house occupied by General Cornwallis as his headquarters at Yorktown did not belong to General Nelson. It belonged to his uncle, Thomas Nelson, the 65–year–old former Deputy Secretary for the Colony of Virginia, who became known as "Secretary Nelson." Secretary Nelson was in his home with Cornwallis during its occupation and during the bombardment on the house on October 9th. His nephew, General Nelson, became so concerned for his uncle's safety that a truce was arranged. Secretary Nelson was allowed to leave the house with a slave at noon on October 10, 1781. The house did not withstand the siege and ultimately was reduced to rubble. General Cornwallis removed to a sunken grotto at the edge of the garden for protection.

[100] Embrasure —a small opening in a parapet or a protective wall or earth defense along the top of a trench or other place of concealment for troops.

[101] An incendiary, anti–personnel projectile designed to burn fiercely and produce poisonous fumes.

[102] Abatis is a type of fortification traditionally made from trees and bushes and designed to slow and disrupt enemy troop movements.

[103] French Lt. General Comte de Rochambeau's (1725–1807) suite at the surrender of Cornwallis at Yorktown, included: Admiral Comte de Barras (1719–1793), Admiral Comte de Grasse (1723–1788), Brigadier General Marquis de Choisy, Major General Marquis de St. Simon, Major General Viscount de Viomenil, and Major General Baron de Viomenil, among other lower ranking officers.

[104] Lt. General Charles O'Hara (1740–1802) was General Cornwallis' adjutant and second in command at Yorktown.

[105] Major General Benjamin Lincoln (1733–1810), from Hingham, Massachusetts, joined the 3rd Regiment of the Suffolk County militia at the age of 21 and was active in the French and Indian War but saw no action. He again was active in the militia during the siege of Boston in 1775 and in the defense of New York in 1776, being promoted to a major general. He was commissioned a major general in the Continental Army by Congress in 1777 based on the recommendation of General George Washington. He was involved in the Battle of Saratoga, and in 1778 assigned to the southern theatre, where after a brief siege of Charleston, South Carolina, he was forced to surrender to British Lt. General Henry Clinton. He was later exchanged for British Major General William Phillips in November 1780 and was therefore able to participate in the Virginia campaign of 1781, where he played a significant role in the Siege of Yorktown. He was mounted on his horse next to French General Rochambeau when he was approached by British General O'Hara, who either mistook him for General Washington, or desired to surrender to a French officer rather that to Washington and the Americans.

[106] "Arms akimbo" implies a posture that communicates defiance, confidence, aggressiveness, or arrogance.

[107] Lieut. William Price, previously in the 3rd Continental Artillery Regiment, was probably assigned to 2nd Continental Artillery Regiment, as was Private Stoddard.

[108] Having or showing signs of a fever, in which there are alternating periods of chills, fever, and sweating.

[109] Captain Charles Asgill (1762–1823) was a British officer who was selected to be hung in retaliation for an American soldier who was hung by loyalists creating a perplexing situation for General George Washington, the circumstances which were known as "The Asgill Affair."

New Jersey militia soldier, Capt. Joshua "Jack" Huddy, was given to a group of loyalists by British General Henry Clinton for the reported purpose of a prisoner swap. Instead, the loyalists hung Capt. Huddy, and placed a sign around his neck that said, "Up Goes Huddy for Phillip White." Phillip White, a loyalist farmer and irregular soldier, was killed on March 30, 1782 while in New Jersey militia captivity. Huddy was hung in retaliation on April 12, 1782, at Sandy Hook, New Jersey.

General Washington then ordered that a British officer of the same rank as Capt. Huddy, being held prisoner in Lancaster, Pennsylvania, be hung in retaliation for the hanging of Capt. Huddy. Captain Charles Asgill was selected by lottery. He with 12 other officers drew papers from a hat. His piece of paper read, "unfortunate." Capt. Asgill was then transferred from Lancaster, Pennsylvania to Chatham, New Jersey.

By June General Washington had already expressed his desire to see Capt. Asgill's life spared, and to request Capt. Asgill be treated "with every tender Attention and politeness." On November 5, 1782, by an Act of the Continental Congress, General Washington set Capt. Asgill free, which is the outcome he sincerely desired. Capt. Asgill was released and returned to England.

[110] Captain Joshua "Jack" Huddy (1735–1782) was born in New Jersey. After an adult life of troubles, divorce and questionable behavior, Huddy joined the patriot cause and was placed in command of a small group of New Jersey irregular militia. Huddy and his militia engaged in raids and executions of suspected loyalists. In February 1782, he was stationed at Toms River, New Jersey on Barnegat Bay, at a blockhouse used for the production of salt, an important commodity for curing meat and fish in colonial America. On March 24, 1782, a small group of irregular forces of the Associated Loyalists, a group headed by William Franklin, son of Benjamin Franklin, attacked the salt works and captured Huddy. He was initially turned over to the British, but General Henry Clinton was deceived into returning him into the hands of the loyalist gang, in the command of Capt. Richard Lippincott, under the pretense of a prisoner exchange. Instead, he was diverted to Midddletown Point on Sandy Hook Bay and hung in retaliation for the death of Phillip White, a member of their group, who was killed while in the captivity of the irregular New Jersey militia.

[111] Louis Joseph of France, born October 22, 1781, was the second child and oldest son of King Louis XVI of France. Through his birthright, he was the "heir apparent" to the King, the crown prince, and was therefore known as the Dauphin of France. The prince died of tuberculosis in 1789.

[112] A "Grand Arbor and Colonnade" was created at West Point for the event on the evening of May 31, 1782. It was built from the trees in the area and was about 220 feet in length, 80 feet wide, and supported by 118 log pillars. It was attractively decorated with boughs, or interwoven tree branches, flowers, garland, fleur–de–lis and other elements significant of the American–French alliance. The first announcement from General Washington to the troops regarding the party came on May 28, 1782 from "Head–Quarters, Newburgh."

[113] The Colonnade was created by French Major Villefranche, an engineer of great ability, using about 1,000 men and built in 10 days.

[114] General Washington and Martha Washington, Governor George Clinton of New York and his wife Sarah, Major General Henry Knox and his wife Lucy, were among the dignitaries and invited guests that attended. Most attendees were from New York and New Jersey and traveled up the Hudson River and arrived at West Point by barge.

[115] There were 13 cannons used. An excerpt of their orders, "Inspector–Generals Order, May 30, 1782," reads, "The discharge of thirteen cannon from the Park, after the first toast, will be followed by a similar discharge from the Garrison at Stoney Point."

[116] Garland decorating the Colonnade.

[117] Fort Putnam was the name for the military garrison and original wood and earthen redoubt built by Col. Rufus Putnam's 5th Massachusetts Regiment in 1778. It sat 500 feet above sea level with a sweeping view of the Hudson River. Fort Putnam was the largest fortification within a series of fortifications and redoubts making up West Point's defenses.

[118] This refers to a near mutiny of the Army that occurred at Newburgh, New York, on the Hudson River, north of West Point, the site of General Washington's Headquarters, which became known as the "Newburgh Conspiracy." Major Stoddard's commentary on the plight of the officers of the Army at the end of the war, and the people he pointed to as being involved in circulating the anonymous letters threatening a mutiny, is worth covering in more detail for the reader's understanding and clarity. See the introduction more information on the Newburgh Conspiracy.

[119] John Armstrong, Jr. (1758–1843), born in Carlisle, Pennsylvania, was an aide to Major General Horatio Gates in March 1783. Armstrong initially served in a Pennsylvania militia regiment in 1775 before being appointed as an aide–de–camp to General Hugh Mercer, who died at the Battle of Princeton in January 1777. He resigned from the military that year for health concerns. In 1782, Armstrong was offered a commission as a major by General Gates and served as his aide from 1782 until the end of the war. After the war, he was a member of the Confederation Congress representing Pennsylvania for one year, and served briefly as a U.S. senator from New York. During the War of 1812, he was commissioned a brigadier general. He was then appointed secretary of war by President James Madison in January 1813 and served in that capacity until September 1814.

[120] Major General Horatio Gates (1727–1806) of the Continental Army was a former British major who made Virginia his home in 1772. In 1775, Gates was commissioned a brigadier general by the Continental Congress, and he went on to become one of the most controversial figures of the American Revolution: He claimed credit for the victory over the British at the Battle of Saratoga, when in fact he acted with a great deal of timidity; he was involved with a cabal of men, while he was head of the Board of War, and while the Army was in a desperate situation at Valley Forge, who conspired to discredit General Washington and replace Washington with Gates in 1777; and he was responsible for his army's disastrous defeat at the Battle of Camden in South Carolina in 1780. The defeat at Camden, and the blame placed on him for the loss, had a detrimental effect on his military career. He never held a field command again. He rejoined Washington's staff at Newburgh, New York in 1782 until the end of the war.

[121] Dr. William Eustis (1753–1825) of Cambridge, Massachusetts, served as a surgeon with the artillery regiment of General Henry Knox in 1775, and in 1777, was placed in command of a military hospital in New York and served there until the end of the war. He served in the Massachusetts state legislature from 1788–1794, and was a surgeon in the Massachusetts militia during Shays' Rebellion. He was appointed secretary of war in the Madison administration, a position he did not distinguish himself in during his tenure. He resigned in December 1812. President Madison then appointed him as minister to the Netherlands from 1814–1818. He was elected governor of Massachusetts in 1823. For more information on his role in the Newburgh Conspiracy, see the introduction section.

[122] Dr. David Townsend (1753–1829) of Boston, Massachusetts, was a volunteer surgeon and surgeon's mate in Col. David Brewer's Massachusetts Regiment during the beginning of the American Revolution. He was appointed senior surgeon in the Hospital Department in April 1777 and served in that capacity until end of the war. Dr. Townsend was identified by Dr. John Armstrong Jr. as a participant in the Newburgh plot and conspiracy.

[123] Captain Patrick Phelon (1750–1791) was from Salem, Essex County, Massachusetts, and served in several different infantry regiments during the American Revolution. He was assigned to the defense of West Point at the end of the war, and was honorably discharged from Jackson's First American Regiment on June 20, 1784. On March 4, 1791 he was appointed a captain in the 2nd United States Regiment of Infantry. He was killed during a bayonet charge on November 4, 1791 while participating in Major General Arthur St. Clair's campaign against a confederation of American Indians, known as the Northwest Indian War. He is buried in a mass grave at Fort Recovery, Ohio.

[124] Major General Arthur St. Clair (1737–1818) was born in Scotland but settled in Pennsylvania in 1764. He was given a commission as a colonel in the Continental Army in the 3rd Pennsylvania Regiment in 1776. He was promoted to major general in February 1777 and served for the entire war. After the war he served a one–year term as president of the Continental Congress, during which time the Northwest Ordinance of 1787 was passed, which created the Northwest Territory. He served as the first governor of the Northwest Territory between 1788 and 1802. In March 1791, St. Clair was commissioned as a major general and placed in command of the United States Army. He led a punitive expedition against the confederation of Indians in what became known as the Northwest Indian War. On November 4, 1791, his two infantry regiments and an artillery battalion, camped on a hill in Mercer County, Ohio, came under attack by combined Indian tribes under the leadership of the Indian chief Little Turtle. The battle was the largest defeat of the American Army by Native American Indians in history, with 623 American soldiers killed in action compared to 50 Indian dead. The event became known as "St. Clair's Defeat."

[125] It is interesting to note that Dr. Eustis was serving as secretary of war during the year 1812 when Major Stoddard wrote this autobiography. Major Stoddard received and faithfully carried out orders from Dr. Eustis as secretary of war during this time.

[126] Meaning; hard money in the form of coin, not paper currency.

[127] Meaning; liquors obtained after repeated distillations from fermented vegetables.

[128] Meaning; changing circumstances of fortune.

[129] As a farmer.

[130] Marcus Tullius Cicero was a Roman soldier, lawyer, statesman, scholar, philosopher and writer. He was a contemporary of Julius Caesar and considered the greatest orator of his time. His writings and orations were translated from Latin into English.

[131] In a letter Amos sent to Mr. Loammi Baldwin on May 19, 1788, Amos stated, "I have taught a school about a year and a half." This teaching employment must have been near his father's home in Lanesborough in the fall of 1783 after his discharge from the Continental Army and before moving to Boston to work for Charles Cushing at the Clerk's Office of the Supreme Judicial Court at the end of 1784.

[132] Literary works, especially essays and poetry, valued for their aesthetic rather than their informative or moral content.

[133] Rev. Prof. Hugh Blair (1718–1800) was born in Edinburgh, Scotland. He was the minister of the Church of Scotland and became best known for *Sermons*, a five–volume discourse on Christian morality. He taught at the University of Edinburgh where he was appointed Professor of Rhetoric in 1760 and Regius Professor of Rhetoric and Belles Lettres in 1762. Blair was an important figure of the Scottish Enlightenment.

[134] A sporty, open carriage popular in the late eighteenth and early nineteenth century.

[135] Oliver Wendell, Esq. (1733–1818) was Judge of Probate for Suffolk County, Massachusetts.

[136] Nathaniel Appleton (1731–1798) of Cambridge, Massachusetts, a graduate of Harvard College in 1749, was Commissioner of Loans for Massachusetts from 1775 until 1789, and served in the same capacity in the United States Continental Loan Office until his death.

[137] Supreme Judicial Court of Massachusetts, in Boston, Massachusetts.

[138] Charles Cushing, Esq. (1733–1810) from Scituate, Massachusetts, was one of two clerks for the Supreme Judicial Court of Massachusetts in Boston. He was the brother of William Cushing, Chief Justice of the Supreme Judicial Court for Massachusetts, and later, Associate Justice of the Supreme Court of the United States from 1789 until 1810.

[139] Wages, benefits or other benefit received as compensation for holding some office or employment.

[140] The Boston Massacre, March 5, 1770.

[141] *Common Sense* was the title of a pamphlet written in 1776 by Thomas Paine that challenged the authority of the British government and the royal monarchy. It was the most widely sold and distributed publication in the history of the American colonies.

[142] The literary work of Charles Rollin (1641–1741), a French historian and educator, *Ancient History* (Histoire Ancienne)," 12 volumes published in Paris between 1730 and 1738.

[143] Theodore Sedgwick (1746–1813) was born in West Hartford, Connecticut in 1746. He attended Yale College but was expelled before graduation for disciplinary reasons. He opened a law practice in Sheffield, Massachusetts in 1767 and was Sheffield's representative to the Massachusetts Legislature in 1782–83. He served in the state Senate in 1784–85. In 1786, he moved his family to Stockbridge, Massachusetts, where he became a leader in the Massachusetts militia to suppress Shays' Rebellion. Theodore Sedgwick was elected to the United States Senate representing Massachusetts in 1796 and served until 1799. He then served in the United States House of Representatives as Speaker of the House from 1799 until 1801.

[144] A public sale at auction.

[145] Col. Henry Jackson (1747–1809) of Boston, Massachusetts, a veteran American Revolution general, and a close personal friend of Secretary of War Henry Knox, set about raising a regiment in Massachusetts on behalf of the Continental Congress. However, Congress never provided sufficient funding and his federal troops never took to the field.

[146] Col. David Humphrey (1752–1818), as a member of the Connecticut General Assembly, raised a regiment of State militia in December 1786 to help deal with the turmoil created by Shays' insurgency in Massachusetts. By the time he arrived with his 120–man force, the Massachusetts militia, led by General Benjamin Lincoln, had the situation under control. This was the only use of federal troops during Shays' Rebellion.

[147] Neither Colonel Jackson nor Colonel Humphrey had much success in their recruiting efforts, and these "Congress Regiments" never participated in any actions. The commanders lacked in both money and in the quality of the recruits they enlisted. It is clear that Amos Stoddard was probably the best recruit they never commanded. It also explains why his service during Shays' Rebellion goes unrecorded: He was recruited into a federal regiment organized by Col. Jackson that never took the field and was absorbed into the Massachusetts militia apparently upon his own volition.

[148] Major General Benjamin Lincoln (1733–1810) was appointed by Governor James Bowdoin of Massachusetts to lead the Massachusetts militia during Shays' Rebellion in 1786. During the American Revolution he fought in the Battle of Saratoga in 1777; he cooperated with French forces in a losing battle at the Siege of Savannah, Georgia; and in March 1780, after a siege by the British, he was compelled to surrender his army to British General Cornwallis at Charleston, South Carolina. He was later exchanged for British Major General William Phillips in November 1780. He returned to field command and led an army to Virginia, and was instrumental at the Siege of Yorktown. He was present at the surrender of Cornwallis' army at Yorktown in October 1781. Lincoln was then appointed by the Continental Congress as the first secretary of war in 1781, a post he held until the end of the war. Major General Lincoln's humane and wise leadership during Shays' Rebellion was largely responsible for the minimal loss of life during that insurrection.

[149] Revolutionary War Brigadier General Jonathan Warner (1744–1803) of Hardwick, Worcester County, Massachusetts was a brigadier general under Major General Benjamin Lincoln at the Battle of Saratoga and a major general in the Massachusetts militia during Shays' Rebellion.

[150] Revolutionary War Colonel William Shepard (1737–1817) of Westfield, Hampshire County, Massachusetts was a major general of Massachusetts militia during Shays' Rebellion. He ordered his defenders of the Springfield Armory to fire their cannons loaded with grapeshot against the insurgents, killing two, in the only significant military engagement loss of life during the insurrection. He later served in the United States House of Representatives from Massachusetts from 1787–1803.

[151] Revolutionary War Major General John Paterson (1744–1808) of Lenox, Berkshire County, Massachusetts was a major general of the Massachusetts militia during Shays' Rebellion. He fought at Trenton, Princeton, Saratoga and Monmouth during the Revolutionary War. He was a brigadier general under Major General Benjamin Lincoln at the Battle of Saratoga. He later moved to Lisle, New York and served in the United States House of Representatives.

[152] A military or naval uniform for use on other than formal occasions.

[153] Greenwich, Massachusetts no longer exists due to the creation of the Quabbin Reservoir in 1938. The town of Hardwick, adjacent to the former town of Greenwich, is known to have been the town of residence of Simeon Hazeltine, sometimes spelled Hayselton. No record has been found of Hazeltine owning a tavern in the area. Pelham, Massachusetts, the home of Capt. Shays, was located to the west of the former town of Greenwich and of Hardwick. The site of Shays' house is now a part of the Quabbin Reservoir area, but is not under water, and its foundation can still be seen today.

[154] Simeon Hazeltine (1734–1821) commanded a company as a captain in Col. John Fellows' Provincial Regiment in 1775 during the American Revolution. He was residing in Hardwick, Massachusetts at the time of Shays' Rebellion. On January 19, 1787, Massachusetts Governor Bowdoin issued a warrant for his arrest for taking up arms and being one of the leaders in the insurrection. Hazeltine was so deeply involved in the Shays' Rebellion that he left Hardwick and removed to Sandgate, Vermont, a town he represented in the General Assembly in 1794. Simeon Hazelton and his wife are buried at the Sandgate, VT cemetery.

[155] A junior officer.

[156] This may possibly be Conkey's Tavern in Pelham, Massachusetts, a well–known watering hole for Daniel Shays and a gathering place of Shays' supporters, or it could possibly be a tavern operated by Shays' friend and neighbor, Nehemiah Hines, known as Hinds (*sic*) Tavern, on East Hill in Pelham. Both served as meeting places and gathering places for insurgents during Shays' Rebellion in 1786–7. Today, the sites of Conkey's Tavern and Hinds Tavern, as well as Shays' farm, are a part of a watershed area as a result of the creation of the Quabbin Reservoir in 1938.

[157] James Hathaway (1727–1817) of Spencer, Massachusetts was a selectman of Spencer in 1785–6, and a representative to the General Court (the Massachusetts State Legislature) between1787 and 1793. His minor role in Shays' Rebellion appears to be unrecorded other than the incident documented by Major Stoddard.

[158] Daniel Shays (1747–1825) served in the American Revolution beginning in 1775 as a sergeant. Sergeant Shays soon became Lieutenant Shays. He fought at Bunker Hill and at Ticonderoga. By 1777, Shays was given a captain's commission in the 5th Massachusetts Regiment of the Continental Army. He fought at the Battle of Saratoga in New York and participated in the night bayonet charge under the command of General Anthony Wayne at Stony Point, New York in 1779. General Lafayette himself honored Captain Shays (and other officers under his command) with a ceremonial sword as a mark of his personal esteem. However, Shays good reputation with fellow officers and soldiers was severely tarnished after he sold the sword presented to him by General Lafayette to a tavern owner in order to pay off his mounting debts. His personal debt situation reflected the situation faced by many former soldiers and officers and led to his leading a group of angry, like–minded veterans against the government in recourse, in what became known as "Shays' Rebellion."

[159] Orange, or "Orringh," Stoddard (1742–1824) was born in Litchfield County, Connecticut. He later removed to Stockbridge, Massachusetts in 1758 and married there in 1765. Orringh (as he apparently like to spell his name) served in the American Revolution beginning in Thomas William's Company, Colonel Paterson's Regiment, of the Massachusetts militia in 1775. He later became the captain of his own company in Colonel Joseph Vose's 1st Massachusetts Regiment which became part the Continental Army 1st Infantry Regiment. He was present at Valley Forge in the winter of 1777–8 leading his company in Glover's Brigade, Col. Vose's 1st Infantry Regiment, within the division under the overall command of Major General de Kalb. He fought at the Battle of Monmouth Courthouse in June 1778. Capt. Orringh Stoddard and the 1st Infantry Regiment were present at West Point in 1779–80, and Amos Stoddard may have met his "distant cousin" Orringh Stoddard there at that time.

[160] This may possibly be Royall Tyler (1757–1826) who served as an aide–de–camp to General Lincoln about this time.

[161] No newspaper publication of the complete letter has been found. However, two newspaper articles, one published on January 23, 1787 in The New–Hampshire Spy, and another published on February 1, 1787 in The Pennsylvania Packet and Daily Advertiser, were found. They are titled, "*Extract of a letter from an officer on the recruiting service, dated at Northampton the10th*" which reflects the date of the letter's original publication.

These two published excerpts are partial representations of the actual letter written by Amos Stoddard to which he refers. In these extracts, he is not identified as being the author of the letter. The original and complete letter was apparently published in a Northampton newspaper on January 10, 1787. The original letter, written to Major General Benjamin Lincoln, has not been found among General Lincoln's papers and appears to have been lost.

[162] Lenox, Massachusetts, near his home in Lanesborough, Massachusetts.

[163] His father, Anthony Stoddard (1734–1785), died November 16, 1785 in Lanesborough, Berkshire County, Massachusetts.

[164] The right of succession belonging to the firstborn child.

[165] Amos Stoddard, Philo Stoddard, Anthony Stoddard, Curtis Stoddard, Simeon Curtis Stoddard, and Eliakim Stoddard.

[167] Anthony Stoddard is likely the male sibling deceased prior to 1812. He was born in 1769 but no death record has been found. All other male siblings are accounted for in 1812.

[168] Phebe died in 1800 at the age of 36; Lavinia died in 1802 at the age of 34.

[169] Major Azariah Egleston (1757–1822) was born in Sheffield, Berkshire County, Massachusetts. He enlisted at Pittsfield in the Massachusetts militia, Paterson's Regiment, Noble's Company, on April 29, 1775. He was present at the Battle of Bunker Hill in Boston that year. He crossed the Delaware with Washington on Christmas Eve, 1776 and was in the advance guard commanded by John Stark that attacked the Hessians at Trenton the next morning. He fought at the Battle of Saratoga. He was in the 1st Massachusetts Infantry Regiment, commanded by Col. Vose, at Valley Forge in 1777–78. He was stationed at West Point as quartermaster until the end of the war. In 1785, he married the daughter of Major General John Paterson, whom he had served with throughout the war.

[170] Theodore Sedgwick (1746–1813) is previously mentioned in note 134.

[171] Brigadier General John Fellows (1735–1808), from Sheffield, Berkshire County, Massachusetts, was a first lieutenant in the South Berkshire Regiment of Massachusetts militia under Colonel John Ashley in 1771. He led the provincial regiment as part of the Lexington Alarm of April 19, 1775. Fellows represented Sheffield and Great Barrington in the First and Second Provincial Congresses in 1774 and 1775. In 1775 he received a commission as a colonel and in 1776 he was appointed a brigadier general in the Massachusetts militia. He commanded at the Battle of Saratoga in 1777 and served as an aide on General Washington's staff. John Fellows became High Sheriff for Berkshire County, Massachusetts after the war.

[172] Petersham, Worcester County, Massachusetts, located north of Hardwick, and northeast of Pelham, is a small Massachusetts town that was centrally involved with the events surrounding Shays' Rebellion and was the site of one of the last confrontations between government forces under the command of General Lincoln and those under the command of Daniel Shays.

[173] John Hubbard (1742–1796) of Sheffield, Berkshire County, Massachusetts. Hubbard joined the Massachusetts militia as an ensign in Capt. Lemuel Barnard's North Sheffield Company, Colonel John Ashley's Regiment, in July 1771, and later was commissioned a First Lieutenant in William Bacon's Company, Col. John Fellow's Regiment, in 1775. John Hubbard served in the Massachusetts legislature in 1786.

[174] Major General John Paterson. See note 151.

[175] These men were: Judge Timothy Edwards (1738–1813) of Stockbridge, the eldest son of Jonathan Edwards, and Judge Jaheel Woodbridge, also of Stockbridge. As the son of Rev. Jonathan Edwards, who was the grandson of Rev. Solomon Stoddard of Northampton, Judge Timothy Edwards was actually related to Amos Stoddard. Whether Major Stoddard knew this or not is not known.

[176] See Brigadier General John Fellows, note 171.

[177] Goal, also spelled Gaol, is an old English word for jail.

[178] General John Ashley (1736–1799), of Sheffield, Massachusetts, graduated from Yale College in 1758. As a colonel, he was in command of the South Berkshire Regiment of Massachusetts militia at the Battle of Saratoga under Brigadier General John Paterson in 1777. He rose to be a major general in the Massachusetts militia during the American Revolution. He served as a colonel in the Massachusetts militia during Shays' Rebellion.

[179] Perez Hamlin (1748–1826) was born at Sharon, Connecticut and died at the age of 78 in Auburn, Cayuga County, New York. Hamlin served during the Revolution as a private in Colonel William B. Whiting's 17th Regiment, Albany County, New York militia. During the skirmish at Stockbridge Hamlin was seriously wounded and captured in the fight. He was tried and convicted of treason and sentenced to death, but escaped from jail.

[180] Solomon Gleason, Jr. (1762–1787), or Glezon, a 25–year–old man from Stockbridge who was apparently taken as a prisoner by the insurgents, was killed by a single shot to the throat. He was the same age as Amos Stoddard at the time.

Ephraim Porter (1762–1787), from Great Barrington, who served in Thomas Ingersoll's Company, Col. Ashley's Regiment of the Berkshire County, Massachusetts militia during the Revolutionary War, and who was now again a soldier in the Massachusetts militia, was also killed. He was initially wounded and later died of his wounds. This is why his death was not known or reported by Major Stoddard.

[181] This was Hugo Burghardt (1770–1822) who was from Great Barrington, Massachusetts. While at home from studies at Yale in his senior year on account of illness, he was wounded by insurgents during their raid on Stockbridge during Shays' Rebellion. After graduation in 1787, he practiced medicine with Dr. Erastus Sergeant. He began practice in Richmond, Massachusetts and was well esteemed there for thirty years. He received an honorary degree of M.D. from Harvard University in 1812. He died in 1822 at the age of 52 years.

It should be noted here that Dr. Erastus Sergeant was also one of the prisoners taken by the insurgents at Stockbridge, along with Solomon Gleason, and was witness to the events of February 27, 1787 described by Major Stoddard and in which Hugo Burghardt was shot by the insurgents. Dr. Sergeant provided his account of that day in a letter he wrote to Major General William Shepard on March 5, 1787: http://www.digitalamherst.org/items/show/777

[182] Major General Benjamin Lincoln (1733–1810). See note 148.

[183] The Honorable William Cushing (1732–1810), Chief Justice of the Supreme Judicial Court for Massachusetts, was the brother of Charles Cushing, Esq. (1734–1810) who hired Amos Stoddard as a court clerk and in whose home he resided prior to accepting a commission in the militia to suppress the rebellion. See note 138.

[184] Unknown.

[185] This must be Major General Artemas Ward (1727–1800) of Shrewsbury, Massachusetts, one of the four original major generals in the Continental Army under General George Washington. He was second in command to General Washington. He resigned his commission in March 1777 due to his health. He later served in the United States House of Representatives from 1791 until 1795.

[186] Major William Lyman (1755–1811) was born in Northampton, Massachusetts and was a 1776 graduate of Yale College. He served with the rank of major as an aide to Major General William Shepard during Shays' Rebellion. William Lyman represented Massachusetts in the United States House of Representatives from 1793 until 1797.

[187] Captain Thomas Ingersoll (1750–1812), born in Westfield, Massachusetts in 1749, was a lieutenant in Col. Miles Powell's Regiment in 1779, and in 1781 commanded a company in Col. Ashley's Regiment of the Berkshire County, Massachusetts militia. After participating in suppressing the rebellion in 1786–7, Ingersoll, a wealthy merchant, lost his fortune due to the economic depression, and removed to Canada where he died at the age of 63.

[188] Meaning; subject to no further debate or dispute.

[189] Possibly James Lovell (1737-1814) or his son James Lovell, Jr. (1758–1850)

[190] In a letter Amos sent to Mr. Loammi Baldwin on May 19, 1788, Amos wrote:

> *"Clerk's Office, Cambridge, May 19, 1788*
>
> *Sir,*
>
> *I understand that you will soon want some body to teach a School in Wolburn. Should this be the case, and no better opportunity offers, I beg leave to solicit your consideration. I have before taught a School about a year and a half.*
>
> *As I am at present, (or soon shall be) out of business, I would teach a school as cheap, perhaps, as any body; and should endeavor to render myself worthy of that trust."*

What compelled Amos to write this letter in the spring of 1788 just after rejoining Charles Cushing in the clerk's office after his exploits during Shays' Rebellion is not known. He does not mention any conflict which would have caused him his loss of employment. Obviously, things worked out in the clerk's office and he went on and continued "driving the quill" for the next three years. It is an interesting letter considering his destiny.

[191] This was Reverend Ephraim Judson (1736–1813), a native of Woodbury, Connecticut, who graduated from Yale College in 1763. Reverend Judson began preaching in Norwich, Connecticut and became the ninth minister of the church in Taunton in 1780. He was dismissed in 1790 by a church council and removed to Sheffield, Massachusetts where he died in February, 1813.

[192] Amos' great–grandfather was the aforementioned Reverend Anthony Stoddard (1678–1760) of Woodbury, Connecticut.

[193] Seth Padelford, Esq. (1751–1810) was born in Taunton, Massachusetts, and graduated from Yale College in 1770. He received an honorary law degree from Brown University in 1778. He was a lawyer and Judge of Probate in Taunton, Massachusetts.

[194] Newly–elected President George Washington appointed Benjamin Lincoln the first collector for the Port of Boston in February 1789. Lincoln bought a mansion on State Street which served as the first customs house and his home. This location was not far from the old merchant shop of Anthony Stoddard (1606-1687).

[195] James Sullivan, (1744–1808), born in Berwick, Maine, was a lawyer, judge and politician in Massachusetts. He served as the state's attorney general for 27 years and as governor of the state from 1807 until his death in 1808.

[196] Untraceable.

[197] Meaning; self–indulgent

[198] Nicholas Stoddard was buried in Lewisham, Kent, England on December 21, 1765. Major Stoddard here refers to a "Son" of Nicholas Stoddard as being a "natural son" but not a legitimate son and heir who did not "long survive his reputed father." He also stated Nicholas Stoddard died a bachelor. It can therefore be inferred that this son was born outside of wedlock and therefore not entitled to inherit his estate. A potentially critical piece of information in the form of a single word was lost due to the missing paper on the page. The word [illegitimate] is therefore inserted based on the clues provided.

[199] This refers to John Stoddard (1730–1795) who was born in Woodbury, Connecticut and resided in Waterbury, Connecticut. He was the older brother of Major Stoddard's father Anthony Stoddard, and the eldest son of Eliakim Stoddard, Major Stoddard's grandfather. The editor of this volume descends from this John Stoddard.

[200] Untraceable.

[201] Meaning; to formally make or acknowledge a transfer of something.

[202] A Scottish expression: "Possession is eleven points in the law, and they say there are but twelve."

[203] This is a mistake of memory on the part of Major Stoddard. Since over 20 years had passed since Major Stoddard was in England, the name "Bowman" is incorrectly stated. It is Bowerman, or Bowreman, of Brooke Parish, from Isle of Wight, to whom he is referring.

There is no record of a Mary Stoddard being married to a Bowerman, or Bowreman of the Isle of Wight. The only Mary Stoddard that has been found was the daughter of Sir Nicholas Stoddard, who died in 1649 and is buried with other family members in Lewisham, Kent, England. There is no record that she was ever married.

The estate of Nicholas Stoddard, after long litigation in the Court of Chancery, was adjudged to the heir of a female line, William Bowreman of Brook, or Newport, on the Isle of Wight. William Bowreman then sold or transferred the estate to Robert Dyneley in 1792. William Bowreman, of the Isle of Wight, died in 1793.

[204] A system of inheritance in which a deceased person's land is divided equally among all male heirs.

[205] Robert Dyneley (1732–1805), a lawyer, of Bloomsbury Square, London, England, and Mottingham, Kent, England, was born in Castley, North Yorkshire, England and died in Eltham, Kent, England. Dyneley purchased the former estate of Nicholas Stoddard from William Bowreman of the Isle of Wight in 1792.

A Thomas Graham, Esq, represented a William Bowreman in a case involving property in Lewisham, Kent, in a case at Nisi Prius decided by Lord Keynon in 1798. This is possibly the Graham referred to in the letter received by Major Stoddard in 1791.

206 John Stoddard lived in Waterbury, Connecticut

207 Honorable William Cushing (1732–1810) was Associate Judge of the Supreme Court of the United States at the time, nominated by President George Washington on September 24, 1789 and confirmed by the Senate two days later. He administered the Oath of Office at George Washington's second inauguration on March 4, 1793.

208 It has been established that Major Stoddard is mistaken about the year. He arrived in December 1790 and spent eight months during 1791 in London, England. See the introduction for more information on this time-line.

209 Deal is a town in Kent, England which lies on the English Channel, eight miles northeast of Dover. In 58 BC, Julius Caesar became governor and military commander of the Roman province of Gaul, consisting mostly of modern France and Belgium today. The coast near Deal is considered the possible landing site of Julius Caesar's two arrivals in Britain with his legions after crossing the English Channel in 55 and 54 BC.

210 Meaning; to move fast in a straight line as if driven by the wind.

211 Meaning; a ship in a storm that has taken down all of her sails; a ship with or under bare poles.

212 Isle of Wight is an island in the English Channel, about four miles from the shore of the County of Hampshire, England.

213 Meaning; a person who cultivates the land; a farmer.

214 Thomas Russell (1749–1796), of Boston, Massachusetts, was a wealthy lawyer and merchant. He was apparently personally involved in financial matters with the bank, Lane, Son & Fraser of London. He died at the age of 47 in 1796, three years after Lane, Son & Fraser failed in 1793.

215 Lane, Son and Fraser, the principals being John Lane and Thomas Fraser, was a London–based merchant bank that was involved in pre–Revolutionary Anglo–American trade. The bank fell into bankruptcy in1793. There seem to have been some scandalous real estate transactions and deals involving this bank and a number of important men from Massachusetts, including Thomas Boylston and Thomas Russell. One such real estate deal was referred to as the Boylston Tract. Thomas Boylston had been a partner in Lane, Son and Frazer since 1784 and had moved to London. As a result of the bank's default, he was arrested in February 1793 and sentenced to debtor prison, where he died in 1798.

216 Mr. Stainsbury is unidentified and untraceable.

217 Sir John Mitford (1748–1830), the second son of John Mitford of Southampton, England, was admitted to the bar in 1777. He became a member of Parliament in 1788. After representing Amos Stoddard in 1791, he was appointed Solicitor–General in 1793. He was chosen Speaker of the House of Commons between1801–1802 and appointed Lord Chancellor of Ireland in 1802 when he was given peerage as 1st Baron Redesdale, of Redesdale in the County of Northumberland. He died at the age of 81 in 1830.

218 This is the text of a handwritten note from Henry Stoddard (1788–1869) of Dayton, Ohio. The note is attached in the middle of numbered page 53 of the autobiography manuscript. The preceding page was numbered "52" while the following page is numbered "55."

Henry Stoddard is credited with finding and preserving the papers of Amos Stoddard, including the autobiography manuscript. According to William Cothren (1819–1898), a close friend of Henry Stoddard, from his book, "*History of Ancient Woodbury, Vol. II,*" the papers of Major Stoddard were found after years of searching, in his military trunk "at the house of a nephew in Mahoning County, Ohio." This nephew was Daniel Stoddard (1808–1850), the son of Eliakim Stoddard (1784–1815) who was the brother of Major Amos Stoddard. Eliakim Stoddard was living in Boardman, Mahoning County, Ohio at the time of Major Stoddard's death at Fort Meigs, Ohio on May 11, 1813. Henry Stoddard likely discovered the papers at the time of Daniel Stoddard's death at his home in Boardman, Mahoning County, Ohio in 1850.

219 It appears that a Mr. Duncan is working for Amos Stoddard in the role of a "forensic" document examiner of the heraldry records. He apparently uncovered the fraudulent marriage record document between a "Colonel Bowerman" and "Mary Stoddard." His identity is untraceable.

[220] Bloomsbury Square Gardens is located near Holborn Underground Station, Russell Square, and the British Museum in central London.

[221] A court that tries questions of fact before one judge; The original court; The "Court of original jurisdiction" is often substituted for the term "nisi prius."

[222] Lloyd Kenyon (1732–1802) was a British politician and barrister. He served as a member of Parliament between 1780 and 1788. In 1784, he became Master of the Rolls, and in 1788, he was appointed Lord Chief Justice, a position he held until his death in1802. He received a peerage in 1788 and became 1st Baron Kenyon.

[223] Warren Hastings (1732–1818) was an English statesman. In 1774, he was appointed Governor–General of Bengal and the first governor of India. He resigned 10 years later, but in 1786, he was accused of crimes and misdemeanors during his time as governor of India by his primary accuser in the House of Commons, Edmund Burke. After a lengthy trial that lasted seven years, the House of Lords acquitted Hastings in April 1795.

[224] The Quebec Bill, or the Constitutional Act of 1791, divided the province of Quebec, Canada into two separate colonies: One with representation for English–speaking settlers, and one with representation for French–speaking settlers. Since French–speaking settlers greatly outnumbered the English–speaking, this was a compromise to accommodate the cultural diversity of the inhabitants in establishing representative government in the new province of Quebec. The bill was introduced in the House of Commons by William Pitt in March of 1791, secured approval in May, and came into effect in Canada on December 26, 1791.

[225] Edmund Burke (1729–1797) was a member of Parliament, author, and perhaps the best political thinker and orator of his time. He is best remembered for his support for the grievances of American colonies, catholic emancipation, his prosecution of Warren Hastings in the House of Commons, and his objections towards the French Revolution. Adam Smith, the famed economist, said that Burke was "the only man I ever knew who thinks on economic subjects exactly as I do, without any previous communications having passed between us." Edmund Burke is known as the father of modern British conservationism.

[226] Charles James Fox (1749–1806) was a member of Parliament who enjoyed a political career spanning from the age of nineteen in 1768 until he died at age 57 in 1797. He was known as a forceful and eloquent speaker of the Whig party. He and Edmund Burke, while polar opposites in their personal lives and in their personal conduct, shared many of the same political values and opinions. They clearly divided over the issue of the French Revolution, which led to their heated debates over the issue of a divided Quebec in 1791.

[227] Rufus King (1755–1827) was born in Scarborough, Maine, then a part of Massachusetts, and was a graduate of Harvard College in 1777. He was well known and respected for his parliamentary eloquence. King was a member of the constitutional convention in Philadelphia in 1787–8, and the Massachusetts convention that ratified the Federal Constitution in February 1788. King served as United States Senator from New York twice: From 1789 to1796 and from 1813 until 1825. He was appointed to the post of United States Minister to Great Britain in 1825 by President John Quincy Adams and served until 1826.

[228] Fisher Ames (1758–1808), from Dedham, Massachusetts, was a graduate of Harvard College. He served as a member of the Massachusetts convention that ratified the Federal Constitution, and was a member of the United States House of Representatives from 1789–1797.

[229] Thomas Erskine (1750–1823), a successful lawyer, politician, and orator, was famous for defending bookseller John Stockdale for publishing a pamphlet defending Warren Hastings in 1789 (he was acquitted), and for defending Thomas Paine, who was charged with seditious libel for his publishing the second part of his book, "*Rights of Man*" in 1792 (Paine was found guilty in absentia). Erskine's political future was seriously damaged for defending Paine. However, he was made a peer and appointed Lord Chancellor in 1806, becoming 1st Baron Erskine.

[230] Vauxhall Gardens and Ranelagh Gardens were the most famous of the London pleasure gardens around the time Amos Stoddard visited London.

[231] Guillotine

[232] Dr. Edward Tatham, D.D. (1749–1834) in the spring of 1791 published *"Letters to the Right Hon. Edmund Burke on Politics"* in support of Burke's book *"Reflections on the Revolution in France"* published in November 1790. Thomas Paine then published *"The Rights of Man"* in 1791 in response to Burke's *"Reflections."* The publication of *"Letters to Burke,"* consisting of two letters written in March and April 1791, is likely the pamphlet to which Major Stoddard refers. Thomas Paine supported the French Revolution while Edmund Burke and Dr. Tatham were against it. Amos Stoddard initially supported the French Revolution but obviously later had a change of heart about it as well as Paine's views on it.

[233] The name of the composition written by Amos Stoddard in London in 1791 is titled, *"The Political Crisis: Or, a Dissertation on the Rights of Man,"* which was published by and printed for J.S. Jordan, No. 166, Fleet–Street, London. Copies are held in various collections, and there are even new reprints available today. The author of that composition has remained unidentified—until now. See the introduction for more information and images.

[234] Trafalgar Square in central London

[235] Meaning; in Christian theology, a state of eternal punishment and damnation.

Citations and References for Introduction

[1] Francis B. Heitman, *Historical Register of the United States Army, from its organization September 29, 1789 to September 29, 1889* (Washington The National Tribune, 1890), p. 619

[2] National Archives, *Founders Online*, From John Adams to United States Senate, 28 May 1798, http://founders.archives.gov/documents/Adams/99-02-02-2513

[3] Albert Matthews, Ed., *Publications of the Colonial Society of Massachusetts, Vol. XII* (Boston, 1911), p. 282–83, Footnote 2

[4] Sharlene Ida Stoddard, *Family of Wells and Eunice Stoddard* (Northwood, IA April 1995), p. 692

[5] Clifford K. Shipton, *Sibley's Harvard Graduates, Vol. IV, 1690–1700, Biographical Sketches of Those Who Attended Harvard College in the Classes of 1690–1700* (Cambridge, Harvard University Press, 1933), p. 381–87

[6] William Cothren, *History of Ancient Woodbury, Connecticut, from the First Indian Deed in 1659 to 1854, Volume I* (Waterbury, Bronson Brothers, 1854), p. 456–60

[7] Ibid

[8] *Boardman Cemetery*, Boardman, Mahoning County, Ohio; December 25, 1815; http://genealogytrails.com/ohio/mahoning/cem_boardman.html

[9] Sharlene Ida Stoddard, *Family of Wells and Eunice Stoddard* (Northwood, IA April 1995), p. 662

[10] Herman M. Moos, Ed., *The American Law Record, 1873–1874, Vol. II, United States Circuit Court for the Southern District of Ohio*, Amasa Bunnell and Others vs Henry Stoddard and Asa P. Stoddard (Cincinnati, 1874), p. 145–162

[11] *The Federal Cases, Comprising Cases Argued and Determined in the Circuit and District Courts of the United States, Book 4* (St. Paul, 1894), p. 671

[12] H.S. Knapp, *History of the Maumee Valley* (Toledo, 1877), p. 676

[13] Wilfrid Hibbert, *Major Amos Stoddard, First Governor of Upper Louisiana and Hero of Fort Meigs*, The Historical Society of Northwestern Ohio, Bulletin No. 2, Volume 2 (April 1930), p. 10

[14] Larry L. Nelson, *Men of Patriotism, Courage & Enterprise: Fort Meigs and the War of 1812* (Heritage Books, 2003), p. 102–111

[15] Harlow Lindley, Ed., *Fort Meigs and the War of 1812: Orderly Book of Cushing's Company and Personal Diary of Captain Daniel Cushing*, The Ohio Historical Society (Columbus, 1975), p.126

[16] William Cothren, *History of Ancient Woodbury, Connecticut, from the First Indian Deed in 1659 to 1854, Volume I* (Waterbury, Bronson Brothers, 1854), p. 714

[17] Franklin Prindle, *The Prindle Genealogy: Embracing the Descendants of William Pringle* (New York, 1906), p. 156

[18] Angie Rhodes, Missouri Historical Museum, Repository Summary, *Amos Stoddard Papers, 1796–1812* (April, 2001)

[19] *Mt. Vernon Register–News*, Mt Vernon, Illinois, Thursday, September 18, 1958, p. 16

[20] Frank Conover, *Centennial Portrait and Biographical Record of the City of Dayton* (A.W. Bowden & Co., 1897), p. 279–80

[21] Augustus Waldo Drury, *History of the City of Dayton and Montgomery County, Ohio, Volume 2* (Chicago, 1909), p.23

[22] Woodland Cemetery and Arboretum, Dayton, Montgomery County, Ohio; *Find A Grave Memorial# 41894210*, Grave marker

[23] L.P. Allen, *The Genealogy and History of the Shreve Family from 1641* (Greenfield, Il, 1901), p. 276

[24] Augustus Waldo Drury, *History of the City of Dayton and Montgomery County, Ohio, Volume 2* (Chicago, 1909), p.20–24

[25] *The Federal Cases, Comprising Cases Argued and Determined in the Circuit and District Courts of the United States, Book 4* (St. Paul, 1894), p. 668

[26] Missouri Historical Society, *Glimpses of the Past, Vol. II, May–September, No. 6–10* (St. Louis, 1935), Gen. Henry Dearborn to Capt. Stoddard, Nov. 7, 1803, p. 79

[27] Ibid, Charles Gratiot to Amos Stoddard; Amos Stoddard to Charles Gratiot, Sept. 30, 1804, p. 121–22

[28] William Cothren, *History of Ancient Woodbury, Connecticut, from the First Indian Deed in 1659 to 1872, Volume II* (Woodbury, William Cothren, 1872), p. 1554

[29] W. Fletcher Johnson, *Life of Wm. Tecumseh Sherman* (1891), p.23–7

[30] William Tecumseh Sherman, *Memoirs of General William Tecumseh Sherman, Vol. I* (New York, D. Appleton & Company, 1891), p. 88–9

[31] William Cothren, *History of Ancient Woodbury, Connecticut, from the First Indian Deed in 1659 to 1872, Volume II* (Woodbury, William Cothren, 1872), p. 1556–57

[32] Fred C. Fisk, *The Stoddard Manufacturing Company*, The Wheelmen, Number 31 (November 1987), p. 16–23

[33] William Cothren, *History of Ancient Woodbury, Connecticut, from the First Indian Deed in 1659 to 1854, Volume I* (Waterbury, Bronson Brothers, 1854), p. 459–60

[34] Stephen K. Williams, *Cases Argued and Decided in the Supreme Court of the United State, 5,6,7,8 Howard, Book 12, Mills v. Stoddard et al, 1850* (Rochester, 1901), p. 1106–115

[35] *The Federal Cases, Comprising Cases Argued and Determined in the Circuit and District Courts of the United States, Book 4, Case No. 2135* (St. Paul, 1894), Bunnell et al v. Stoddard et al, Circuit Court of the South District of Ohio, Oct. 24, 1866, p. 667–83

[36] William Cothren, *History of Ancient Woodbury, Connecticut, from the First Indian Deed in 1659 to 1854, Volume I* (Waterbury, Bronson Brothers, 1854), p. 136, 141

[37] *Publications of the Colonial Society of Massachusetts, Volume 12* (Boston, 1911), p. 282–83

[38] Franklin Bowditch Dexter, *Biographical Sketches of the Graduates of Yale College with Annals of the College History, October 1701–May 1745* (New York, 1885), p. 597

[39] William Cothren, *History of Ancient Woodbury, Connecticut, from the First Indian Deed in 1659 to 1854, Volume I* (Waterbury, Bronson Brothers, 1854), p. 398

[40] Sharlene Ida Stoddard, *Family of Wells and Eunice Stoddard* (Northwood, IA April 1995), p. 688

[41] Jeanne Stoddard, *The Stoddards of Rushton Spencer* (London, 1979), p. 5

[42] Ibid, p.24–29

[43] Sharlene Ida Stoddard, *Family of Wells and Eunice Stoddard* (Northwood, IA April 1995), p. 689

[44] Francis Russell Stoddard, Jr., *The Stoddard Family, Being an Account of Some of the Descendants of John Stoddar of Hingham, Massachusetts Colony* (New York, 1912), p. 13

[45] David Williams Patterson, *John Stoddard of Wethersfield, Conn. and his Descendants, 1642–1872* (Succasunna, NJ, 1873), p. 12

[46] Sharlene Ida Stoddard, *Family of Wells and Eunice Stoddard* (Northwood, IA April 1995), p. 689

[47] Ibid, p. 690

[48] Ibid

[49] John Langdon Sibley, M.A., *Biographical Sketches of Graduates of Harvard University, Volume I, 1642–1658* (Cambridge, 1873), P. 28–48

[50] John Ward Dean, Ed., *The New England Historical and Genealogical Register…for the Year 1884, Volume 38* (Boston, 1884), p. 194–97

[51] Sharlene Ida Stoddard, *Family of Wells and Eunice Stoddard* (Northwood, IA April 1995), p. 691

[52] Ibid

[53] Ibid, p. 692

[54] Ibid, p. 693–94

[55] Ibid, p.695

[56] Ibid, p.674

[57] Ibid, 674–75

[58] Ibid, p. 675

[59] Ibid

[60] Ibid

[61] Ibid, p. 675–76

[62] James Russell Trumbull, *The History of Northampton, Massachusetts from Its Settlement in 1654* (Northampton, 1902), p .54

[63] Ibid, p .52–66

[64] John Langdon Sibley, M.A., *Biographical Sketches of Graduates of Harvard University, Volume 2, 1659–1677, Class of 1662* (Cambridge, 1881), p. 111–22

[65] Ibid, p. 115

[66] Rev. Benjamin Colman, *A Sermon Preached at the Lecture in Boston Upon the Death of the Learned and Venerable Solomon Stoddard* (Boston, 1729), Appendix

[67] Williston Walker, *The American Church History Series, Volume 3* (New York, Charles Scribner's Sons, 1894), p. 179–182

[68] Ibid

[69] Sharlene Ida Stoddard, *Family of Wells and Eunice Stoddard* (Northwood, IA April 1995), p. 678

[70] Ibid, p. 680–81

[71] Litchfield Historical Society, *Database of Students of Litchfield Law School*, The Ledger, Aaron Burr, http://www.litchfieldhistoricalsociety.org/ledger/students/479

[72] James Abercrombie, D.D., *A Sermon, Occasioned by the Death of Major Gen. Alexander Hamilton* (Philadelphia, 1804), Title Page

[73] David Robertson, *Trial of Aaron Burr for Treason, Vol. II* (New York, James Cockcroft & Company, 1875), p.550

[74] Sharlene Ida Stoddard, *Family of Wells and Eunice Stoddard* (Northwood, IA April 1995), p. 682

[75] Ibid, p. 667–68

[76] William Cothren, *History of Ancient Woodbury, Connecticut, from the First Indian Deed in 1659 to 1854, Volume I* (Waterbury, Bronson Brothers, 1854), p. 135–138

[77] Sharlene Ida Stoddard, *Family of Wells and Eunice Stoddard* (Northwood, IA April 1995), p. 667–674

[78] Thomas Townsend Sherman, *Sherman Genealogy, Including Families of Essex, Suffolk and Norfolk, England* (New York, Tobias Wright, 1920), p.134

[79] Sharlene Ida Stoddard, *Family of Wells and Eunice Stoddard* (Northwood, IA April 1995), p. 672

[80] William Cothren, *History of Ancient Woodbury, Connecticut, from the First Indian Deed in 1659 to 1879, Genealogical Statistics of the Same, Volume III* (Woodbury, Conn., William Cothren, 1879), p. 238

[81] Ibid, p. 229

[82] Ibid, p. 308

[83] Ibid, p. 242

[84] Gary Boughton, Photo of Headstone, Woodbury, CT. South Cemetery, *Find A Grave Memorial #45316631* (2009)

[85] Sharlene Ida Stoddard, *Family of Wells and Eunice Stoddard* (Northwood, IA April 1995), p. 670

[86] Corporal Anthony Stoddard, CT 16397; Private Eli Stoddard, CT 16445, *Valley Forge Muster Roll*, http://valleyforgemusterroll.org/

[87] Edward Deacon, *Some of the Ancestors of Rodman Stoddard of Woodbury, Conn. and Detroit, Mich.* (Bridgeport, Connecticut, 1893), p. 43–4

[88] Ensign John Strong, CT16387, *Valley Forge Muster Roll*, http://valleyforgemusterroll.org/

[89] William Cothren, *History of Ancient Woodbury, Connecticut, from the First Indian Deed in 1659 to 1854, Volume I* (Waterbury, Bronson Brothers, 1854), p. 205

[90] Joseph Plumb Martin, CT16333, *Valley Forge Muster Roll*, http://valleyforgemusterroll.org/

[91] Joseph Plumb Martin, *A Narrative of some of the Adventures, Dangers and Sufferings of a Revolutionary Soldier* (Hallowell, Maine 1830), p. 66–7

[92] Ira Smith, CT16096, *Valley Forge Muster Roll*, http://valleyforgemusterroll.org/

[93] Joseph Perkins Beach, *History of Cheshire, Connecticut, from 1694 to 1840* (Cheshire, Conn. 1912), p. 231

[94] William Cothren, *History of Ancient Woodbury, Connecticut, from the First Indian Deed in 1659 to 1879, Genealogical Statistics of the Same, Volume III* (Woodbury, Conn., William Cothren, 1879), p. 238

[95] William Cothren, *History of Ancient Woodbury, Connecticut, from the First Indian Deed in 1659 to 1854 Volume I* (Waterbury, Bronson Brothers, 1854), p. 785

[96] Ibid, p. 137–141

[97] William Cothren, *History of Ancient Woodbury, Connecticut, from the First Indian Deed in 1659 to 1872, Volume II* (Woodbury, William Cothren, 1872), p. 1032–33

[98] Ibid, p. 971–72

[99] Sharlene Ida Stoddard, *Family of Wells and Eunice Stoddard* (Northwood, IA April 1995), p. 661

[100] Ibid, p. 665

[101] Ibid, p. 663–666

[102] Woodbury Land Deed Record; *Eliakim Stoddard, Deed Recorded March 22, 1736*, Volume 5, Page 79

[103] Sharlene Ida Stoddard, *Family of Wells and Eunice Stoddard* (Northwood, IA April 1995), p. 661, 665

[104] Eliakim Stoddard, *Record of Probate, Dated March 31, 1752*, Woodbury, Connecticut

[105] Woodbury Land Deed Record, *Asa Stoddard*, Volume 30, Page 7

[106] Ibid, *William Mosely*, Volume 31, Page 55

[107] William Cothren, *History of Ancient Woodbury, Connecticut, from the First Indian Deed in 1659 to 1854 Volume I* (Waterbury, Bronson Brothers, 1854), p. 334

[108] Woodbury Land Deed Record, *Abijah Hatch*, Volume 33, Page 175; Volume 34, Page 222

[109] Ibid, *Aaron Hitchcock, Nathan Preston*, Volume 36, Page 22

[110] William Cothren, *History of Ancient Woodbury, Connecticut, from the First Indian Deed in 1659 to 1872, Volume II* (Woodbury, William Cothren, 1872), p. 1016

[111] William Cothren, *History of Ancient Woodbury, Connecticut, from the First Indian Deed in 1659 to 1854 Volume I* (Waterbury, Bronson Brothers, 1854), p. 335

[112] American Antiquarian Society, Worcester, MA, Ashley Cataldo, Assistant Curator, *Elisha Hatch Day Book, 1814–15*

[113] William Cothren, *History of Ancient Woodbury, Connecticut, from the First Indian Deed in 1659 to 1872, Volume II* (Woodbury, William Cothren, 1872), p. 1002–03

[114] William Cothren, *History of Ancient Woodbury, Connecticut, from the First Indian Deed in 1659 to 1879, Genealogical Statistics of the Same, Volume III* (Woodbury, William Cothren, 1879), p. 241

[115] William Cothren, *History of Ancient Woodbury, Connecticut, from the First Indian Deed in 1659 to 1854 Volume I* (Waterbury, Bronson Brothers, 1854), p. 591

[116] Ibid, p. 333–34

[117] Woodbury Land Deed Record, *Lucius Foote*, Volume 45, Page 220

[118] William Cothren, *History of Ancient Woodbury, Connecticut, from the First Indian Deed in 1659 to 1872, Volume II* (Woodbury, William Cothren, 1872), p. 1392–94

[119] Ibid, p. 1002–03

[120] Woodbury Land Deed Record, *Elijah Smith and George Lewis*, Volume 42, Page 72; Volume 44, Page 291

[121] William Cothren, *History of Ancient Woodbury, Connecticut, from the First Indian Deed in 1659 to 1872, Volume II* (Woodbury, William Cothren, 1872), p. 1003

[122] Ibid, p. 1010

[123] Ibid, p.1019

[124] Ibid, p.1020

[125] Woodbury Land Deed Record, *Frederick Kelly*, Volume 48, Page 133

[126] William Cothren, *History of Ancient Woodbury, Connecticut, from the First Indian Deed in 1659 to 1879, Genealogical Statistics of the Same, Volume III* (Woodbury, William Cothren, 1879), p. 241

[127] Ibid, p. 246

[128] William Cothren, *History of Ancient Woodbury, Connecticut, from the First Indian Deed in 1659 to 1872, Volume II* (Woodbury, William Cothren, 1872), p. 1003

[129] Library of Congress, *Maps, Clark's Map of Litchfield County, Connecticut; 1859*; https://www.loc.gov/item/2001620489/

[130] Woodbury Land Deed Record, *Vincent Judson*, Volume 44, Page 194

[131] Ibid, *Levi Curtis*, Volume 53, Page 502

[132] Sharlene Ida Stoddard, *Family of Wells and Eunice Stoddard* (Northwood, IA April 1995), p. 668

[133] Sophia Smith–Martin, *Mack Genealogy: The Descendants of John Mack of Lyme, Connecticut* (Hartford, Conn.,1903), p. 27

[134] Editorial Staff, *Genealogical and Family History of the State of Connecticut, Volume II* (New York, 1911), p. 1054

[135] Litchfield Historical Society, *Database of Students of Litchfield Law School*, The Ledger, Richard Smith, http://www.litchfieldhistoricalsociety.org/ledger/students/2381

[136] Ibid, Nathan Smith, http://www.litchfieldhistoricalsociety.org/ledger/students/2380

[137] Ibid, Nathaniel Smith, http://www.litchfieldhistoricalsociety.org/ledger/students/2383

[138] William W. Williams, *The National Magazine; A Monthly Journal of American History, Volume 3* (Cleveland, 1885), p. 442

[139] Litchfield Historical Society, *Database of Students of Litchfield Law School*, The Ledger, Nathaniel Smith, http://www.litchfieldhistoricalsociety.org/ledger/students/2383

[140] Sharlene Ida Stoddard, *Family of Wells and Eunice Stoddard* (Northwood, IA April 1995), p. 662

[141] Ibid

[142] William Cothren, *History of Ancient Woodbury, Connecticut, from the First Indian Deed in 1659 to 1879, Genealogical Statistics of the Same, Volume III* (Woodbury, Conn., William Cothren, 1879), p. 243

[143] William Thomas Davis, *Bench and Bar of the Commonwealth of Massachusetts, Volume 2* (Boston, 1895), p. 150

[144] John Anthon, *American Precedents of Declarations…*,(New York, 1810), Appendix, p. 570

[145] Joseph Gardner Swift, *Memoirs of Gen. Joseph Gardner Swift, 1800–1865* (Worcester, 1890), p. 19

[146] Almon D. Hodges, Jr., *Genealogical Record of the Hodges Family of New England* (Boston, 1896), p. 250

[147] Emma Huntington Nason, *Old Hallowell on the Kennebec* (Augusta, Maine, 1909), p.36, 137

[148] *Lincoln County Probate Records 1760–1800* (June 1796), p.305

[149] Peleg W. Chandler, Ed., *The Law Reporter, Volume 5, Obituary Notices* (Boston, 1843), p. 528

[150] *Act and Laws of the Commonwealth of Massachusetts, Vol. 9* (Boston, 1896), p. 266

[151] Ibid, p. 608

[152] Emma Huntington Nason, *Old Hallowell on the Kennebec* (Augusta, Maine, 1909), p.61–2

[153] *Act and Laws of the Commonwealth of Massachusetts, Vol. 9* (Boston, 1896), p. 266, 608, 738

[154] Amos Stoddard, *A Masonic Address, Delivered before the Worshipful Master, Officers and Brethren, of the Kennebeck Lodge, in the New Meeting–house, Hallowell, Massachusetts; June 24th, anno lucis 5797* (Hallowell, Printed by Brother Howard S. Robinson, 1797)

[155] Brother Amos Stoddard, Captain in the Artillery of the United States, *An Oration, Delivered in the Meeting House of the First Parish in Portland, Monday, June 24th, 5799: At the Request, and in the Presence of the Portland Lodge of Free and Accepted Masons, in Celebration of the Anniversary Festival of St. John the Baptist* (Portland, Printed by Baker & George, 1799)

[156] *A Catalogue of Books in the Library of the American Antiquarian Society* (Worcester, 1837), p. 35

[157] Amos Stoddard, *A Masonic Address, Delivered in St. John's Church, Portsmouth, June 24, 5802: at the Request, and in the Presence of the Most Worshipful, The Grand Lodge of New Hampshire, in Celebration of the Anniversary Festival of St. John, the Baptist* (Portsmouth, NH, 1802)

[158] Amos Stoddard, *An oration, delivered before the citizens of Portland, and the Supreme Judicial Court of the Commonwealth of Massachusetts, on the fourth day of July, 1799: being the anniversary of American independence* (Portland, Printed and Sold by E.A. Jenks, 1799)

[159] National Archives, *Founders Online*, From John Adams to United States Senate, 28 May 1798, http://founders.archives.gov/documents/Adams/99-02-02-2513

[160] Thomas H.S. Hamersly, *Complete Army Register of the United States for 100 Years (1779 to 1879)*, (Washington, 1881), p. 50

[161] Arthur Wade, *Artillerists and Engineers, The Beginnings of American Seacoast Fortifications, 1794–1815* (Coast Defense Study Group, 2011), p.50

[162] National Archives, *Founders Online*, To Alexander Hamilton from Amos Stoddard, 9 July 1799, http://founders.archives.gov/documents/Hamilton/02-01-02-0661

[163] Andro Linklater, *An Artist in Treason, The Extraordinary Double Life of General James Wilkinson* (New York, Walker Publishing Company, 2009), p. 113–16

[164] Ibid, p. 116–18

[165] Ibid, p.134–39

[166] Ibid, p.161

[167] Ibid, p. 185–87

[168] Ibid, p. 191–96

[169] Joseph Gardner Swift, *Memoirs of Gen. Joseph Gardner Swift, 1800–1865* (Worcester, 1890), p. 49

[170] Andro Linklater, *An Artist in Treason, The Extraordinary Double Life of General James Wilkinson* (New York, Walker Publishing Company, 2009), p. 191–96

[171] Ibid, All

[172] Marion Mills Miller, *Great Debates in American History, Vol. 9* (New York, Current Literature Publishing Company, 1913), p. 182–201

[173] *Papers of the War Department, 1784–1800*, Letter from Amos Stoddard to Samuel Hodgdon, Esq., March 10, 1799, http://wardepartmentpapers.org/document.php?id=30736

[174] National Archives, *Founders Online*, To Alexander Hamilton from Amos Stoddard, 3 March 1799, http://founders.archives.gov/documents/Hamilton/02-01-02-0084

[175] *Papers of the War Department, 1784–1800*, Letter from Amos Stoddard to Samuel Hodgdon, Esq., March 4, 1799, 1784–1800, http://wardepartmentpapers.org/document.php?id=30679

[176] Ibid, Letter from Amos Stoddard to Samuel Hodgdon, Esq., April 15, 1799, http://wardepartmentpapers.org/document.php?id=31316

[177] Ibid, Letter from Amos Stoddard to Samuel Hodgdon, Esq., July 18, 1799, http://wardepartmentpapers.org/document.php?id=33695

[178] Logan Esarey, *Governors Messages and Letters, Messages and Letters of William Henry Harrison, Vol. II, 1812–1816* (Indianapolis, 1922), Letter from Secretary of War to Harrison, September 10, 1812, p.135–36

[179] Arthur Wade, *Artillerists and Engineers, The Beginnings of American Seacoast Fortifications, 1794–1815* (Coast Defense Study Group, 2011), p.248

[180] National Archives, *Founders Online*, To Alexander Hamilton from Amos Stoddard, 6 November, 1799, http://founders.archives.gov/documents/Hamilton/02-01-02-1585

[181] William Simmons to Secretary of War, Accountants Office Letterbook, Certificate of Payment to Capt. Amos Stoddard for Travel and Related Expenses, January 6, 1800, *Papers of the War Department, 1784–1800*, http://wardepartmentpapers.org/document.php?id=37407

[182] Arthur Wade, *Artillerists and Engineers, The Beginnings of American Seacoast Fortifications, 1794–1815* (Coast Defense Study Group, 2011), p.247

[183] University of New Hampshire, Douglas and Helena Milne Special Collections & Archives Department, *United States Oracle and Portsmouth Advertiser*, May 8, 1802

[184] Francis B. Heitman, *Historical Register of the United States Army, from its organization September 29, 1789 to September 29, 1889* (Washington, The National Tribune, 1890), p. 23

[185] Ibid

[186] War Department Archives, *Secretary of War Letters Received, Letter Book II, Jan. 3, 1803 – Jan. 7, 1806*, Letter #5 Received January 7, 1803

[187] William L. Clements Library, The University of Michigan, *Henry Burbeck Papers*, Letter from Amos Stoddard to Henry Burbeck, Pittsburgh, January 19, 1803, Photocopy

[188] Gerhard Peters and John T. Woolley, *The American Presidency Project*, Thomas Jefferson, Confidential Message to Congress Regarding the Lewis and Clark Expedition, January 18, 1803, http://www.presidency.ucsb.edu/ws/?pid=65820

[189] Reuben Gold Thwaites, *Journals of the Lewis & Clark Expedition, 1804–1806, Volume I* (New York, Dodd, Mead & Company, 1904), p. xxvi

[190] Hunter Miller, *Treaties and Other International Acts of the United States of America, Vol. II, Documents 1–40, 1776–1818* (Washington : Government Printing Office, 1931), p. 498

[191] Reuben Gold Thwaites, *Journals of the Lewis & Clark Expedition, 1804–1806, Volume I* (New York, Dodd, Mead & Company, 1904), p. xxxi

[192] Clarence Edwin Carter, *Territorial Papers of the United States, Vol. VII, The Territory of Indiana, 1800–1810* (Washington, 1948), The Secretary of War to Thomas H. Cushing, March 10,1803, p. 95–6

[193] Ibid, The Secretary of War to Thomas H. Cushing, 9th & 10th March, 1803 (Washington, 1948), p. 94–6

[194] War Department Archives, *Secretary of War Letters Received, Letter Book II, Jan. 3, 1803 – Jan. 7, 1806*, Letter #22, 26, 28 & 30; Received March 10, 22, 24, & 30, 1803

[195] Missouri Historical Museum, *Daniel Bissell Papers*, Box 1, Folder 1, 1770–1805, War Department to Daniel Bissell, Russell Bissel, Amos Stoddard, War Department, July 2, 1803, Photocopy

[196] National Archives, *Founders Online*, Purchase of Louisiana, July 5, 1803, http://founders.archives.gov/documents/Hamilton/01-26-02-0001-0101

[197] Stephen E. Ambrose, *Undaunted Courage: Meriwether Lewis Thomas Jefferson and the Opening of the American West* (New York, Simon and Schuster, 1996), p. 13

[198] *The Thomas Jefferson Papers at the Library of Congress*, Thomas Jefferson to Meriwether Lewis, June 20, 1803, https://www.loc.gov/item/mtjbib012509/

[199] Clarence Edwin Carter, *Territorial Papers of the United States, Vol. VII, The Territory of Indiana, 1800–1810* (Washington, 1948), The Secretary of War to Amos Stoddard, January 19,1803, p. 85–6

[200] Reuben Gold Thwaites, *Journals of the Lewis & Clark Expedition, 1804–1806, Volume I* (New York, Dodd, Mead & Company, 1904), p. xxix

[201] Ibid, p. xxx

[202] *The Thomas Jefferson Papers at the Library of Congress*, Meriwether Lewis to Thomas Jefferson, July 26, 1803, https://www.loc.gov/item/mtjbib012636/

[203] Clarence Edwin Carter, *Territorial Papers of the United States, Vol. XIII, The Territory of Louisiana–Missouri, 1803–1806*, (Washington, 1948), The Secretary of War to Russel Bissell and Amos Stoddard, July 19 & 27, 1803, p. 3–5

[204] Elin Woodger and Brandon Toropov, *Encyclopedia of the Lewis & Clark Expedition* (New York, 2004), p. 193

[205] Clarence Edwin Carter, *Territorial Papers of the United States, Vol. XIII, The Territory of Louisiana–Missouri, 1803–1806* (Washington, 1948), The Secretary of War to Amos Stoddard, July 19, 1803, p. 3–4

[206] Ibid, The Secretary of War to Russell Bissell and Amos Stoddard, July 27, 1803, p. 4–5

[207] Clarence Edwin Carter, *Territorial Papers of the United States, Vol. VII, The Territory of Indiana, 1800–1810* (Washington, 1948), Indenture between the Department of War and John Edgar, September 4, 1803, p. 154–5

[208] Missouri Historical Museum, *Amos Stoddard Papers*, DS Meriwether Lewis, Receipt for Public Powder, December 1, 1803, Photocopy

[209] James B. Garry, *Weapons of the Lewis & Clark Expedition* (Norman, Oklahoma, Arthur H. Clark Company, 2012), p. 168

[210] Missouri Historical Museum, *Amos Stoddard Papers*, ALS from H. Dearborn to Capt. Amos Stoddard, War Department, November 7, 1803, Photocopy

[211] Ibid, AS from William C.C. Claiborne to Amos Stoddard, New Orleans, January 24, 1804, Photocopy

[212] Richard W. Stewart, Ed., *American Military History: The United States Army and the Forging of a Nation, 1775–1917* (Washington D.C, 2005), p. 124

[213] Major Amos Stoddard, *Sketches, Historical and Descriptive, of Louisiana* (Philadelphia, 1812), p. 71

[214] Ibid, p. 102

[215] Ibid

[216] Robert Julius Rombauer, *The Union Cause in St. Louis in 1861: An Historical Sketch* (St. Louis, 1909), p. 74

[217] Missouri Historical Society, *Glimpses of the Past, Vol. II, May–September, No. 6–10* (St. Louis, 1935), Capt. Stoddard's Address to the People of Upper Louisiana, St. Louis, March 10, 1804, p. 88

[218] Ibid, Stoddard to Gen. Dearborn, St. Louis, 10th March, 1804, p.92

[219] Ibid, Stoddard to Claiborne, St. Louis, 26 March 1804, p. 98–9

[220] Ibid, Stoddard to Dearborn, St. Louis, 3d June 1804, p. 104–6

[221] Clarence Edwin Carter, *Territorial Papers of the United States, Vol. XIII, The Territory of Louisiana–Missouri, 1803–1806* (Washington, 1948), The Secretary of War to Amos Stoddard, April 7,1804, p.17–8

[222] Missouri Historical Museum, *Amos Stoddard Papers*, Meriwether Lewis to Amos Stoddard, St. Louis, May 16, 1804

[223] Missouri Historical Society, *Glimpses of the Past, Vol. II, May–September, No. 6–10* (St. Louis, 1935), Stoddard to Claiborne, St. Louis, 19 May 1804, p. 102–3

[224] Ibid, Stoddard to Dearborn, St. Louis, June 3, 1804, p. 110–11

[225] Ibid, Stoddard to His Mother, Mrs. Samuel Benham, St. Louis, June 16, 1804, p. 112–13

[226] Clarence Edwin Carter, *Territorial Papers of the United States, Vol. XIII, The Territory of Louisiana–Missouri, 1803–1806,* (Washington, 1948), The Secretary of War to Thomas H. Cushing, March 1, 1804, p.16–7

[227] Thomas H.S. Hamersly, *Complete Army Register of the United States for 100 Years (1779 to 1879),* (Washington, 1881), p. 53

[228] Clarence Edwin Carter, *Territorial Papers of the United States, Vol. XIII, The Territory of Louisiana–Missouri, 1803–1806,* (Washington, 1948), The Secretary of War to Amos Stoddard, May 4, 1804, p.20–1

[229] Ibid, p.23

[230] Andro Linklater, *An Artist in Treason, The Extraordinary Double Life of General James Wilkinson* (New York, Walker Publishing Company, 2009), p. 191–92

[231] Harvard University, Houghton Library, Ebeling Vol. 3, *Kennebunk Intelligencer*, January 14, 1797, Digital Media Note: This published, political treaties has never been previously attributed to Amos Stoddard

[232] Massachusetts Historical Society, *Charles Edward French Autograph Collection*, Amos Stoddard to General Dearborn, Hallowell, 10 September 1797, Digital Media

Clarence Edwin Carter, *Territorial Papers of the United States, Vol. XIII, The Territory of Louisiana–Missouri, 1803–1806,* (Washington, 1948), The Secretary of War to Amos Stoddard, May 4, 1804, p.23–4, and Footnote 59

[234] Andro Linklater, *An Artist in Treason, The Extraordinary Double Life of General James Wilkinson* (New York, Walker Publishing Company, 2009), p. 196–99, 202–06, 208–9

[235] Walter Lowrie, Ed., *American State Papers, Documents, Executive and Legislative, of the Congress of the United States, Class X, Miscellaneous, Volume 1* (Washington, Gales and Seaton, 1834), p. 571–73

[236] Clarence Edwin Carter, *Territorial Papers of the United States, Vol. XIII, The Territory of Louisiana–Missouri, 1803–1806,* (Washington, 1948), The Secretary of War to Thomas H. Cushing, March 1, 1804, p.16–7

[237] Andro Linklater, *An Artist in Treason, The Extraordinary Double Life of General James Wilkinson* (New York, Walker Publishing Company, 2009), p. 198–201, 208–13, 216–17

[238] Missouri Historical Society, *Glimpses of the Past, Vol. II, May–September, No. 6–10* (St. Louis, 1935), Stoddard to Gov. William Henry Harrison, St. Louis, June 3rd, 1804, p. 107–9

[239] Logan Esarey, *Governors Messages and Letters, Messages and Letters of William Henry Harrison, Vol. II, 1812–1816* (Indianapolis, 1922), Letter from Jefferson to Harrison, Washington, March 31, 1804, p.94

[240] Ibid, Letter from Harrison to Jefferson, Vincennes, June 24, 1804, p.96

[241] Clarence Edwin Carter, *Territorial Papers of the United States, Vol. XIII, The Territory of Louisiana–Missouri, 1803–1806*, (Washington, 1948), The President to the Secretary of War, June 6, 1804, p.24–5, including Footnotes

[242] Ibid

[243] National Archives, *Founders Online*, From Thomas Jefferson to William Henry Harrison, 14 July 1804, http://founders.archives.gov/documents/Jefferson/99-01-02-0073

[244] Clarence Edwin Carter, *Territorial Papers of the United States, Vol. XIII, The Territory of Louisiana–Missouri, 1803–1806*, (Washington, 1948), The Secretary of War to Thomas H. Cushing, March 1, 1804, p. 16–7, Footnote 33

[245] Missouri Historical Museum, *Amos Stoddard Papers*, DS William Henry Harrison, Appointment of Amos Stoddard as Justice of the Peace, Vincennes, Indiana Territory, October 1, 1804

[246] Library of Congress, Amos Stoddard to Thomas Jefferson, October 29, 1804, https://www.loc.gov/item/mtjbib013937/

[247] Ibid, Amos Stoddard to Thomas Jefferson, March 24, 1805, https://www.loc.gov/item/mtjbib014515/

[248] Donald Jackson, Ed., *Letters of the Lewis and Clark Expedition, with Related Documents, 1783–1854* (Urbana, Il, University of Illinois Press, 1962), p. 231–234

[249] Missouri Historical Museum, *Amos Stoddard Papers*, LS or DS Meriwether Lewis to Captain Amos Stoddard, St. Louis, May 16, 1804

[250] Clarence Edwin Carter, *Territorial Papers of the United States, Vol. XIII, The Territory of Louisiana–Missouri, 1803–1806*, (Washington, 1948), James Bruff to James Wilkinson, September 29th, 1804 p.56–61

[251] Ibid, James Wilkinson to The Secretary of War, Nov. 2nd 1804, p. 56

[252] War Department Archives, *Secretary of War Letters Received, Letter Book II, Jan. 3, 1803 – Jan. 7, 1806*, Letter #140 Received February 20, 1804

[253] National Archives, *Founders Online*, From Thomas Jefferson to Henry Dearborn, 30 August 1804, http://founders.archives.gov/documents/Jefferson/99-01-02-0299

[254] Clarence Edwin Carter, *Territorial Papers of the United States, Vol. XIII, The Territory of Louisiana–Missouri, 1803–1806*, (Washington, 1948), Governor Wilkinson to Seth Hunt, St. Louis, Augt 22nd, 1805, p. 213–14

[255] Ibid, Seth Hunt to Governor Wilkinson, St Louis Augt 31st 1805, p. 214

[256] Ibid, Governor Wilkinson to the Secretary of War, St. Louis Sepr 8th 1805, p. 204–05

[257] Ibid, Court of Inquiry RE: Amos Stoddard, September 5, 1805, p. 194

[258] Ibid, Governor Wilkinson to the Secretary of War, St. Louis Sepr 8th 1805, p. 204–05

[259] Ibid, Court of Inquiry RE: Amos Stoddard, September 5, 1805, p. 194, Inc. Footnote 96

[260] Ibid, Governor Wilkinson to the Secretary of War, St. Louis, Septr 22nd 1805, p. 227–28

[261] Ibid, The Secretary of War to Governor Wilkinson, War Department, Augt 5th 1805, p. 178–79

[262] Ibid, Governor Wilkinson to the President, St. Louis, Oct. 22nd 1805, p. 243

[263] Andro Linklater, *An Artist in Treason, The Extraordinary Double Life of General James Wilkinson* (New York, Walker Publishing Company, 2009), p.122–23; 202–09; 211–12; 214–16

[264] Logan Esarey, *Governors Messages and Letters, Messages and Letters of William Henry Harrison, Vol. II, 1812–1816* (Indianapolis, 1922), Harrison to Secretary of War, St. Louis, October 18, 1805, p.170

[265] Clarence Edwin Carter, *Territorial Papers of the United States, Vol. XIII, The Territory of Louisiana–Missouri, 1803–1806*, (Washington, 1948), Governor Wilkinson to The Secretary of War, St. Louis, October 22nd 1805, p. 243–44

[266] Major Amos Stoddard, *Sketches, Historical and Descriptive, of Louisiana* (Philadelphia, 1812), p. 429

[267] William R. Swagerty, *The Indianization of Lewis and Clark, Vol I* (Norman, OK, The Arthur H Clark Company, 2012), p. 621–22

[268] Ibid

[269] The National Archives, *Letters Received by the Office of the Adjutant General, 1805–1821*, Publication No. M566, Record Group 94, To Thomas H. Cushing from Amos Stoddard, September 29, 1806

[270] Ibid, To Thomas H. Cushing from Amos Stoddard, November 1, 1806

[271] William L. Haskin, *The History of the First Regiment of Artillery, from Its Organization in 1821, to January 1, 1876* (Portland, 1879), p. 268

272 The National Archives, *Letters Received by the Office of the Adjutant General, 1805–1821*, Publication No. M566, Record Group 94, To Thomas H. Cushing from Amos Stoddard, Carlisle Barracks, Pennsylvania, November 8, 1806

273 Clarence Edwin Carter, *Territorial Papers of the United States, Vol. XIII, The Territory of Louisiana–Missouri, 1803–1806*, (Washington, 1948), James Taylor to Secretary of State James Madison, New Port, Kentucky, Feby 8th 1807, p. 91–3

274 William L. Clements Library, The University of Michigan, *Henry Burbeck Papers*, Letter from Amos Stoddard to Henry Burbeck, Fort Adams, M.T., November 18, 1806, Photocopy

275 National Archives, Records of U.S. Army, War Department, 1st Artillery Regiment 1802–1814, GR–98, E. 94, *Orderly Book of the Company of Captain Amos Stoddard, November 1807–June 1808*, Digital Media

276 Ibid

277 Ibid

278 National Archives, *Founders Online*, To Thomas Jefferson from Henry Dearborn, 24 November 1807, http://founders. archives.gov/documents/Jefferson/99-01-02-6841

279 Thomas H.S. Hamersly, *Complete Army Register of the United States for 100 Years (1779 to 1879)*, (Washington, 1881), p. 56

280 National Archives, Records of U.S. Army, War Department, 1st Artillery Regiment 1802–1814, GR–98, E. 94, *Orderly Book of the Company of Captain Amos Stoddard, November 1807–June 1808*, Digital Media

281 Ibid

282 *The Modern British Drama in Five Volumes, Volume Third, Comedies* (London, 1811), p. 638

283 The New–York Historical Society, Patricia D. Klingenstein Library, *Records of the United States Military Philosophical Society*, Letter from Amos Stoddard to William Popham, Fort Adams, January 26, 1808

284 Arthur Wade, *Artillerists and Engineers, The Beginnings of American Seacoast Fortifications, 1794–1815* (Coast Defense Study Group, 2011), p. 230–34

285 Major Amos Stoddard, *Sketches, Historical and Descriptive, of Louisiana* (Philadelphia, 1812), Title Page

286 New–York Historical Society, *Papers of The United States Military Philosophical Society, MS. Minutes and Records, Including Membership Lists, Correspondence and Papers Written for the Society, 1802–1813, in Four Volumes*, New York, Digital Media

287 National Archives, Records of U.S. Army, War Department, 1st Artillery Regiment 1802–1814, GR–98, E. 94, *Orderly Book of the Company of Captain Amos Stoddard, November 1807–June 1808*, Digital Media

288 Ibid

289 Ibid

290 Ibid

291 Major Amos Stoddard, *Sketches, Historical and Descriptive, of Louisiana* (Philadelphia, 1812), p. 134

292 Missouri Historical Museum, *Amos Stoddard Papers*, ALS Capt. Meriwether Lewis to Major Amos Stoddard, Fort Pickering, Chickasaw Bluffs, September 22, 1809, Digital Media

293 Missouri Historical Museum, *George Sibley Papers*, ALS John Sibley to Major Amos Stoddard, Natchitoches, April 2, 1812, Digital Media

294 *Meriwether Lewis to Thomas Jefferson, September 23, 1806*, Library of Congress, https://www.loc.gov/item/mtjbib016499/

295 Missouri Historical Museum, *Amos Stoddard Papers*, ALS Capt. Meriwether Lewis to Major Amos Stoddard, Fort Pickering, Chickasaw Bluffs, September 22, 1809, Digital Media

296 Missouri Historical Society, *Glimpses of the Past, Vol. II, May–September, No. 6–10* (St. Louis, 1935), Stoddard to Dearborn, St. Louis, June 3, 1804, p. 110–11

297 Ibid

298 National Archives, *Founders Online*, John Brahan to Thomas Jefferson, 18 October 1809, http://founders.archives.gov/documents/Jefferson/03-01-02-0476

299 Mark Bennitt, Editor-in-Chief, *History of the Louisiana Exposition* (St. Louis, Universal Exposition Publishing Company, 1905), Previously Unpublished Letter Exhibited at the Louisiana Purchase Exposition by the Missouri Historical Society, p. 73–4

300 William L. Clements Library, The University of Michigan, *Henry Burbeck Papers*, Letter from Amos Stoddard to Henry Burbeck, Fort Columbus, N.Y., December 28, 1809, Photocopy

301 The New–York Historical Society, Patricia D. Klingenstein Library, *NYHS Membership Records, 1810 and 1814*, Digital Media

302 Major Amos Stoddard, *Sketches, Historical and Descriptive, of Louisiana* (Philadelphia, 1812), Title Page

[303] National Archives and Records Administration, U.S. *Electoral College, Historical Election Results*, http://www.archives. gov/federal-register/electoral-college/scores.html

[304] National Archives, *Founders Online*, To James Madison from William Eustis, 18 March 1809, http://founders.archives. gov/documents/Madison/03-01-02-0070

[305] Thomas H.S. Hamersly, *Complete Army Register of the United States for 100 Years (1779 to 1879)*, (Washington, 1881), p. 51–2

[306] Department of War, Letters Sent, *Secretary of War to Henry Burbeck*, War Department, June 12, 1810

[307] Arthur Wade, *Artillerists and Engineers, The Beginnings of American Seacoast Fortifications, 1794–1815* (Coast Defense Study Group, 2011), p. 248

[308] Lewis Miller, William L. Clements Library, The University of Michigan , Manuscripts Division, Finding Aids, *Henry Burbeck Papers*, 1735–1866, Biography, (July 2015) www.clements.umich.edu

[309] Gaillard Hunt, Ed., *Journals of the Continental Congress, 1774–1789, Vol. XXIV,1783, January 1–August 29* (Washington, 1922), p. 291–93

[310] Major Edward C. Boynton, *General Order of George Washington…Issued at Newburgh on the Hudson, 1982–1883* (Harrison, Harbor Hill Book, 1973), p. 69–70

[311] Joseph Plumb Martin, *A Narrative of some of the Adventures, Dangers and Sufferings of a Revolutionary Soldier* (Hallowell, Maine 1830), p. 208

[312] Richard H. Kohn, The William and Mary Quarterly, Vol. 27, No. 2, *The Inside History of the Newburgh Conspiracy: America and the Coup D'Etat* (1970), p.188–220

[313] Edward C. Skeen and Richard H. Kohn, The William and Mary Quarterly, Vol.31 No. 2, *The Newburgh Conspiracy Reconsidered* (1974), p. 273–98

[314] Richard H. Kohn, The William and Mary Quarterly, Vol. 27, No. 2, *The Inside History of the Newburgh Conspiracy: America and the Coup D'Etat* (1970), p.205

[315] Gaillard Hunt, Ed., *Journals of the Continental Congress, 1774–1789, Vol. XXIV,1783, January 1–August 29* (Washington, 1922), p. 295–97

[316] Ibid, p. 297–98

[317] Ibid, p. 298–99

[318] Ibid, p. 306–10

[319] Massachusetts Historical Society, *George Washington, Newburgh Address, 15 March 1783*, http://www.masshist.org/database/1742

[320] John E. Ferling, *The First of Men: A Life of George Washington* (New York, Oxford University Press, 1988), p. 311

[321] Gaillard Hunt, Ed., *Journals of the Continental Congress, 1774–1789, Vol. XXIV,1783, January 1–August 29* (Washington, 1922), p. 311

[322] James Abercrombie, D.D., *A Sermon, Occasioned by the Death of Major Gen. Alexander Hamilton* (Philadelphia, 1804), Title Page

[323] Richard Brookhiser, *James Madison*, (New York, Basic Books, 2011), p. 121

[324] David Robertson, *Trial of Aaron Burr for Treason, Vol. II* (New York, James Cockcroft & Company, 1875), p.88

[325] National Archives, Department of War, *Letter from Amos Stoddard to Henry Burbeck*, Fredericktown, 20th Oct, 1811

[326] National Archives, *Founders Online*, James Madison from Peter Gansevoort, 29 November 1811, http://founders.archives.gov/documents/Madison/03-04-02-0047

[327] Andro Linklater, *An Artist in Treason: The Extraordinary Double Life of General James Wilkinson* (New York, Walker & Company, 2009), p.293–94

[328] Ibid, p. 315

[329] National Archives, *Founders Online*, To James Madison from William Eustis, 3 December 1812 http://founders.archives.gov/documents/Madison/03-05-02-0387

[330] Edmund F. Brown, *The Reference Book of the United States* (Washington, 1841), p. 18

[331] Byron Farwell, *The Encyclopedia of Nineteenth–Century Land Warfare: An Illustrated World View* (New York, W.W. Norton & Company, 2001), p. 862

[332] Edward C. Skeen and Richard H. Kohn, The William and Mary Quarterly, Vol. 31 No. 2, *The Newburgh Conspiracy Reconsidered* (1974), p. 275, Footnote 10

[333] Joseph Gardner Swift, *Memoirs of Gen. Joseph Gardner Swift, 1800–1865* (Worcester, 1890), p. 79

[334] Ibid, p. 124

335 National Archives, Department of War, *Letter from Major Amos Stoddard to Col. Henry Burbeck*, Fort Columbus, 15ᵗʰ Febʸ 1810

336 Ibid, *Letter from Major Amos Stoddard to Col. Henry Burbeck*, Fort Columbus, 8ᵗʰ March 1810

337 National Archives, Department of War, *Letter from Secretary of War William Eustis to Col. Henry Burbeck*, War Department, June 12ᵗʰ 1810

338 William L. Clements Library, The University of Michigan , Manuscripts Division, Finding Aids, *Henry Burbeck Papers*, 1735–1866, Correspondent Inventory (July 2015) www.clements.umich.edu

339 The National Archives, *Letters Received by the Office of the Adjutant General, 1805–1821*, Publication No. M566, Record Group 94, To Thomas H. Cushing from Amos Stoddard, November 1, 1806

340 National Archives, *Founders Online*, Thomas Jefferson to Amos Stoddard, 10 January 1811, http://founders.archives.gov/documents/Jefferson/03-03-02-0217

341 Christine Coalwell, Monticello Research Department, *Jefferson's Library of the Americas*, https://www.monticello.org/site/jefferson/books-american-geography-thomas-jeffersons-library

342 Missouri Historical Museum, *George Sibley Papers*, ALS John Sibley to Major Amos Stoddard, Natchitoches, April 2, 1812, Digital Media

343 Major Amos Stoddard, *Sketches, Historical and Descriptive, of Louisiana* (Philadelphia, 1812), p. 332

344 National Archives, Founders Online, To James Madison from William Eustis, 14 September 1811, Footnote 4, http://founders.archives.gov/documents/Madison/03-03-02-0547

345 Thomas John Chew Williams, *History of Frederick County, Maryland, Volume 1* (Frederick, L.R. Titsworth & Co., 1910), p. 163

346 National Archives, Department of War, *Letter from Amos Stoddard to Col. Henry Burbeck*, Fredericktown, 20ᵗʰ Octʳ 1811

347 National Archives, *Founders Online*, To James Madison from Peter Gansevoort, 29 November 1811, http://founders.archives.gov/documents/Madison/03-04-02-0047

348 William L. Clements Library, The University of Michigan, *Henry Burbeck Papers*, Letter from Amos Stoddard to Henry Burbeck, Frederick Town, 10ᵗʰ Novʳ. 1811, Photocopy

349 Ibid, Letter from Amos Stoddard to Henry Burbeck, Frederick Town, 24ᵗʰ December 1811, Photocopy

350 Joseph Gardner Swift, *Memoirs of Gen. Joseph Gardner Swift, 1800–1865* (Worcester, 1890), p. 98

351 Ibid

352 William L. Clements Library, The University of Michigan , Manuscripts Division, Finding Aids, *Henry Burbeck Papers*, 1735–1866, Correspondent Inventory (July 2015) www.clements.umich.edu

353 John C. Fredriksen, Ed., *The War of 1812 U.S. War Department Correspondence, 1812–1815* (Jefferson, NC, McFarland & Company, Inc, 2016), p. 372, No. 9528

354 William L. Clements Library, The University of Michigan , Manuscripts Division, Finding Aids, *Henry Burbeck Papers*, 1735–1866, Correspondent Inventory (July 2015) www.clements.umich.edu

355 National Archives, Department of War, *Letter from Major Amos Stoddard to Col. Henry Burbeck*, Fort Columbus, 10ᵗʰ Febʸ 1812

356 William L. Clements Library, The University of Michigan , Manuscripts Division, Finding Aids, *Henry Burbeck Papers*, 1735–1866, Correspondent Inventory (July 2015) www.clements.umich.edu

357 Donald E. Graves, *The First Official Artillery Manuals, 1810–1812*, The War of 1812 Magazine, Issue 15, May 2011. Used with Permission of the Author

358 William L. Clements Library, The University of Michigan, *Henry Burbeck Papers*, Letter from Amos Stoddard to Henry Burbeck, Frederick Town, 24ᵗʰ December 1811, Photocopy

359 Robert S. Quimby, *The U.S. Army in the War of 1812: An Operational and Command Study* (Michigan State University Press, East Lansing, 1997), p. 75–78

360 USNA, RG 107, Micro 221, Reel 48, *Amos Stoddard to William Eustis*, 14 February 1812

361 John C. Fredriksen, Ed., *The War of 1812 U.S. War Department Correspondence, 1812–1815* (Jefferson, NC, McFarland & Company, Inc, 2016), p. 372, No. 9529

362 Donald E. Graves, *The First Official Artillery Manuals, 1810–1812*, The War of 1812 Magazine, Issue 15, May 2011. Used with Permission of the Author.

363 John C. Fredriksen, Ed., *The War of 1812 U.S. War Department Correspondence, 1812–1815* (Jefferson, NC, McFarland & Company, Inc, 2016), p. 372, No. 9530

364 Printed by Pelsue & Gould, No. 3 New–street, New York, 1812

[365] Donald E. Graves, *The First Official Artillery Manuals, 1810–1812*, The War of 1812 Magazine, Issue 15, May 2011. Used with Permission of the Author.

[366] G. Auchinleck, *A History of the War Between Great Britain and the United States of America* (Toronto, MacLear and Co., 1855), p. 42–3

[367] Duke University, David M. Rubenstein Rare Book & Manuscript Library, History of Medicine Collections, *Philip Turner Papers*, Major Amos Stoddard to Dr. Phillip Turner, Washington, 9 July 1812, Digital Media

[368] John C. Fredriksen, Ed., *The War of 1812 U.S. War Department Correspondence, 1812–1815* (Jefferson, NC, McFarland & Company, Inc, 2016), p. 372, No. 9533

[369] Ibid, p. 404, No.10353, 10356

[370] William L. Clements Library, The University of Michigan , *Henry Burbeck Papers*, Letter from Amos Stoddard to Henry Burbeck, Washington City, 23d Augt 1812, Photocopy

[371] John R. Elting, *Amateurs, to Arms!: A Military History of the War of 1812* (Da Capo Press, Inc., 1995), p.27, 30

[372] Logan Esarey, *Governors Messages and Letters, Messages and Letters of William Henry Harrison, Vol. II, 1812–1816*, Letter from Secretary of War to General Hull, War Department, September 26th 1812, (Indianapolis, 1922), p.191

[373] Ibid, p. 33–34

[374] Milo Milton Quaife, *Chicago and the Old Northwest*, 1673–1835 (Chicago, 1913), p. 216

[375] John Brannan, *Official Letters of the Military and Naval Officers of the United States During the War with Great Britain, 1812, 13,14, & 15*, Captain N. Heald to Thomas H. Cushing, Esq., Pittsburg, October 23, 1812 (Washington City, 1823), p. 84–5

[376] William L. Clements Library, The University of Michigan , *Henry Burbeck Papers*, Letter from Amos Stoddard to Henry Burbeck, Washington City, 23d Augt 1812, Photocopy

[377] Ibid, Letter from Amos Stoddard to Henry Burbeck, Washington City, 29th Augt 1812, Photocopy

[378] Ibid

[379] Harold Allison, *The Tragic Saga of the Indiana Indians* (Paducah, Turner Publishing Company, 1986), p. 202

[380] Logan Esarey, *Governors Messages and Letters, Messages and Letters of William Henry Harrison, Vol. II, 1812–1816* (Indianapolis, 1922), Letter from Harrison to Secretary of War, September 24, 1812, p.151

[381] John C. Fredriksen, Ed., *The War of 1812 U.S. War Department Correspondence, 1812–1815* (Jefferson, NC, McFarland & Company, Inc, 2016), p. 404, No. 10359, 10360

[382] Logan Esarey, *Governors Messages and Letters, Messages and Letters of William Henry Harrison, Vol. II, 1812–1816* (Indianapolis, 1922), Letter from Secretary of War to Harrison, September 10, 1812, p.129

[383] Ibid, p. 136–7

[384] George W. Cullum, *Biographical Register of the Officers and Graduates of the U.S. Military Academy at West Point, Vol. I, Second Edition* (New York, 1868), p. 99

[385] John C. Fredriksen, Ed., *The War of 1812 U.S. War Department Correspondence, 1812–1815* (Jefferson, NC, McFarland & Company, Inc, 2016), p. 373, No. 9535

[386] William L. Clements Library, The University of Michigan, *Henry Burbeck Papers*, Letter from Amos Stoddard to Henry Burbeck, Pittsburgh, 21. Septr 1812, Photocopy

[387] John C. Fredriksen, Ed., *The War of 1812 U.S. War Department Correspondence, 1812–1815* (Jefferson, NC, McFarland & Company, Inc, 2016), p. 373, No. 9535, 9536, 9537

[388] Logan Esarey, *Governors Messages and Letters, Messages and Letters of William Henry Harrison, Vol. II, 1812–1816* (Indianapolis, 1922), Secretary of War to Harrison, War Department, September 26, 1812, p.155

[389] John C. Fredriksen, Ed., *The War of 1812 U.S. War Department Correspondence, 1812–1815* (Jefferson, NC, McFarland & Company, Inc, 2016), p. 373, No. 9539, 9540

[390] William L. Clements Library, The University of Michigan, *War of 1812 Collection*, Letter from Maj. Amos Stoddard to Lieut. Bryson, Pittsburgh, Nov. 15,1812, Photocopy

[391] Ibid, Letter from Amos Stoddard to Capt. James R. Butler, Pittsburgh, September 18, 1812, Photocopy

[392] Logan Esarey, *Governors Messages and Letters, Messages and Letters of William Henry Harrison, Vol. II, 1812–1816* (Indianapolis, 1922), H. Johnson to Harrison, Fort Fayette [Pittsburgh], November 3, 1812, p.193–200

[393] Ibid, Harrison to Secretary of War, Head Quarters, Franklinton, 17 Nov 1812, p. 221–22

[394] John C. Fredriksen, Ed., *The War of 1812 U.S. War Department Correspondence, 1812–1815* (Jefferson, NC, McFarland & Company, Inc, 2016), p. 373, No. 9541

[395] For a secondary opinion on militia behavior at this time, see: National Archives, *Founders Online*, To James Madison from Joseph Wheaton, 10 December 1812 (Abstract), http://founders.archives.gov/documents/Madison/03-05-02-0403

[396] John C. Fredriksen, Ed., *The War of 1812 U.S. War Department Correspondence, 1812–1815* (Jefferson, NC, McFarland & Company, Inc, 2016), p. 373, No. 9542

[397] The National Archives, *Letters Received by the Office of the Adjutant General, 1805–1821*, Publication No. M566, Record Group 94, To Brigadier General Thomas H. Cushing from Amos Stoddard, Pittsburgh, November 18, 1812

[398] Ibid, To Brigadier General Thomas H. Cushing from Amos Stoddard, Pittsburgh, December 12, 1812

[399] *Report of the Adjutant General of the State of Kentucky, Soldiers of the War of 1812*, Roll of Captain Alney McLean's Company, First Regiment Kentucky Mounted Militia (Frankfort, Kentucky, 1891), p. 2

[400] National Archives, *Founders Online*, Isaac A. Coles to Thomas Jefferson, 8 January 1813, http://founders.archives.gov/documents/Jefferson/03-05-02-0460-0002

[401] John C. Fredriksen, Ed., *The War of 1812 U.S. War Department Correspondence, 1812–1815* (Jefferson, NC, McFarland & Company, Inc, 2016), p. 372–73, No. 9534

[402] The Western Reserve Historical Society, *Tract No. 92, Part II, Northern Ohio During the War of 1812, from Manuscripts in the Collection of*, (Cleveland, 1913), p. 71

[403] Ibid, p. 74–5

[404] H.S. Knapp, *History of the Maumee Valley* (Toledo, 1877), p. 676

[405] National Archives, Department of War, *Letter from Amos Stoddard to Henry Burbeck*, Cleveland, 14th Jany 1813

[406] George Washington Cullum, *Campaigns of the War of 1812–15, Against Great Britain: Sketched and Criticized, with Brief Biographies of the American Engineers* (New York, James Miller, 1879), Bvt. Lieut.–Colonel Eleazor D. Wood, Journal of the Northwestern Campaign of 1812–13 under Major–General William H. Harrison, p. 364

[407] Ibid, p. 4–7

[408] H.S. Knapp, *History of the Maumee Valley* (Toledo, 1877), p. 676

[409] Logan Esarey, *Governors Messages and Letters, Messages and Letters of William Henry Harrison, Vol. II, 1812–1816* (Indianapolis, 1922), Letters from Harrison to Secretary of War, and Others, Head Quarters N.W. Army, Miami Rapids, 20th Day – 23rd January 1813, p.316–331

[410] National Archives, *Founders Online*, William Henry Harrison to James Monroe, 26 January 1813, http://founders.archives.gov/documents/Madison/03-05-02-0533

[411] George Washington Cullum, *Campaigns of the War of 1812–15, Against Great Britain: Sketched and Criticized, with Brief Biographies of the American Engineers* (New York, James Miller, 1879), Bvt. Lieut.–Colonel Eleazor D. Wood, Journal of the Northwestern Campaign of 1812–13 under Major–General William H. Harrison, p. 366

[412] Larry L. Nelson, *Men of Patriotism, Courage & Enterprise: Fort Meigs and the War of 1812* (Heritage Books, 2003), p. 38

[413] Dallas Tabor Herndon, *The High Lights of Arkansas History* (The Arkansas History Commission, 1922), p. 15

[414] H.S. Knapp, *History of the Maumee Valley* (Toledo, 1877), p. 676

[415] Harlow Lindley, Ed., *Fort Meigs and the War of 1812: Orderly Book of Cushing's Company and Personal Diary of Captain Daniel Cushing*, The Ohio Historical Society (Columbus, 1975), p.97

[416] George Washington Cullum, *Campaigns of the War of 1812–15, Against Great Britain: Sketched and Criticized, with Brief Biographies of the American Engineers* (New York, James Miller, 1879), Bvt. Lieut.–Colonel Eleazor D. Wood, Journal of the Northwestern Campaign of 1812–13 under Major–General William H. Harrison, p. 370

[417] Ibid. p. 371

[418] Ibid. p. 16–17

[419] Logan Esarey, *Governors Messages and Letters, Messages and Letters of William Henry Harrison, Vol. II, 1812–1816* (Indianapolis, 1922), Letter from Harrison to Secretary of War, Head Quarters (Camp Meigs) Miami Rapids, 24th Feby 1813, p.368

[420] Ibid

[421] Joseph H. Larwill, *Journal of Joseph H. Larwill Relating to Occurrences Transpired in the Service of the U States Commencing April 5, 1812*, (Unpublished Transcription, Burton Historical Collection, Detroit Public Library), p. 57–8

[422] George Washington Cullum, *Campaigns of the War of 1812–15, Against Great Britain: Sketched and Criticized, with Brief Biographies of the American Engineers* (New York, James Miller, 1879), Bvt. Lieut.–Colonel Eleazor D. Wood, Journal of the Northwestern Campaign of 1812–13 under Major–General William H. Harrison, p. 378–79

[423] Joseph H. Larwill, *Journal of Joseph H. Larwill Relating to Occurrences Transpired in the Service of the U States Commencing April 5, 1812*, (Unpublished Transcription, Burton Historical Collection, Detroit Public Library), p. 60

[424] Ibid, p 70–1

[425] Ibid, 71

[426] Harlow Lindley, Ed., *Fort Meigs and the War of 1812: Orderly Book of Cushing's Company and Personal Diary of Captain Daniel Cushing*, The Ohio Historical Society (Columbus, 1975), p.105–06

[427] George Washington Cullum, *Campaigns of the War of 1812–15, Against Great Britain: Sketched and Criticized, with Brief Biographies of the American Engineers* (New York, James Miller, 1879), Bvt. Lieut.–Colonel Eleazor D. Wood, Journal of the Northwestern Campaign of 1812–13 under Major–General William H. Harrison, p. 379–80

[428] Described as such on Marker giving history of the namesake of Stoddard County, located on the grounds of the Stoddard County Courthouse, Bloomfield, Missouri

[429] Wilfrid Hibbert, *Major Amos Stoddard, First Governor of Upper Louisiana and Hero of Fort Meigs*, The Historical Society of Northwestern Ohio, Bulletin No. 2 (April 1930)

[430] Logan Esarey, *Governors Messages and Letters, Messages and Letters of William Henry Harrison, Vol. II, 1812–1816* (Indianapolis, 1922), Letter from Harrison to Secretary of War, Various, p.104, 173–78, 183–85

[431] George Washington Cullum, *Campaigns of the War of 1812–15, Against Great Britain: Sketched and Criticized, with Brief Biographies of the American Engineers* (New York, James Miller, 1879), Bvt. Lieut.–Colonel Eleazor D. Wood, Journal of the Northwestern Campaign of 1812–13 under Major–General William H. Harrison, p. 380–81

[432] Ibid, p. 382–83

[433] Harlow Lindley, Ed., *Fort Meigs and the War of 1812: Orderly Book of Cushing's Company and Personal Diary of Captain Daniel Cushing*, The Ohio Historical Society (Columbus, 1975), p.3, 110

[434] Logan Esarey, *Governors Messages and Letters, Messages and Letters of William Henry Harrison, Vol. II, 1812–1816*, Letter from Harrison to Gov. Shelby & Secretary of War, April 9th and April 15th, 1813 (Indianapolis, 1922), p.416–18

[435] Harlow Lindley, Ed., *Fort Meigs and the War of 1812: Orderly Book of Cushing's Company and Personal Diary of Captain Daniel Cushing*, The Ohio Historical Society (Columbus, 1975), p.3

[436] Ibid, p. 112

[437] George Washington Cullum, *Campaigns of the War of 1812–15, Against Great Britain: Sketched and Criticized, with Brief Biographies of the American Engineers* (New York, James Miller, 1879), Bvt. Lieut.–Colonel Eleazor D. Wood, Journal of the Northwestern Campaign of 1812–13 under Major–General William H. Harrison, p. 383

[438] Harlow Lindley, Ed., *Fort Meigs and the War of 1812: Orderly Book of Cushing's Company and Personal Diary of Captain Daniel Cushing*, The Ohio Historical Society (Columbus, 1975), p. 112

[439] Ibid, p. 4

[440] Ibid, 113

[441] George Washington Cullum, *Campaigns of the War of 1812–15, Against Great Britain: Sketched and Criticized, with Brief Biographies of the American Engineers* (New York, James Miller, 1879), Bvt. Lieut.–Colonel Eleazor D. Wood, Journal of the Northwestern Campaign of 1812–13 under Major–General William H. Harrison, p. 383

[442] Harlow Lindley, Ed., *Fort Meigs and the War of 1812: Orderly Book of Cushing's Company and Personal Diary of Captain Daniel Cushing*, The Ohio Historical Society (Columbus, 1975), p.6

[443] Logan Esarey, *Governors Messages and Letters, Messages and Letters of William Henry Harrison, Vol. II, 1812–1816* (Indianapolis, 1922), Harrison to Secretary of War, Head Quarters N.W. Army Camp Meigs (Miami Rapids), [About April 15, 1813], p. 417–18

[444] Harlow Lindley, Ed., *Fort Meigs and the War of 1812: Orderly Book of Cushing's Company and Personal Diary of Captain Daniel Cushing*, The Ohio Historical Society (Columbus, 1975), p. 8

[445] Wilfrid Hibbert, *Major Amos Stoddard, First Governor of Upper Louisiana and Hero of Fort Meigs*, The Historical Society of Northwestern Ohio, Bulletin No. 2 (April 1930)

[446] George Washington Cullum, *Campaigns of the War of 1812–15, Against Great Britain: Sketched and Criticized, with Brief Biographies of the American Engineers* (New York, James Miller, 1879), Bvt. Lieut.–Colonel Eleazor D. Wood, Journal of the Northwestern Campaign of 1812–13 under Major–General William H. Harrison, p. 384

[447] Ibid, p. 383

[448] Harlow Lindley, Ed., *Fort Meigs and the War of 1812: Orderly Book of Cushing's Company and Personal Diary of Captain Daniel Cushing*, The Ohio Historical Society (Columbus, 1975), p. 115

[449] Ibid

[450] George Washington Cullum, *Campaigns of the War of 1812–15, Against Great Britain: Sketched and Criticized, with Brief Biographies of the American Engineers* (New York, James Miller, 1879), Bvt. Lieut.–Colonel Eleazor D. Wood, Journal of the Northwestern Campaign of 1812–13 under Major–General William H. Harrison, p. 386

[451] Ibid, 389–90

[452] Logan Esarey, *Governors Messages and Letters, Messages and Letters of William Henry Harrison, Vol. II, 1812–1816* (Indianapolis, 1922), Letter from Harrison to Secretary of War, Head Quarters Lower Sandusky, 13th May 1813, p.446–47

[453] Ibid, Letter from Harrison to Secretary of War, Head Quarters Franklinton, May 19th 1813, p. 455

[454] Ibid, Letter from Secretary of War to Harrison, War Department, May 8th 1813, p. 434

[455] Ibid, Letter from Harrison to Secretary of War, Head Quarters Franklinton, May 18th 1813, p. 453

[456] Harlow Lindley, Ed., *Fort Meigs and the War of 1812: Orderly Book of Cushing's Company and Personal Diary of Captain Daniel Cushing*, The Ohio Historical Society (Columbus, 1975), p. 116

[457] Ibid

[458] George Washington Cullum, *Campaigns of the War of 1812–15, Against Great Britain: Sketched and Criticized, with Brief Biographies of the American Engineers* (New York, James Miller, 1879), Bvt. Lieut.–Colonel Eleazor D. Wood, Journal of the Northwestern Campaign of 1812–13 under Major–General William H. Harrison, p. 390

[459] Harlow Lindley, Ed., *Fort Meigs and the War of 1812: Orderly Book of Cushing's Company and Personal Diary of Captain Daniel Cushing*, The Ohio Historical Society (Columbus, 1975), p. 120

[460] Ibid

[461] Larry L. Nelson, *Men of Patriotism, Courage & Enterprise: Fort Meigs and the War of 1812* (Heritage Books, 2003), p. 76

[462] George Washington Cullum, *Campaigns of the War of 1812–15, Against Great Britain: Sketched and Criticized, with Brief Biographies of the American Engineers* (New York, James Miller, 1879), Bvt. Lieut.–Colonel Eleazor D. Wood, Journal of the Northwestern Campaign of 1812–13 under Major–General William H. Harrison, p. 394–96

[463] Larry L. Nelson, *Men of Patriotism, Courage & Enterprise: Fort Meigs and the War of 1812* (Heritage Books, 2003), p. 80

[464] Logan Esarey, *Governors Messages and Letters, Messages and Letters of William Henry Harrison, Vol. II, 1812–1816* (Indianapolis, 1922), Letter from Harrison to Secretary of War, Head Quarters Camp Meigs, 5th May 1813 (Indianapolis, 1922), p.431–32

[465] Ibid, Letter from Harrison to Secretary of War, Head Quarters Camp Meigs, 9th May 1813, p. 438–40

[466] Ibid, Harrison and Proctor, Agreement for Exchange of Prisoners, May 7, 1813, p. 433–34

[467] Ibid, Harrison, General Orders, 9th May 1813; Harrison to Secretary of War, Head Quarters, Camp Meigs, 9th May 1813; p. 435–40

[468] John Brannan, *Official Letters of the Military and Naval Officers of the United States During the War with Great Britain, 1812, 13,14, & 15*, General Orders, Head Quarters, Fort Meigs, May 9th, 1813 (Washington City, 1823), p. 154–56

[469] George Washington Cullum, *Campaigns of the War of 1812–15, Against Great Britain: Sketched and Criticized, with Brief Biographies of the American Engineers* (New York, James Miller, 1879), Bvt. Lieut.–Colonel Eleazor D. Wood, Journal of the Northwestern Campaign of 1812–13 under Major–General William H. Harrison, p. 402–03

[470] Harlow Lindley, Ed., *Fort Meigs and the War of 1812: Orderly Book of Cushing's Company and Personal Diary of Captain Daniel Cushing*, The Ohio Historical Society (Columbus, 1975), p. 120

[471] Logan Esarey, *Governors Messages and Letters, Messages and Letters of William Henry Harrison, Vol. II, 1812–1816* (Indianapolis, 1922), Letter from Harrison to Secretary of War, Head Quarters, Lower Sandusky, May 13th 1813, p.447

[472] Ibid, Letter from Harrison to Secretary of War, Head Quarters, Franklinton, May 18th 1813 (Indianapolis, 1922), p.453–54

[473] Harlow Lindley, Ed., *Fort Meigs and the War of 1812: Orderly Book of Cushing's Company and Personal Diary of Captain Daniel Cushing*, The Ohio Historical Society (Columbus, 1975), p. 120

A NOTE ON BIBLIOGRAPHICAL SOURCES

The bibliography is broken-down into three parts: primary, secondary and online sources. The primary sources are either widely referenced throughout the book or large sections are excerpted. Copious endnotes have been used throughout the introduction to identify where a bibliography source was used in the text —either as the idea for the text, in the paraphrasing of the source text, or as an excerpt of the original text. Secondary sources are publications (or reputable websites) generally only referenced once or twice. They are used to identify the source of a stated fact and to demonstrate to the reader the attempted factualness of the information presented.

The genealogy information in the Introduction has primarily been taken from the excellent work of Sharlene Ida Stoddard of Northwood, Iowa, from her book, *Family of Wells and Eunice Stoddard*, published in April 1995. In her book Sharlene provides "fifty-eight pages of information on the ancestors of Wells Stoddard." Wells Stoddard was the great-grandson of Eliakim Stoddard (Amos Stoddard's grandfather). This editor also descended from Wells and Eunice Stoddard.

Sharlene Stoddard's information is derived from her reconciliation of nearly all the previously published Stoddard family genealogies which are included in this bibliography whether they were used or not. She also collaborated with other active Stoddard genealogists —many of who have since passed. It is because of the efforts of all of these fine kinsmen that we are able to tell a factually–complete story of Major Amos Stoddard's ancestral beginnings.

Another primary source is the aforementioned seminal work, *History of Ancient Woodbury* series by William Cothren, a comprehensive history of the founding of Woodbury, Connecticut. It is arguably the greatest historical recording of any city from colonial America which happens to also encompass the ministerial career of Reverend Anthony Stoddard and includes records of many of his descendants —including Major Amos Stoddard. What makes Cothren's work even more interesting was that he was not even born in Woodbury and his family was not from Woodbury. He only settled in Woodbury and started a law practice there in 1844 —just 10 years before his first volume was published in 1854.

Sharlene Stoddard extensively referenced William Cothren's invaluable *History of Ancient Woodbury* series. This is what makes her work so valuable: she has already done the work of cross–referencing all of the previously–published sources. Sharlene also did extensive research of her own —traveling and scouring the country and finding many original records, mostly on film, thereby adding new information, confirming old information and correcting errors. Her genealogical work is of the highest quality and standard.

The Missouri Historical Museum contributed significantly to the primary source material used for this book. This publication would not have been possible without the photocopies of the autobiography manuscript and the original documents and letters cited within the introduction. For simplicity, many letters from their *Amos Stoddard Papers* collection are cited as being from their 1935 publication, *Glimpses of the Past*, but this editor was also provided with photocopies of all of those documents and letters contained within that article as well.

Clarence Edwin Carter's *Territorial Papers of the United States* series and Logan Esarey's *Governors Messages and Letters* are widely quoted for the period 1803 to 1813. The letters contained within each give us a first–hand perspective of the thoughts of the people involved in the events as they unfolded.

The staff of the William Clements Library at the University of Michigan supplied much of the primary source material for this book in the form of photocopies of letters from the *Henry Burbeck Papers* collection. There is no substitute for original source documentation. The *Orderly Book of the Company of Captain Amos Stoddard* from the National Archives was extremely helpful in documenting his time at Fort Adams and Fort Dearborn in 1808.

Sketches, Descriptive and Historical, of Louisiana by Major Amos Stoddard was frequently excerpted and referenced. It also proved invaluable in disclosing evidence as to Major Amos Stoddard's whereabouts in 1808-9.

The Memoirs of General Joseph Gardner Swift is also widely referenced and quoted. It is interesting to note General Swift shares his recollection of Capt. Amos Stoddard from when he was yet a young man in 1799 but fails to mention Major Amos Stoddard's attendance and participation with him at the trial of General James Wilkinson in 1811.

John C. Fredriksen's book, *The War of 1812: U.S. War Department Correspondence, 1812-1815*, was invaluable for filling–in gaps of Major Amos Stoddard's presence and activities prior to and during the War of 1812. The alternative would have required spending many tedious hours at the National Archives going through microfilm.

Excerpted passages from Joseph Plumb Martin's book, A *Narrative of some of the Adventures, Dangers, and Sufferings of a Revolutionary Soldier*, while not used in providing information on our subject, were used to provide background.

An Artist in Treason: The Extraordinary Double Life of General James Wilkinson by Andro Linklater provided extensive and invaluable background information for the motivations and the behavior of General Wilkinson, as well as towards the political climate in the government and within the Army at the time. Any reader who desires a more in–depth source of information about this turbulent period in American history is encouraged to read this well–researched work.

Material from the *Journal of Bvt. Lt.–Col Eleazor Darby Wood*, the *Diary of Capt. Daniel Cushing*, and the *Orderly Book of Cushing's Company of Artillery*, while extensively cited in many other works of this period, were excerpted and used where it particularly pertained to the subject. These sources provide an invaluable first–hand account leading up to and including the siege of Fort Meigs during the first nine days of May 1813.

All other works are noted to be secondary sources. While some may be referenced more than twice, they did not significantly contribute to the writing of the introduction of Major Amos Stoddard. They mostly serve as citations of the facts provided. While in some cases this could be considered excessive (and even unnecessary) they provide reference to other material which some readers may appreciate. An example of the most significant of these are Wilfrid Hibbert's *Major Amos Stoddard, First Governor of Upper Louisiana and Hero of Fort Meigs*; Larry Nelson's *Men of Patriotism, Courage & Enterprise: Fort Meigs and the War of 1812*; and the *Trial of Aaron Burr for Treason* by David Robertson.

Only trusted and reputable online resources were used. *Founders Online* by the National Archives and *Papers of the War Department 1784 to 1800* by George Mason University are excellent examples of some of the best resources for original documentation of the period found on the Web.

Bibliography

Primary Sources:

Carter, Clarence Edwin. *Territorial Papers of the United States, Vol. VII, The Territory of Indiana, 1800-1810.* Washington, 1948.

—. *Territorial Papers of the United States, Vol. XIII, The Territory of Louisiana - Missouri, 1803-1806.* Washington, 1948.

Cothren, William. *History of Ancient Woodbury, Connecticut, from the First Indian Deed in 1659 to 1854, Volume I.* Waterbury: Bronson Brothers, 1854.

—. *History of Ancient Woodbury, Connecticut, from The First Indian Deed in 1659 To 1872, Volume II.* Woodbury, Conn.: William Cothren, 1872.

—. *History of Ancient Woodbury, Connecticut, from the First Indian Deed in 1659 to 1879, Genealogical Sketches of the Same, Volume III.* Woodbury: William Cothren, 1879.

Cullum, George Washington. *Campaigns of the War of 1812-15, against Great Britain: Sketched and Criticized, with brief Biographies of the American Engineers.* New York: James Miller, 1879.

—. *Biographical Register of the Officers and Graduates of the U.S. Military Academy at West Point, Vol. 1, Second Edition, 1802-1840.* New York: D. Van Nordstrand, 1868.

Esarey, Logan. *Governors Messages and Letters, Messages and Letters of William Henry Harrison, Vol. II, 1812-1816.* Indianapolis: Indiana Historical Commission, 1922.

Fredriksen, John C. *The War of 1812: U.S. War Department Correspondence, 1812-1815.* Jefferson: McFarland & Company, Inc., 2016.

Lindley, Harlow. *Fort Meigs and the War of 1812: Orderly Book of Cushing's Company and Personal Diary of Captain Daniel Cushing.* Columbus, 1975.

Linklater, Andro. *An Artist in Treason, The Extraordinary Double Life of General James Wilkinson.* New York: Walker Publishing Company, 2009.

Lionberger, Issac; Drumm, Stella "Transfer of Upper Louisiana." In *Glimpses of the Past - Volume II, May-September, Numbers 6-10,* by Missouri Historical Society, 78-120. St. Louis: Missouri Historical Society, 1935.

Martin, Joseph Plumb. *A Narrative of some of the Adventures, Dangers and Sufferings of a Revolutionary Soldier.* Hallowell: Glazier, Masters, and Co., 1830.

Stoddard, Major Amos. *Sketches, Historical and Descriptive, of Louisiana.* Philadelphia: Amos Stoddard, 1812.

Stoddard, Sharlene Ida. *Family of Wells and Eunice Stoddard.* Northwood, IA: Self-Published, April, 1995.

Swift, General Joseph Gardner. *The Memoirs of General Joseph Gardner Swift, 1800-1865.* Worcester, 1890.

The Amos Stoddard Papers. Missouri Historical Museum, St. Louis, Missouri

The Henry Burbeck Papers. William L. Clements Library, University of Michigan, Ann Arbor, Michigan.

Orderly Book of the Company of Captain Amos Stoddard, National Archives, College Park, Maryland.

Secondary Sources:

A Record of the Streets, Alleys, Places, Etc. in the City of Boston. Boston: City of Boston, 1910.

Abercrombie, James. *A Sermon Occasioned by the Death of Major Gen. Alexander Hamilton.* Philadelphia, 1804.

Acts and Laws of the Commonwealth of Massachusetts, Volume 9. Wright & Potter, 1896.

Adams, Henry. *History of the United States: The Second Administration of James Madison, 1813-1817*. New York: Charles Scribner's Sons, 1911.

Albin, John. *A New, Correct, and Much-improved History of the Isle of Wight*. London: Scratcherd and Whitaker, Booksellers, 1795.

Allen, L.P. *The Genealogy and History of the Shreve Family from 1641*. Greenfield: Self-Published, 1901.

Allison, Harold. *The Tragic Saga of the Indiana Indians*. Paducah: Turner Publishing Company, 1986.

Ames, Fisher. *The Influence of Democracy on Liberty, Property, and the Happiness of Society, Considered*. London: John Parker, Esq., 1835.

Anthon, John. *American Precedents of Declarations,...* New York: Stephen Gould, 1810.

Auchinleck, G. *A History of the War Between Great Britain and the United States of America*. Toronto: MacLear & Co., 1855.

Beach, Joseph Perkin. *History of Cheshire, Connecticut from 1694 to 1840*. Cheshire: Lady Fenwick Chapter, D.A.R., 1912.

Bell, Carol. *Approaching Jonathan Edwards*: The Evolution of a Persona. Burlington: Ashgate, 2015.

Birkhimer, William Edward. *Historical Sketch of the Organization, Administration, Matérial and Tactics of the Artillery, United States Army*. Washington, D.C. : James J. Chapman, 1884.

Boatner, Mark Mayo. *Encyclopedia of the American Revolution*. New York: D. McKay Co., 1966.

Boucher, Rev. James E. *Letters, Archaeological and Historical: Relating to the Isle of Wight, Volume 1*. London: Henry Frowde, 1896.

Boynton, Capt. Edward C. *History of West Point*. London: Sampson Low, Son & Marston, 1864.

Boynton, Major Edward C. *General Orders of George Washington...issued at Newburgh on the Hudson, 1782-1783*. Harrison: Harbor Hill Books, 1973.

Brannan, John. *Official Letters of the Military and Naval Officers of the United States During the War with Great Britain, 1812, 13, 14, & 15*. Washington, 1823.

Brookhiser, Richard. *James Madison*. New York: Basic Books, 2011.

Brown, Edmund F. *The Reference Book of the United States*. Washington, 1841.

Calder, Isabel M. *Letters & Papers of Ezra Stiles, President of Yale College, 1778-1795*. New Haven: Yale University Library, 1933.

Colmen, Reverend Benjamin. *A Sermon Preached at the Lecture in Boston Upon the Death of the Learned and Venerable Solomon Stoddard*. Boston: Boston Weekly News-Letter: No. 112, 1729.

Conover, Frank. *Centennial Portrait and Biographical Record of the City of Dayton and Montgomery County, Ohio*. A.W. Bowden & Co., 1897.

Cubbison, Douglas R. *Historic Structures Report, Logistical and Quartermaster Operations at Fortress West Point, 1778-1783*. Prepared for West Point Museum, West Point, NY: U.s. Military Academy, 2006.

Davis, William Thomas. *Bench and Bar of the Commonwealth of Massachusetts, Volume 2*. Boston, 1895. Deacon, Edward. *Some of the Ancestors of Rodman Stoddard of Woodbury, Conn. and Detroit, Mich*. Bridgeport, 1893.

Deacon, Edward. Some of the Ancestors of Rodman Stoddard of Woodbury, Conn. and Detroit, Mich. Bridgeport, 1893.

Dean, John Ward, Ed. *The New England Historical and Genealogical Register, for the Year 1884, Volume 38*. Boston: By the Society, 1884.

Denny, Major Ebenezer. *Military Journal of Major Ebenezer Denny*. Philadelphia: J.B. Lippincott & Co., 1859.

Dexter, Franklin Bowditch. *Biographical Sketches of the Graduates of Yale College with Annals of the College History, October 1701-May 1745*. New York: Henry Holt and Company, 1885.

Drury, Augustus Waldo. *History of the City of Dayton, Montgomery County, Ohio, Volume 2*. Chicago, 1909.

Egleston, Thomas. "Major Azariah Egleston of the Revolutionary Army." In *New York Genealogical and Biographical Record, July 1892: Vol. XXIII, No. 3*.

—. *The Life of John Paterson, Major-General in the Revolutionary Army*. New York: G.P. Putnam's Sons, 1898.

Elmer, Ebenezer. *An Elogy on Francis Barber, Esq*. New York: Charles F. Heartman, Originally Published at Chatham in 1783; Reprinted in 1917.

Elting, John R. *Amateurs to Arms!: A Military History of the War of 1812*. Da Capo Press, Inc., 1995.

Farwell, Byron. *The Encyclopedia of Nineteenth-Century Land Warfare: An Illustrative View*. New York: W.W. Norton & Company, 2001.

Fisk, Fred C. "The Stoddard Manufacturing Company." In *The Wheelman, Number 21, November 1897*, by Ed. Russell Mamone, 16-23. The Wheelman, 1987.

Fiske, John. *The Critical Period of American History, 1783-1789*. Boston and New York: Houghton, Mifflin and Company , 1889.

Gardner, Frank A. "Colonial John Fellows Regiment." In *The Massachusetts Magazine, July Vol. II, No 3, 1909*: 141-161.

Garry, James B. *Weapons of the Lewis & Clark Expedition*. Norman: Arthur H. Clark Company, 2012.

Genealogical and Family History of the State of Connecticut, Volume II. New York, 1911.

Graham, Col. James J. *Memoir of General [Samuel] Graham*. Edinburgh: Privately Printed by R.& R. Clark, 1862.

Graves, Donald E. "The First Official Artillery Manuals, 1810-1812." In *The War of 1812 Magazine, Issue 15, May 2011, Part 9*, Online Magazine. Napoleon Series Website, 2011.

Gregory, R.R.C. *The Story of Royal Eltham*. Eltham: Kentish District Times Company, Ltd., 1909.

Hamersly, Thomas H.S. *Complete Army Register of the United States for 100 Years (1779 to 1879)*. Washington: Thomas H.S. Hamersly, 1881.

Hamilton, Alexander, and Editors Julius Goebel Jr. and Joseph H. Smith. *The Law Practice of Alexander Hamilton, Documents and Commentary, Vol. IV*. New York and London: Columbia University Press, 1980.

Haskin, William L. *The History of the First Regiment of Artillery, from its Organization in 1821, to January 1, 1876*. Portland, 1879.

Hasted, Edward. *The History and Topographical Survey of the County of Kent, Volume 1*. Canterbury: Printed by W. Bristow, on the Parade, 1797.

Hatch, Charles E. "Affair Near James Island." In *The Virginia Magazine of History and Biography, July Vol. 53, 1945*: 172-196.

Hatch, Louis Clinton. *The Administration of the American Revolutionary Army, Vol. X*. New York: Longmans, Green, And Co., 1904.

Heitman, Francis B. *Historical Register of Officers of the Continental Army During the War of the Revolution, April, 1775, to December, 1783*. Washington, D.C., 1893.

—. *Historical Register of the United States Army, from Its Organization, September 29, 1789 to September 29, 1889*. Washington: The National Tribune, 1890.

Herbert Wood Kimball, Compiler. *Register of Members, Sons of the American Revolution*. Springfield, Mass.: Massachusetts Society, 1907.

Herndon, Dallas Tabor. *The High Lights of Arkansas History*. Little Rock: Arkansas History Commission, 1922.

Hibbert, Wilfrid. "Major Amos Stoddard, First Governor of Upper Louisiana and Hero of Fort Meigs." In *The Historical Society of Northwestern Ohio, Bulletin No. 2, April 1930*. The Historical Society of Northwestern Ohio, 1930.

Historical Localities in Northampton. Northampton: Gazette Printing Co., 1904.

History of Litchfield County, Connecticut. Philadelphia: J.W. Lewis & Company, 1881.

History of the County of Berkshire, Massachusetts. Pittsfield, 1829.

Hodges, Almon D. *Genealogical Record of the Hodges Family of New England*. Boston, 1896.

Hunt, Gaillard. *Journals of the Continental Congress, 1774-1789, Vol. XXIV, 1783, January 1-August 29*. Washington, 1922.

Johnson, W. Fletcher. *Life of Wm. Tecumseh Sherman, Vol. I*. New York: D. Appleton & Company, 1891.

Johnston, George. *History of Cecil County, Maryland*. Elkton, MD: Published by the Author, 1881.

Johnston, Henry Phelps. *The Yorktown Campaign and The Surrender of Cornwallis, 1781*. New York: Harper and Brothers, 1881.

Journals of the American Congress, from 1774 to 1788; Vol IV, April 1, 1782 to November 1, 1788 inclusive. Washington: Way and Gideon, 1783.

Knapp, H.S. *History of the Maumee Valley*. Toledo, 1877.

Kohn, Edward C. Skeen and Richard H. "The Newburgh Conspiracy Reconsidered." In *The William and Mary Quarterly, Vol. 31, No. 2*, 273-298. Williamsburg: Omohundro Institute of Early American History and Culture, 1974.

Kohn, Richard H. "The Inside History of the Newburgh Conspiracy; America and the Coup D'Etat." In *The William and Mary Quarterly, Vol. 27, No. 2*, 188-220. Williamsburg: Omohundro Institute of Early American History and Culture, 1970.

Lincoln, James Minor. *The Papers of Capt. Rufus Lincoln of Wareham, Mass*. Unknown: Privately Printed, 1904.

Lockhart, Paul D. *The Drillmaster of Valley Forge: The Baron de Steuben and the Making of the American Army*. New York: Harper Collins, 2008.

Lowrie, Walter. *American State Papers, Documents, Executive and Legislative, of the Congress of the United States, Class X, Miscellaneous, Volume 1*. Washington: Gales and Seaton, 1834.

Lysons, Daniel. *The Environs of London: An Historical Account of the Towns. Villages and Hamlets, Counties of Kent, Essex, and Herts*. London: T. Cadwell and W. Davies, 1811.

Lytle, Richard M. *The Soldiers of America's First Army, 1791*. Lanham, MD: The Scarecrow Press, Inc., 2004.

Mark Bennitt, Editor-in-Chief. *History of the Louisiana Exposition*. St. Louis: Universal Exposition Publishing Company, 1905.

Massachusetts Soldiers and Sailors of the Revolutionary War: A Compilation of the Archives. Boston: Wright and Potter Printing Company, 1907. Matthews, Albert. *Publications of the Colonial Society of Massachusetts, Vol. XII*. Boston: Colonial Society of Massachusetts, 1911.

Miller, Hunter. *Treaties and Other International Acts of the United States of America, Vol. II, Documents 1-40, 1776-1818*. Washington, 1931.

Miller, Marion Mills. *Great Debates in American History, Vol. 9*. New York: Current Literature Publishing Company, 1913.

Moore, Frank. *American Eloquence: A Collection of Speeches and Addresses…Vol. II.* New York: D. Appleton and Company, 1895. Moos, Herman M. *The American Law Record, 1873-1874, Volume II.* Cincinnati, 1874.

Muhlenberg, Henry A. *The Life of Major-General Peter Muhlenberg.* Philadelphia: Carey and Hart, 1849.

Nason, Emma Huntington. *Old Hallowell on the Kennebec.* Augusta, 1909.

Nelson, Larry L. *Men of Patriotism, Courage & Enterprise: Fort Meigs and the War of 1812.* Heritage Books, 2003.

Page, William. *A History of the County of Hampshire: Volume 5.* London: Victoria County History, 1912.

Paige, Lucius R. *History of Hardwick, Massachusetts.* Boston: Houghton, Mifflin and Company, 1883.

Parmenter, Charles Oscar. *History of Pelham, Mass: From 1738 to 1898, Including the Early History of Prescott.* Amherst: Press of Carpenter & Morehouse, 1898.

Parsons, Usher. *The Life of Sir William Pepperrell, Bart.* Boston: Little, Brown and Company, 1855.

Patterson, David Williams. *John Stoddard of Wethersfield, Conn., and his Descendants, 1642-1872, A Genealogy.* Succasunna, 1873.

Peck, Brainerd T. "The Stoddard and Waller Families." In *The American Genealogist, 1968*: 50-60.

Peleg W. Chandler, Ed. *The Law Reporter, Volume 5.* Boston: Bradbury, Soden, and Company, 1843.

Powell, Colonel William Henry. *List of Officers of the Army of the United States, 1779-1900.* New York: H.R. Hamersly & Co., 1900.

Prindle, Franklin. *The Prindle Genealogy: Embracing the Descendants of William Prindle.* New York: Self-Published, 1906.

Prior, James Esq. *Memoir of the Life and Character of the Right Hon. Edmund Burke….* Philadelphia: Abraham Small, 1825.

Publications of the Colonial Society of Massachusetts, Volume 12. Boston: Colonial Society of Massachusetts, 1911.

Quaife, Milo Milton. *Chicago and the Old Northwest, 1673-1835.* Chicago, 1913.

Rhees, William J. *Register of the District of Columbia Society, Sons of the American Revolution.* Washington: District of Columbia Society, 1896.

Richard W. Stewart, Ed. *American Military History: The United States Army and the Forging of a Nation, 1775-1917.* Washington: Center of Military History - United States Army, 2005.

Roberts, William McKay and W. *John Hoppner, R.A.* . London: P.& D. Polnaghi & Co., 1909.

Robertson, David. *Trial of Aaron Burr for Treason, Volume II.* New York: James Cockcroft & Company, 1875.

Rolls of Connecticut Men in the French and Indian War, 1755-1762, Volume 1. Hartford: Connecticut Historical Society, 1903.

Rombauer, Robert Julius. *The Union Cause in St. Louis in 1861: An Historical Sketch.* St. Louis, 1909.

Sanderson, Gen. Thomas W. *20th Century History of Youngstown and Mahoning County, Ohio.* Chicago: Biographical Publishing Company, 1907.

Scott, Henry Edwards. *The New England Historical and Genealogical Register.* Boston: N.E. Historic Genealogical Society, 1913.

Sewell, Samuel. *Diary of Samuel Sewell.* Boston: Massachusetts Historical Society, 1878.

Sherman, Thomas Townsend. *Sherman Genealogy, Including Families of Essex, Suffolk, and Norfolk England,…* New York: Tobias Wright, 1920.

Shipton, Clifford K. *Sibley's Harvard Graduates, Vol. IV, 1690-1700, Biographical Sketches of Those Who Attended Harvard College in the Classes of 1690-1700.* Boston: Harvard University Press, 1933.

Sibley, John Langdon. *Biographical Sketches of Graduates of Harvard University in Cambridge, Massachusetts, Volume I, 1642-1658*. Cambridge: University Press, 1873.

Smith, J.E.A. *The History of Pittsfield (Berkshire County) Massachusetts*. Springfield: C.W. Bryan & Co., 1876.

Smith-Martin, Sophia. *Mack Genealogy: The Descendants of John Mack of Lyme, Connecticut*. Hartford: The Tuttle Company, 1903.

Spaulding, J.A. *Illustrated Popular Biography of Connecticut*. Hartford: J.A. Spaulding, 1891.

Stoddard, Elijah Woodward. A*nthony Stoddard of Boston, Mass. and his descendants: 1639-1873. A Genealogy*. New York: Press of Poole & Maclauchlan, 1873.

Stoddard, Francis Russell. *The Stoddard Family, Being an Account of Some of the Descendants of John Stoddar of Hingham, Massachusetts Colony*. New York: Self-Published, 1912.

Stoddard, Jeanne. *The Stoddards of Rushton Spencer. A Short Account of the Ancestors of Anthony Stoddard of Boston*. London: Rushton Spencer-Stoddard Memorial Fund, 1979.

Stone, Edward Martin. *Our French Allies, in the Great War of the American Revolution, 1778-1782*. Providence: Providence Press Company, 1884.

Steuben, Baron Friedrich Wilhelm de. *Regulations for the Order and Discipline of the Troops of the United States*. Hartford: Printed by Hudson and Goodwin, 1782.

Swagerty, William R. *The Indianization of Lewis and Clark, Vol. I*. Norman: The Arthur H. Clark Company, 2012.

The Federal Cases, Comprising Cases Argued and Determined in the Circuit and District Courts of the United States, Book 4. St. Paul: West Publishing Company, 1894.

Thwaites, Reuben Gold. *Journals of the Lewis & Clark Expedition, 1804-1806*. New York: Dodd, Mead & Company, 1931.

Trumbull, James Russell. The History of Northampton, Massachusetts from Its Settlement in 1654. Northampton: Self-Published, 1902.

Turell, Ebenezer. *The Life and Character of Rev. Benjamin Colman, D.D.* Boston: Rogers & Fowle, 1749.

Wade, Arthur. *Artillerists and Engineers, The Beginnings of American Seacoast Fortifications, 1794-1815*. McClean: Coast Defense Study Group - CDSG Press, 2011.

Walker, Williston. *The American Church History Series, Volume 3*. New York: Charles Scribner's Sons, 1894.

Walters, Raymond. *Albert Gallatin: Jeffersonian Financier and Diplomat*. New York: The MacMillan Company, 1957.

Western Massachusetts, A History, 1636-1925, Vol I. New York and Chicago: Lewis Historical Publishing Company, Inc, 1926.

Williams, Stephen K. *Cases Argued and Decided in the Supreme Court of the United States, 5,6,7,8, Howard, Book 12*. Rochester, 1901.

Williams, Thomas John Chew. *History of Frederick County, Maryland, Volume 1*. Frederick: L.R. Titsworth & Company, 1910.

Willis, William. *The History of Portland, from 1632 to 1864: With a Notice of Previous Settlements, Colonial Grants, and Changes of Government in Maine*. Portland: Bailey & Noyes, 1865.

Winsor, Justin. *The Memorial History of Boston, including Suffolk County, Massachusetts, 1660-1880*. Boston: James R. Osgood and Company, 1882.

Woodger, Elin, and Brandon Toropov. *Encyclopedia of the Lewis & Clark Expedition*. New York, 2004.

Online Sources:

About Harvard: Harvard at a Glance; History. 2016. http://www.harvard.edu/about-harvard/harvard-glance/history (accessed September 11, 2016).

Feng, Patrick. *The Battle of the Wabash: The Forgotten Disaster of the Indian Wars.* https://armyhistory.org/the-battle-of-the-wabash-the-forgotten-disaster-of-the-indian-wars/ (accessed September 11, 2016).

George Washington Papers, 1741–1799, Library of Congress. 1999 16, February. https://memory.loc.gov/ammem/gwhtml/gwhome.html (accessed September 11, 2016).

Goodway, Frank. *American Participants at the Battles of Saratoga .* August 1997. http://saratoganygenweb.com/batlst.htm (accessed September 11, 2016).

Historic Building of Massachusetts. September 17, 2016. http://mass.historicbuildingsct.com/?p=6452 (accessed September 17, 2016).

King Solomon's Lodge #7. http://www.kingsolomonslodge7.org/ (accessed September 11, 2016).

Lafayette's Virginia Campaign 1781. March 15, 2001. http://www.xenophongroup.com/mcjoynt/laf_va.htm (accessed September 11, 2016).

Leitch, Alexander. *Edwards, Jonathan: A Princeton Companion, Princeton University Press.* 1978. https://etcweb.princeton.edu/CampusWWW/Companion/edwards_jonathan.html (accessed September 11, 2016).

Litchfield Historical Society - The Ledger. 2010. http://www.litchfieldhistoricalsociety.org/ledger/ (accessed September 11, 2016).

National Archives. *Founders Online.* http://founders.archives.gov/ (accessed September 11, 2016).

Papers of the War Department 1784-1800. 2016. http://wardepartmentpapers.org/ (accessed September 11, 2016).

Simon, Margaret. *Genealogy Trails History Group.* 1974. http://genealogytrails.com/ohio/mahoning/cem_boardman.html (accessed September 11, 2016).

Sedgwick Family Papers. May 2006. http://www.masshist.org/collection-guides/view/fa0248 (accessed September 11, 2016).

The New York State Society of the Cincinnati. February 22, 2015. http://www.nycincinnati.org/NYOfficers.htm (accessed September 11, 2016).

Valley Forge Legacy - The Muster Roll Project. August 28, 2016. http://valleyforgemusterroll.org/ (accessed September 11, 2016).

Index

Quotations

"I have never been depressed so low –raised so high, or whirled about with such a mixture of good and bad fortune" 65, 105

"Thus you perceive that my stars at my birth were unpropitious; — nothing but parental care preserved me" 106

"Licentiousness to society is more pernicious than the sullen gloom of religious bigotry" 106

"Don't you know that I have the blood of the Stoddard's in me!" 20, 105

"You will soon be sick of it" 103, 109

"A set of pale livered beings" 114

"Old Generals are seldom successful" 91, 116

"What a proud day to the United States was that on which a British army marched out of its works, and grounded their arms!" 121

"I endeavored to convince him by my conduct that I was not unworthy of the name I bore" 20, 135

"On a course of business adapted to my means and capacity, and endeavor to become, what is called, settled in life" 13, 136

"Perhaps all is right, as at least one half of us must to the right about before the United States will have a good corps of officers" 80

"A Military man never knows what to depend on. He must always be ready to move when duty calls, and to consider his time and talents as the property of the public." 58, 85

"I hope it will be believed that everything has been done by me, which it was in the power of one man to do" 88

"Truth has a poor chance in a contest with prejudice." 90

G

Gallatin, Albert, 60

Gates, Major General Horatio, 77–9, 122, 151

Germantown, Battle of, 27

Gilchrist, Peter, 32–3,

Gilchrist, Damaris Judson, 32-3

Gimat (or Gemot), Colonel Jean–Joseph Sourbader de, 112, 148

Gleason, Jr., Solomon, 131, 156

Glimpses of the Past, 18

Governor's Island, New York, 74–5

Grand Traverse, 98–9

Greenwich, Massachusetts, 126, 154

Gratiot, Charles, Sr., 18, 53, 57, 62

Gratiot, Jr., Charles, 86, 88, 93

Great Barrington, Massachusetts, 131–34, 156–57

Groton, Connecticut, 46

H

Hackensack, New Jersey, 111, 147

Hallowell, Maine (Massachusetts), 14, 34, 37, 42–3

Hancock, John, 132

Hamilton, Major General Alexander, 24, 43–6, 51, 77, 79, 139, 149

Hanks, Lieut. Porter, 84

Hardwick, Massachusetts, 126, 154

Harrington (Massachusetts), 53

Harrison, President William Henry, 16, 61–2, 64–5, 86–95, 97–102, 104

Harvard University (or College), 14, 20, 22–5,105–6, 144, 153, 157, 160

Hastings, Warren, 139, 160

Hatch, Abijah, 31

Hatch, Elisha, 31

Hathaway, James, 126–7, 155

Haverstraw Bay, New York, 109, 147

Hazeltine, Simeon, 126, 154

Henry Holt & Company, 17–8

Hessian Troops, 121, 156

Hinman, Col. Benjamin, 327, 145

Hodgdon, Samuel, 44–5

Holt, Capt. David, 99

Hooke (or Hook), Moses, 48

House of Representatives, 42, 44, 106, 153–54, 157, 160

Hoyt, Mary, 19

Hubbard, John, 130, 156

Huddy, Joshua, 151

Hull, Brigadier General William, 84–5, 89, 100

Humphrey, Col. David, 126, 154

Hunt, Major Seth, 63

Hurd, Annis, 35

I

Ingersoll, Capt. Thomas, 133–4, 157

Insurgents, 126, 129–32, 134, 154–57

Isle of Wight, 137, 158–59

J

Jackson, Major Daniel, 46

Jackson, Col. Henry, 126, 154

Jamestown (or James Town), Virginia, 116, 149

Jefferson Administration, 18

Jefferson, President Thomas, 44, 47–8, 60–2, 64–5, 68, 70, 74, 77, 79, 81, 86, 91, 149

Johnson, Lieut. Hezekiah, 88, 90, 100

Jones, Joseph, 79

Judson, Damaris, 32

Judson, Esther, 32

Judson, Reverend Ephraim, 20, 30, 157

Judson, Vincent, 33

K

Kaskaskia, Illinois, 47–51, 53, 62, 70, 81

Kelly, Frederick, 33

Kelly's Hotel, 33

Kenniston, Bradbury, 46

Kent, Connecticut, 16, 19, 30, 34

Kenyon, Lloyd 1st Baron Kenyon, 139, 160

Kimball's, Capt. Jesse Company, 28

King Solomon's Lodge #7, 31–4

King, Rufus, 139, 160

Kingsbury, Lieut. Col. Jacob, 67

Kosciusko, Bvt. Brigadier General Tadeusz, 83

L

Lafayette, Major General Marquis de, 13, 17, 127, 147–50, 155

Lane, John, 138

Lane, Son, and Frazer, 138

Lanesborough, Massachusetts, 13, 34, 107, 153, 155

Lawless, Judge Luke E., 15, 18

Larwill, Lieut. Joseph H., 94

Lee, Massachusetts, 130

Leftwich, Brigadier General Joel, 93–4, 96, 98

Lenox, Massachusetts, 129, 153–54

Letters to the Right Hon. Edmund Burke on Politics, 36, 161

Lewis & Clark, 47–8, 51, 53, 57, 62

Lewis, Capt. Meriwether, 47–8, 50–1, 53, 56–7, 62, 69, 70–4

Lewis, George B., 32–3

Lincoln, Major General Benjamin, 121, 126–27, 129, 131–2, 136, 150, 154–58

London, England, 21–2, 36–7, 137–39, 142–43, 158–61

London Bridge, 105, 136

Louisiana Purchase, 18, 52

Louisiana Territory, 18, 47, 52, 61–2, 81

Lyman, Major William, 133, 135, 157

About the Editor

Robert Stoddard resides in San Diego, California with his wife Vera. Robert hails from Aberdeen, Washington. He is a graduate of Golden Gate University in San Francisco, California.

Robert has two children, Spencer Christian Stoddard and Rachael Jade Stoddard, and seven siblings. His father, John Spencer "Jack" Stoddard (1917-1985), was a junior college teacher and basketball coach at Grays Harbor College in Aberdeen. Jack's father, Albert "A.I" Stoddard (1881-1951) of  Cedar Rapids, Linn County, Iowa, was the son of Elijah Willard Stoddard (1850-1936). Elijah Willard Stoddard, born in Marion, Linn County, Iowa, was the son of Wells Stoddard (1806-1853). Wells Stoddard, born in Coventry, Chenango County, New York, migrated to Sandusky, Ohio circa 1835 and then again further west in a covered wagon and settled in Marion, Linn County, Iowa circa 1850. Wells Stoddard was the son of Deacon John Stoddard (1763-1821) of Coventry, New York (but born in Waterbury, Connecticut). Deacon John Stoddard was the son of John Stoddard (1730-1795) of Waterbury, Connecticut (but born in Woodbury). John Stoddard was the eldest son of Eliakim Stoddard (1705-1749) of Woodbury Connecticut and the elder brother of Anthony Stoddard (1734-1785). Anthony Stoddard of Lanesborough, Massachusetts was the father of Major Amos Stoddard (1762-1813). Both Anthony and his son Amos were born in Woodbury, Connecticut.